Lessons

from a

Legendary

Defender

# WHAT WINNERS WON'T TELL YOU

# MALCOLM JENKINS

**SIMON & SCHUSTER**

New York   London   Toronto   Sydney   New Delhi

Simon & Schuster
1230 Avenue of the Americas
New York, NY 10020

First Simon & Schuster hardcover edition October 2023

SIMON & SCHUSTER and colophon are registered
trademarks of Simon & Schuster, Inc.

For information about special discounts for bulk purchases,
please contact Simon & Schuster Special Sales at
1-866-506-1949 or business@simonandschuster.com.

The Simon & Schuster Speakers Bureau can bring authors to
your live event. For more information or to book an event, contact
the Simon & Schuster Speakers Bureau at 1-866-248-3049
or visit our website at www.simonspeakers.com.

Interior design by Lewelin Polanco

Manufactured in the United States of America

1  3  5  7  9  10  8  6  4  2

Library of Congress Cataloging-in-Publication Data has been applied for.

ISBN 978-1-6680-0449-4
ISBN 978-1-6680-0451-7 (ebook)

*This book is dedicated to Coach L, Mr. Lawrence Lester.*
*We should all strive to have an impact as great as yours.*
*Although you are not physically with us, your legacy continues.*

*It is not the critic who counts; not the man who points out how the strong man stumbles, or where the doer of deeds could have done them better. The credit belongs to the man who is actually in the arena, whose face is marred by dust and sweat and blood; who strives valiantly; who errs, who comes short again and again, because there is no effort without error and shortcoming; but who does actually strive to do the deeds; who knows great enthusiasms, the great devotions; who spends himself in a worthy cause; who at the best knows in the end the triumph of high achievement, and who at the worst, if he fails, at least fails while daring greatly, so that his place shall never be with those cold and timid souls who neither know victory nor defeat.*

**—THEODORE ROOSEVELT**

# CONTENTS

# FOREWORD

Malcolm's unique journey to the top of the NFL is one of perseverance and determination. At times, I think players who come into the league with high expectations, like Malcolm, have a harder job than those of us who were late-round draft picks. Malcolm entered the NFL as a first-round pick with the weight of a franchise on his shoulders, and he never faltered in establishing himself as one of the best defensive players in the game and one of the greatest leaders our league has ever seen. Super Bowl rings and All-Pro selections only scratch the surface of what he accomplished every single down that he was on the field. However, what he accomplished off the field is even more inspiring. Malcolm stands for what is right and what is good in this world. He lives a life of integrity, and I am grateful to call him a friend.

One of my vivid memories of playing against Malcolm dates back to Super Bowl LII in Minneapolis. Going into the game, I knew he would be a significant obstacle for our offense in attempting to move the ball down the field and score points. It was later in his career, but in the whirlwind of Super Bowl weeks, I was always more wary of veterans who had been in that moment before. And he had played so many different positions in his career that he was hard to account for. I don't like to relive the final quarter of that game, but thinking back, I was telling my guys to be as aggressive as Malcolm and his teammates were on the opposite line of scrimmage. Our offense played an incredible game that night, nearly perfect, but his unit was up to the task of getting one stop when they needed it. I know his presence on the sidelines and in the huddle was a huge part of making that happen.

As towering as they are, Malcolm's achievements on the field pale in comparison to what he's done off of it. He's gone above and beyond what is expected and has used his platform to make a meaningful impact on the lives of everyone in his community. As the cofounder of the Players Coalition, he was a powerful advocate for social justice, pushing for meaningful change in policies and programs across the country. He's been an influential voice in the conversation surrounding criminal justice reform, voting rights, and educational equality.

During our time together in the NFL Players Association, I was able to witness the passion Malcolm had for these issues. He was never afraid to speak his mind and stand up for what he believed was right. Malcolm helped articulate why it was so important to use our voices as professional athletes and how we could bring attention to systemic issues that affect so many Americans. It is inspiring to see how dedicated he was to creating positive change within our league and society at large.

In addition to his advocacy work, Malcolm has been a dedicated philanthropist, giving back to the communities that helped shape him into the man he is today. Through his foundation, the Malcolm Jenkins Foundation, he provides scholarships and educational resources to underprivileged students in New Orleans, Philadelphia, and his hometown of Piscataway, New Jersey. Malcolm's commitment to the next generation is a testament to his character and a shining example of what it means to be a true leader and live a life of purpose and integrity.

It is not often that you come across an individual who excels in every aspect of their life—professionally, personally, and spiritually. Malcolm Jenkins is one of those rare individuals. This memoir will offer you a glimpse into the life of a man who has truly made a difference, both on and off the field. Through his words, you'll experience highs and lows, triumphs and setbacks, and an unwavering determination that has defined Malcolm's journey throughout his entire life.

*Tom Brady*

# PREFACE

On the morning of March 30, 2022, I wake up alone. It's 5:58 a.m., two minutes before my alarm is set to go off. As my brain floods with the list of things I need to complete, I stare at the ceiling, and exhale.

- I need to take my twelve-year-old Maltese Yorkie, Roxy, on her morning walk.
- I need to wake my two daughters up, and have them washed, dressed, and fed before I take them to school at 7:20 a.m.
- After that, I need to get back home to watch ESPN, because at 8:30 a.m. they will air the interview in which I announce that I'm retiring from NFL football.

After thirteen seasons in the NFL as a two-time Super Bowl champion and a three-time Pro Bowler, playing in 199 games with 1,044 tackles, 51 of them for losses; 35 quarterback hits; 13½ sacks, 11 fumble recoveries; 20 forced fumbles; 110 pass deflections; 21 interceptions; and 8 touchdowns, I am grateful to never have broken a bone or have a major surgery. Though thirty-four years old is young, in a game where every inch counts, I'm old as shit. But what I may have lost in youth I've gained in wisdom.

In 2021, the season before I hung up my cleats for good, I decided, with me at the end of one journey and at the beginning of another, that I wanted to tell a story of my life that properly contextualized my career, shedding light on what drove me—honoring the people who inspired me, and sharing the lessons I learned that made me the man whom you watched play.

When my agent sent my proposal to publishers, we repeatedly received the same "This looks great, we'll get back to you" response followed by radio silence. That was until a recently appointed senior editor gave me feedback. Because I played in this league for as long as I have and wanted the best book possible, I needed somebody who wasn't afraid to tell me, "Yo, homie, this shit is trash."

He wanted to talk to me alone, no agents, no managers, and that conversation sparked the clarity for the book you're about to read. "Anyone can write a linear story about their lives, giving you the play-by-play of every waking year," he told me on our call. "But the legendary books tell a story that lasts in the minds of the readers long after they have finished the final page."

Not knowing the first thing about books, I needed a coach pushing me and pulling on every thread, challenging me to go deeper to help me connect dots even I didn't see; my editor played that position.

One day during training camp, as I typed away at my computer, Saints quarterback Jameis Winston asked me what I was working on.

"I'm writing a memoir."

He smiled.

"I want to be like you when I grow up, man."

Though I knew he was joking, I also recognized his seriousness.

That I was revising my book proposal in the middle of training camp became a point of fascination for my teammates. But every day, in training camp, I kept this routine until I finished the fifty-page proposal and sent it to my editor.

The next day, I got a call.

"This right here is a story."

# 1

# FEAR

*Courage, brother! do not stumble,*
*Though your path be dark as night;*
*There's a star to guide the humble:*
*Trust in God, and do the right.*

**—NORMAN MACLEOD**

The first time my toes touched the Bermuda grass fields at the New Orleans Saints practice facility, it was hotter than a motherfucker. Like walking outside into a steam room, New Orleans is always humid. I normally wouldn't be nervous stepping onto a football field for training camp. But this was the highest level of the game I'd played at that point. This was the NFL.

Though the Saints picked me, first round, fourteenth overall, in the 2009 draft, because my contract was nowhere near done, my agent, Ben Dogra, told me not to go.

The issue with my contract was simple: when you're signed to the NFL, all players' salaries and payment schedules are announced on various sports sites, like ESPN. Just like the fans, I know what everyone is being paid. In my case, being the fourteenth pick, I knew that the thirteenth pick, Brian Orakpo, the defensive end drafted out of Texas by the team now known as the Washington Commanders, signed a five-year deal for $20 million; and the sixteenth pick, Larry English, the linebacker drafted out of Northern Illinois by the San Diego Chargers, signed a five-year deal for $17.8 million. In the case of Brian Cushing, the linebacker drafted immediately after me out of USC by the Houston Texans, he signed a five-year deal for $14 million.

As a draft pick, you expect the player drafted ahead of you to make more than you, and you to make more than the player you're drafted ahead of. Because English was being paid more for the same-length contract than Cushing was, even though he was the lower pick, it was important to me to (1) get to camp as quickly as possible, and (2) be paid between what English and Orakpo received. This was my first business decision: start training camp on time and accept whatever deal they offered or hold out until I was paid my worth. I chose the latter, and it cost me the first eleven days of training camp.

We were to report to camp on July 30, but I didn't step on the field until August 10, the twelfth day of a thirty-five-day preseason schedule. I had twenty-three days to make up for the time lost and catch up with the veterans in front of me. By then Ben had successfully negotiated the terms of my contract: five years for $19 million.

Now I would have to earn every dollar.

The first five days of camp is what you'd call an acclimation period, which allows your body to adjust to the physical demands of training camp. The ten days following is the bulk of training camp, where you are evaluated from sunup to sundown on your performance in practice, your performance in workouts, and your attentiveness in the classroom. The remaining twenty days—give or take—overlaps with the preseason, when you're evaluated more for your performance on the field against other teams. Arriving on the twelfth day meant that while everyone else was making their best effort to climb the depth chart, I was still learning the plays.

On my first day of training camp, Dan Dalrymple, our strength coach, blew the whistle for the team to begin stretching. As we were jogging out onto the field, I heard the excitement of the fans who were there to watch us practice. As I was trotting behind veteran cornerback Jason David, who'd been on the Saints for two seasons and was going into his sixth season in the NFL at that point, a fan yelled, "Thank God Jenkins is here! We can finally get rid of Jason David!"

In college, fans were never at practice except for two open practice sessions held at the stadium every training camp. Fans couldn't see the daily toils and follies of trying to improve your game on the practice field. But in the NFL, almost every day, weather permitting, a couple hundred fans line the edges of the practice field during training camp. Access that ends once the season starts. Beat writers write and post articles about who looked good in practice, who was where on the depth chart, and wrote daily predictions of who would make the team and who might find themselves on the chopping block.

Right then, before the coaches split offense and defense into different position groups, defensive coordinator Gregg Williams called the entire defense into a circle that closed around me. The night before, he'd told me I'd have to do forty up-downs to start practice.

An up-down is essentially a "burpee": you jog in place until you hear a whistle. When the whistle blows, you drop down, do a push-up, stand up, and jump. This wasn't a team bonding moment. Gregg was a mastermind and told me about an experiment that researchers conducted at the University of Wisconsin in 1966. In this experiment, researchers put five monkeys into a large cage. In the middle of the cage, one of the researchers hung a ring of bananas at the top, with a ladder placed underneath for the monkeys to reach them. But whenever one of the monkeys climbed the ladder, the researcher sprayed them with cold water. Not stopping there, the researcher then turned the water on every other monkey who hadn't climbed.

This cycle repeated itself until the monkeys understood to leave the bananas alone. At this point in the experiment, the researcher replaced one of the trained monkeys with a new one. When the new monkey saw the bananas and attempted to climb the ladder, all the other monkeys, in fear of being sprayed again, attacked the new monkey.

The experiment continued until all the original monkeys were rotated out of the cage and all the new monkeys understood the program: leave those bananas alone. After he finished telling me about the experiment, he turned to me with a grin.

"That's how you create culture."

When I stood up during my last burpee, I understood a few things about how Gregg ran his program. Fear was at the very core of his leadership style. He knew how to make us more afraid of letting each other down than we were of any opponent.

The first drill of the day was a team run. This is a period in practice in which the offense's objective is to advance the ball only with run plays, and the defense's objective is to stop those rushing attempts to three yards or less; anything more is considered a win for the offense. The logic is that if you can rush the ball for more than three yards every carry, then you will always get a first down. The simplest and most basic game plan there is. You must first establish if you are strong enough to run or stop the run of your opponent before you try any other approach. The defense ran back to the main field to meet with the offense, who drew up run plays.

Knowing they were run plays, it was our job as the defense to react to those plays—with the emphasis on the defensive line. This drill always got intense because if you played defense for Gregg, stopping the football was a lifestyle. Any ballcarrier running through the defense without their forward momentum being fully stopped was a problem. Most NFL practices are rarely live. We still run at our top speeds, and collide, but because we all understand that the most important thing is keeping our best players in one piece, the goal is for no one to hit the ground. Gregg would literally tell us daily that when he watched the tape from practice, anyone who was constantly on the ground was only communicating, "Cut me."

This created a dilemma for us on the defense. How in the hell am I supposed to stop a ballcarrier's forward momentum without tackling him? And how do I play football with the biggest and best in the world and not hit the ground? Technique! If you cannot play full-speed and still be under control, you are a danger to yourself and the other players around you. We practice getting better, and we show up every day to get better. Injuries prevent players from practicing, which stops them from getting better. A player must learn to play at a high enough rate of speed to challenge their limits with the sobriety of mind to keep from putting their teammates in compromising positions. The most important example of this is staying off the quarterback. Nothing will end your championship dreams faster than some out-to-prove-it-to-the-world rookie who injures your franchise quarterback, Drew Brees, before the season even starts. Imagine playing tag with a person you're not allowed to touch and being evaluated on the hypothetical outcome of your positioning. Quarterbacks were the only players whose jerseys were red. A reminder to stay the fuck off them. But these parameters applied to almost everyone in practice. If we were to lose someone, let it be in a real game, not at practice.

A team run consisted of twenty plays. Starters ran the first four plays, second-stringers ran the next three, then third-stringers ran another three, and then we'd repeat. As I was at the bottom of the depth chart—behind veterans Jabari Greer, Tracy Porter, Randall Gay, Jason David, and Leigh Torrence—my first set of plays in an NFL practice would be with the guys fighting desperately to make the team. Because the rosters will hold only fifty-three spots, the depth charts become real-time standings of who's on the chopping block of the eighty players invited to training camp.

On my first team run rep, Reggie Bush ran the ball to the opposite side of the field. But because Gregg believed in maximum effort, the play wasn't dead until everyone touched him. The second play was a run in my direction, which allowed me to tag the runner sooner than the first play. I had one more play until I was off the field. In anticipating the moment I'd be able to leave the field, I didn't see that our backup quarterback, Mark Brunell, had snapped the ball.

All I saw next was Pierre Thomas sprinting through the middle and into the secondary, unimpeded, toward the goal. Over fans cheering, cameras clicking, Gregg's voice cut through.

"Stop the fucking ball!"

For about forty yards down the field, I ran until I shoved Pierre out-of-bounds. My first three plays were finished. And so was I. Turning to jog off the field, I could no longer feel my legs. I could physically touch them, but I couldn't feel them.

"Quit fucking walking on my field!"

Until my walk sped up to a fat man's trot, more voices swarmed me. Nauseous, I hyperventilated. Trying to get as much access to air as possible, I took my helmet off. When the trainers saw this, they grabbed cold sponges, squeezing the water down my pads to help regulate my body heat. Desperately trying to cool off before I had to get back on the field, I stripped out of my shoulder pads. The defensive back coach, Dennis Allen, checked in.

"Is he up or is he down?"

If you're up, you're expected to perform the given task to the standard of the team. If you're down: get off the field and go to rehab until you're up again. I was down—and out. My opportunity to shine ended with a sponge bath in the cold tubs. The day was over.

When I was six years old, I attended the Chad School, a private, all-Black K–12 school in Newark, New Jersey, that prided itself on teaching its students Black history, culture, and identity. Mainly because of my new teacher, Sister Friar, I hated the school.

Before Sister Friar, I loved the Chad School. Instead of pledging allegiance to America's flag every morning, we'd sing James Weldon Johnson's "Lift Every Voice and Sing." We referred to classmates and teachers as "brother" and "sister."

In preschool, Sister Penny made her teaching atmosphere full of fun. In kindergarten, Sister Beatrice taught us about prominent figures in the Black community—from Malcolm X to Martin Luther King Jr.—and we put on a play in which I portrayed Marcus Garvey. My experience quickly turned into a hell of Sister Friar's making. Suddenly, rules became the focus.

She made Agatha Trunchbull from *Matilda* look like a substitute teacher. If you didn't pay attention, she snapped a yardstick across the top of your arm. When you didn't do what she said, she made you write your offense on the blackboard, like Bart Simpson, till your arm fell off. Her favorite punishment was having a kid stand in the corner with their nose against the wall like a real-life dunce. Her authoritative style, marrying obedience with pain, worked. I was so afraid of her, rather than getting into trouble, I peed on myself when she refused to allow me to use the bathroom during assembly. The difference between Gregg Williams's implementation of fear and Sister Friar's? Gregg had something defensive players wanted: playing time.

In the second quarter of our first preseason game, just four days after my first practice, I found myself at the bottom of the depth chart, watching from the sidelines. Our opponent was the Cincinnati Bengals. It was their third down with four yards to go on the 14-yard line with eleven seconds left in the half. We were up 7–0, and they just called a time-out.

Because their offense was already in field goal range, we knew, as a defense, that they only had enough time to execute one play, making the likelihood of that play being a pass all but guaranteed. Gregg radioed in the orders to our middle linebacker, who spread the word.

"No double moves! Play the goal line."

With the second-stringers in the game, Jason David played the right-side cornerback. As a defender, Jason made a career out of anticipating offensive patterns and jumping between the ball and the receiver for an interception. What he didn't understand: when you gamble, the house always wins. For every interception he snagged, it seemed like he gave up two touchdowns. In a seemingly harmless preseason game on 3rd and 4, I could tell by his stance that Jason was ready to gamble.

When J. T. O'Sullivan snapped the ball, Bengals wide receiver Chris Henry executed the double move Gregg had warned the defense about. After only a few strides, Henry broke toward the end zone. Jason attempted to jump the short route and was caught out of position.

"Touchdown, Bengals!"

Gregg was livid. If Gregg could've cut him right there, he would've. Instead they cut him the next day. In that moment, I saw how the decisions we make on the field have real consequences, and even though my spot on the depth chart was secured for the time being, I understood I could be the next Jason David if I didn't tighten up.

It was 3rd and 5 as my teammates and I lined up for the play. I was ten and the quarterback for my team. Summertime on Third Street in Piscataway, New Jersey, meant we played football from sunrise to sunset. We either played two-hand touch in the street or we played tackle in the rectangular plot of grass next to my house. Because we were all highly competitive in my neighborhood, these games were often heated, but they rarely escalated into physical fights.

All we needed was five yards to get a fresh set of downs, but everyone wanted to run deep and score touchdowns. My younger brother Martin—the tough and fearless middle child who's two years younger than me—was one of the receivers on my team. Because Martin's practical, he knew what to do without me saying a word.

"Set, hike!"

Martin ran five yards and stopped right over the middle with no defense. I dished it to him immediately. At that time, his favorite players to watch were the legendary half- and fullback duo for the Tampa Bay Buccaneers, Warrick Dunn and Mike Alstott. Giving his best Alstott impression, Martin lowered his head, shielded the ball with both hands, and rammed his shoulder into Hassan's chest, dragging him for another five yards.

Hassan was short—with an even shorter temper and a foul mouth. A bad combination on my block. But his secret weapon was his older brother, Hakeem, who was two or so years older than me. Hakeem constantly checked to make sure that you feared him, the type to jump at you just to see you flinch.

Earlier that summer while playing ball, Hassan pushed Martin into a set of hedges that outlined the grass field we played on. Instinctually, I threw a perfect spiral, hitting him in his spine. As he turned around, Hassan's eyes welled with tears.

"I'm going to go get my brother. He gon' fuck you up."

A few minutes later, Hakeem arrived. As he got within about ten yards of me, I attempted to defuse the situation. Before I could finish my sentence, Hakeem cocked back with his right fist and threw a wild haymaker. As I ducked, I had a decision to make: Do I counterpunch him and fight a kid that's older than me or do I run?

Before he could recover from his punch, I was three steps past him, through the bushes, and in the house. From that point on, the other boys in the neighborhood ridiculed me. Even the younger kids had jokes. Whenever I bossed up, they'd say, "Shut up before I go get Hakeem."

Now, after Hassan felt the wrath of Martin's shoulder, he pushed Martin again.

"Ey! Keep your hands to yourself!" I yelled.

"Shut up, bitch," Hassan said, and then spit at me.

Knowing that Hassan was sure to summon his older brother, I cut my losses and went to the house. As I grabbed the handle to the red screen door, I realized it was locked. As I looked up, I saw my father's mother on the other side of the screen.

My grandmother Barbra Jenkins, with her curly short Afro and soft caramel skin, was a retired social worker who worked for DCF in

Child Protective Services. She was tough, independent, and loved to travel. She adorned her home with knickknacks and souvenirs from her adventures around the world. Because she always had pyramids all around her house and the pictures from her trip on her fridge, I think her favorite destination was Egypt. The magnets on her refrigerator showed all the places she had traveled. When arranged in the right order, they created a map of the world. Though her love for me, her oldest grandson, was unconditional, her love never stopped her from teaching me hard lessons.

"Did that boy just spit at you?"

"Yeah, but it didn't land . . ."

"Go punch that boy in the face."

"Huh?"

"Somebody spitting at you is the worst thing they can do. Go punch that boy in the face. Don't come in this house until you do."

The house in question was the same house she and my grandfather had bought in the early sixties, the same house she raised my father in; the same house that, when she and my grandfather got divorced, she converted into a two-family home and rented out the upstairs part to my parents. If she wouldn't give her son a break on rent, I knew she meant what she said.

Emboldened by the request, and, quite frankly, fearing my grandmother more than Hakeem, I about-faced, walked directly down the pathway in my front yard to Hassan, grabbed him by the throat, and punched him in his face.

"I'm going to get my brother!"

After a few hours, Hakeem never materialized, so I thought the coast was clear. To blow off steam, I went down to the basketball court to shoot around. Right on cue, I saw Hakeem, Hassan, and their pudgy third wheel, Skeet, walking down the street, pointing at me.

As they approached me, I kept my cool, ignoring them. The closer they got, the tighter I clenched my fists. They stopped at the edge of the court.

"I thought I told you to keep your hands off my brother," Hakeem said.

"You better tell him to keep his hands off mine."

Sensing that I wasn't going to back down, Hakeem had an appetite for dialogue.

"Yeah, aight, nigga, you heard what I said."

To my surprise, Hakeem turned around and left. That's when I learned that, for fear to win, you have to be afraid, and for that moment, I wasn't.

A few days prior to my second preseason game, where we were set to play the Texans, we arrived in Houston. In the days leading up to the game, we were scheduled to conduct three joint practices with them. On paper, joint practices sound like a good idea. To break up the monotony of training camp, and to get high-quality reps and evaluations, the league allows teams to compete in a controlled practice. Though everyone doesn't play in the actual game, joint practices provide even the bottom-roster player an opportunity to show their value.

What this really turns into is a dick swinging contest between teams and players. "High-quality reps" are replaced with fights, injuries, and overaggressive plays. After two fights broke out between us and the Texans, we only got through two of the three scheduled practices. On one field our offense was in an all-out brawl with their defense and on the other field our defense was in a melee with their offense.

During our downtime one evening, the veteran defensive backs invited the entire group for dinner. Though I wasn't invited to attend the dinner as a guest, as a rookie who was expected to pay for this dinner, my presence was mandatory. For first-round draft picks, this was tradition. As if learning the ins and outs of the playbook weren't enough, we stocked the meeting room fridge with snacks, bought and delivered breakfast upon request, and provided daily entertainment during the dog days of camp. Until this point in training camp, I did what I was told, kept quiet, and stayed out of the way. When I was asked to sing the "Thong Song," I obliged. When they wanted to hear a joke, I yelled, "I'm rich, *biatch*!" in my best Donnell Rawlings voice. I did it all, with humility.

Though having to pay a bill of $10,000 or more—depending on the defiance of the rookie and the ruthlessness of the vets—wasn't uncommon for rookies, the vets took it easy on me by only having me pay for the defensive backs and not the whole defense or whole team. The worst I'd ever heard was Dez Bryant's purported $54,896 dinner bill. This came after Dez openly refused to carry other players' football pads.

Del Frisco's was the restaurant of choice. At a long table in a quiet corner of the restaurant, twelve of us on the Saints' defensive back roster broke bread. Suddenly defensive captain Jonathan Vilma, or "JV" as we called him, and the entire linebacker core arrived, increasing the group from twelve to twenty-one. As they raised their glasses to me for covering the evening's bill, I sat at the head of the table, worried.

After devouring plates of calamari and lobster, the check arrived. Looking at the total, I leaned over to Darren Sharper and Roman Harper.

"Do I have to pay for the linebackers, too?"

Roman smiled.

"Nah, bro, you're *our* rookie. Let their rookies take care of them."

Sharper followed up.

"Nah, we ain't gonna do you like that."

When the waiter returned, I told him that I would only cover the twelve defensive backs I was with. The waiter then dropped another check on the opposite end of the table. Confused, JV grabbed it and looked at me.

"What's this?"

"They said I only had to pay for the DBs."

JV raised his eyebrows, slowly leaned back, and nodded.

"Okay, that's how we're doing it."

When JV no longer directed the question-statement at me, but at Roman and Sharper, I realized they had set me up. When I tried to offer to pay, JV declined, reached into his pocket, paid for the line-backers, and left.

The next day, when the coaches blew the last whistle of practice, the team huddled, Sean Payton made a few comments, and we headed to the locker room. Walking off the field, veteran defensive linemen Will Smith and Paul Spicer walked up on both sides of me and lifted me off the ground. Besides cutting me in the lunch line once, I didn't know Paul, but Will, who was a former Buckeye like me, was like a big brother. This was when JV walked up.

"You too big to pay for dinner, huh? Okay, well, let's see how you feel about it now."

My feet still in the air, Will offered, "We can do this the easy way or the hard way."

It was at this moment that I realized that piles of athletic tape and every watercooler and Gatorade bottle were conveniently positioned by the goalpost at the end of the field.

"I'll walk."

Paul and Will escorted me down to the goalpost, where they, along with JV, taped me flush to it. Thinking that would be it—that they'd leave me taped from head to toe—I then felt something ice-cold rushing from my neck down to my toes. Pouring cold Gatorade, water, and ice over my head, they told me, "Cool off, rook."

After that, they brought the watercoolers with the motorized pumps on them and fixed them inside the collar of my pads. They turned the water on and left it on. And there I stayed, hugging the goalpost on the Houston Texans' indoor practice field, freezing my ass off, until the tape softened enough for me to wriggle free.

In the second quarter of the fourth preseason game, I was lined up across from Dolphins wide receiver Davone Bess. The fourth preseason game means that the starters only play the first series, and the rest of the game is played by all the backup players desperate to solidify their spot on the roster. Because Jabari Greer and Tracy Porter have both cornerback positions on lock, it was clear that, come week 1, I won't be starting.

My last hope to crack the starting lineup was as the third corner, or the "nickel." Due to the versatility and intelligence the position requires, the nickel is an important position. You must be quick and skilled enough to cover wide receivers, tight ends, and running backs. You must be knowledgeable enough to understand how to navigate run plays, and you're closer to the line of scrimmage, which means that you are up against the opposing team's offensive linemen, and because the closer you are to the line of scrimmage, the faster the game happens, your decision-making must be fast.

Gregg emphasized that we needed to fight the desire to be right and only play fast.

"When in doubt, check whup ass!"

Even if you don't know the play, just go somewhere fast with bad intentions. Gregg could coach you to make better decisions, but he expected his players to make fast decisions. While I was skilled with the ability to cover receivers with the physical physique to play in the league, I didn't have the skills to play the nickel position. But here we were.

Coming off the ball, Bess gave me a jab step one way. Eager to get my hands on him—because he was a smaller and quicker receiver than me—I reacted. *If I can get my hands on him early*, I figured, *then I can control him*. But my overreaction to his jab step and the cast I wore on my left wrist from a sprain I got earlier in camp left me grasping at the air.

By the time I recovered, he executed his route off toward the sideline right at the 1st-down marker. And because this is the NFL, the ball was right there, with no chance for me to recover. I dove, only able to get him to step out-of-bounds.

At this point, I attempted to stop everything myself. If you try to stop everything, you stop nothing. If I understood the defense, all I had to do was make sure I secured my left, which was the outside, exactly where he ran that route. In a situation where I had help to my right, playing to the strength of the defense would've helped me, but I lined up with what I came with, which at that point was my competitive nature and natural talent.

Now, one quick out route in a game is to be expected. But when you're desperate to make plays, those frustrations mount up. Instead of making plays, I made a mistake. Later in the game, I lined up at corner across from a familiar face, Brian Hartline, a former teammate at Ohio State. The ball was snapped. I took two shuffles back and saw that it was a run play, and it was coming right to my side.

Similar to how Bess set me up, I set Brian up. Knowing he had to block me, I jab-stepped him to the inside. When he overreacted, I countered back, ducked under him, and now I was free to the ballcarrier, who was coming up quick. Closing my eyes, throwing my arms out, I dove. When I opened my eyes, the ballcarrier was in the end zone. I'd missed the tackle.

As the game went on, more and more players got reps, and I was taken out in the third quarter. Having not much action after that and with the preseason quiet for me, when I walked into the locker room, I was pretty sure that I had done nothing to change my spot on the depth chart. As we approached the season, I was going to have to settle for playing special teams. I felt as if I had failed but I decided to embrace whatever role I was given and would compete my ass off every day until I took the starting spot.

The same summer that my grandmother taught me to defend myself, my father taught me to play the game of football. A new pep in his step, my father was excited to sign me and my middle brother up for Pop Warner football, to teach us the fundamentals of the game.

Almost every boy in the neighborhood stood in a single-file line in my father's backyard. An architect at heart, he saw the backyard as a makeshift training facility. As the summer heat drew sweat that dripped from his ever-growing widow's peak down to his Apollo Creed–like mustache and onto his brown shirt that he worked the yard in, his eagerness beamed.

Using landmarks in the modest-size backyard as a pseudo-obstacle course, he created a game that simulated the routes receivers ran—eight different routes, eight different obstacles. Whoever completed the route first, won.

We walked ten yards away from my father with our backs turned to him, and when he yelled, "Hit," we turned to find the ball ripping quickly toward our faces. We couldn't run away or duck. Before the ball blasted us in the face, we had to focus and catch it. In my career, you can ask any of my teammates or coaches, catching the ball has always been a problem.

Always hard on me when the ball bounced out of my hands, he spared no expense, laughing at me in front of all the other boys.

"You got to come back to the ball, Malcolm. Stop being afraid of it."

Second only to myself, my father was the harshest critic of my game. Immediately after games, he loved to remind me of the tackles I had missed or the interceptions I'd dropped.

"Good game, son . . . But what happened on that play when you let that boy just run you over?"

---

The day after a game, players normally come to the facility on their day off to receive rehab or to work out. While I was setting up my locker in preparation for the season, Pierson Prioleau, the thirteen-year vet, looked worried.

"Man, I got to lay low. Grim Reaper walking around."

The "Grim Reaper" was one of the assistant coaches whose job it was on cut day to find the players that the coaches wanted to let go, notify them that Sean wanted to speak to them, and usher them to the coach's office. If he looked for you, it was not good.

When training camp began, there were eighty players on the roster. By the third preseason game, the roster must be cut to seventy-five players. After the fourth and final preseason game, coaches had two days to cut the roster from seventy-five players to fifty-three. You knew who'd been cut by seeing which lockers were already cleaned out, or witnessing that someone was at his locker with his head down, packing things into a black construction-grade garbage bag.

With the roster now at fifty-three players, the meeting room looked like Thanos had snapped his fingers. Even though I was their first-round draft pick and knew I wouldn't be gone in the first training camp, between my lackluster performance, not being in the starting lineup, and seeing veterans like Pierson nervous, I thought the worst.

But the Monday following the last preseason game, Sean Payton started the meeting upbeat.

"This is who we're taking into the 2009 season. Congratulations. Let's get to work."

# 2

# DISCIPLINE

*We must all suffer one of two pains:*
*the pain of discipline or the pain of regret.*

**—JIM ROHN**

I was at the starting line of a 400-meter race, but this was practice. After my high school health teacher, Mr. Lester, who was also the head track coach and assistant football coach for the varsity team, had pestered me for months to come out, I decided to show up. Besides the fact that track would allow me to work on my speed during the offseason, word on the street was that the cutest honeys ran track.

Figuring out what events I would be best at, Mr. Lester had me try out all of them in the early parts of practice. At that time in my life, a freshman in high school, the farthest I ran was a hundred yards. Four hundred meters was an entire lap around the track, but how hard could it be, right?

Mr. Lester said, "Set." And then I heard the large clap from the two 4x4s to simulate the sound of a gun. The first one hundred meters, I learned from Mr. Lester, was to get up to speed. *Get out of the blocks, open your stride, and get around the first turn of the lap.* Once you get to the back straightaway, on the second one hundred, conserve energy. The only way to maintain speed while reserving energy:

*Sync your breathing with the cadence of your strides; use your arms more than your legs; maintain an even stride that doesn't restrict your breath.*

As you hit that third one hundred meters, you feel the lactic acid in your legs build up, your chest tighten, and with the finish line nowhere in sight, doubt creeps up. But coming around that last turn, when you see the final finish line, you're reenergized. Now it's time to finish strong and give it everything you got. That last one hundred is in front of the bleachers in the stands, and everybody wants to see how you finish. You don't want to cross the finish line looking like you have a refrigerator on your back, so you try your best to finish strong.

Approaching the finish line, I heard Mr. Lester calling out times: 49, 50, 52. After fifty-two seconds and some change, I crossed the line. Not bad for my first attempt. Our best runner, Sir Leslie Ford, ran his 400s at about forty-eight seconds, a full four seconds in front of me.

Soon as I crossed the line, I collapsed onto the track, lying on my back, barely able to breathe. Telling everybody to get up and walk it off, Mr. Lester jogged over. It wasn't until he pointed to a huddle across the field of a few girls, whose job it was to record our times for the records, that my legs regained their strength.

After he blew his whistle, a coach yelled.

"Angle tackles, line them up!"

It was practice on the Piscataway Braves Pop Warner junior pee-wee team. I played Pop Warner football, and attempted to quit both years, but my dad wouldn't let me. *You got to finish what you start,* he'd tell me. So there I stood in line for the drill I hated the most: tackling.

Though these drills were meant to educate kids on the proper technique to tackle safely and effectively, back then usually the volunteer coaches implemented these drills as a litmus test to identify which kids were tough and which ones weren't. Oftentimes those who weren't tough were deployed as practice dummies for the best players on the team. They split us into two lines and, judging by the fact that no one in my line was naturally gifted, or were the favorites, it was obvious that I was on the practice-dummy line.

So I did what any kid that's a little afraid of contact does. I counted how many players were in the other line and made sure that I wasn't matched up with any of the biggest hitters. In fact, I was all the way at the end of the line, hoping that the five or ten minutes that the coaches allocated for this drill might run out by the time I had to go. One by one, I saw the kids in my line get demolished. And after every time, the coaches surrounded the player and enthusiastically asked them if they wanted to go again, to which that player always said yes.

Next in line was my best friend on the team, Calvin Johnson. He lived on the other side of town with both his parents. But I can tell you one thing, he was no crash test dummy. He was one of those kids that you never had to teach the technique of how to strike somebody. He did it naturally. He was doing at the age of nine what I didn't learn to do until I was well into my NFL career. That is a striking six-inch blow. The perfect tackle is like a golf swing: it sounds great when executed. It's about getting a little bit lower than the ballcarrier and at the right moment striking him with a short upward motion of your shoulder, knocking him either backward or off his feet.

When the whistle blew, Calvin took off to the cone situated at a forty-five-degree angle from him and the ballcarrier five yards away from him. They'd both been instructed to run to the cone, to not make any jukes or try to make anybody miss, but to collide and let the strong man win. Well, in this rep, Calvin was a strong man. Like a car crash, you heard the oversized football pads smack into each other as Calvin drove the ballcarrier into the ground, and all the kids and coaches erupted into cheers. Calvin was like that.

He loved every bit of contact and wasn't somebody who closed his eyes or winced right before he made hits. He did it willingly and happily. Next up was Billy. Billy was a kid who was blessed with a ton of heart and a ton of will, but very little God-given talent or size. They blew the whistle, he ran to the cone, and got hit so hard I thought his head would come off his shoulders, still in his helmet. Billy lay there on the ground for a while as we all looked on thinking that he was dead.

But the coaches quickly surrounded him, picked him up on his feet.

"Billy, you want some more?"

"Yes, Coach."

To everybody's cheers and encouragement, Billy got back in line. The players lined up at the cone, the whistle was blown, and Billy met the same exact fate. After his punishment was over, I was up next. My plan to beat the clock failed. So I was going to just do what I had to do. The whistle blew and I ran to the cone. I closed my eyes right before contact and felt two pains. The first pain was being struck by the tackler.

The second pain was hitting the ground. When I opened my eyes, it was over. So I slowly got up and began to head to the back of the line, thinking the worst of it was past me. But the coaches ran up to me the same way they had Billy and surrounded me.

"Jenkins, you want to go again? You want some more?"

Right in his eyes, I looked at the coach.

"No."

The summer before I joined the track team, I strutted down the street with my chest up, head high, feeling good as I walked back home one summer afternoon. The reason why I was feeling good? Because for the first time in my life, I had got some pussy. So of course I wanted to strut my stuff in the neighborhood.

As I walked into the house, I beelined to go upstairs where my bedroom was, skipping the first floor, where the master bedroom was and where I knew my parents would be. But before I could hit the second step, my dad called out.

"Malcolm, come here. We got to talk to you."

I was a kid with good grades. I didn't get in trouble much, so I couldn't imagine what it was that we had to talk about. Surely they didn't know what had happened earlier that day.

In the summers, on Third Street, the neighborhood was full of latchkey kids—kids with parents who had to go to work during the day and often couldn't afford weeks of summer camp—so we were left at home with large portions of time unsupervised. My grandmother had retired and moved to Virginia, so I was in charge. And the first thing I would do was kick my brothers out of the house, invite my boys over, and we'd play video games, watch BET, or spend some quality time with our girlfriends.

My mother was the first to speak.

"I heard that you had girls at the house and that you had unprotected sex."

"Uh, no. I used protection."

Being thirteen, I didn't understand the line of thought my dad went to next.

"What about your career?"

My face screwed up. *What kind of career is he talking about?* I wasn't dreaming about being in the NFL. Also, *I'm not in trouble?* My mom chirped in next with something a little bit more sensible, and she said that I would have plenty of time to experiment with sex, to explore those things when I was older, but that I should really be careful and selective who I share my body with.

Surprised that my parents found out that I had sex in their house and wasn't in trouble, I left with a smirk on my face. Reflecting, I wish I had heeded those warnings, especially my mother's.

Track was over, and so was the school year. And with all that free time, I spent more and more time with my best friend, Calvin. Not only had we played football together from Pop Warner all the way into high school, but we did everything together. Got into some fights. Skipped school a couple times. We were even dating two girls that were also best friends.

I always had his back and he had mine. He was still the punisher when he was off the field. Cool, calm, and collected, the same way he was when he was standing in that line. But when it was time to go or somebody tried him, he had a quick temper and even quicker hands. But even me, I was no longer the kid that was sitting in the line for crash test dummies. I'd had a growth spurt and had a mean disposition for proving my point. So oftentimes, no one messed with him and no one messed with me, because they'd have to see both of us if they did.

But I also knew that things were rapidly changing in both of our lives and there were parts of his life that he kept me far away from. It started out with things like smoking. He knew I didn't smoke. So whenever he and his cousins would pick me up, they usually smoked beforehand or once we got out of the car. They wouldn't hot box while I was in it, just out of respect. Then things escalated when I would catch wind that Calvin and his cousins or friends had robbed somebody or they were rumored to have jumped somebody on a weekend that Calvin told me he was busy.

And even more so when he went to North Carolina for a few weeks to visit his brother and some of his family members there. Word on the street was that Calvin had become a Crip. We had already hung out around a lot of the Crips in Piscataway, just naturally gravitating toward one another. Calvin was there with them, I was there with Calvin, so I was constantly around it. But none of this shit popped off while I was around.

And every summer, Our Lady of Fatima, the local church, threw a fair that had all the kids from Piscataway, but also the surrounding towns, show up. So I was there with Calvin and a few other Crips that were normally hanging around. One, his name was Mike. I saw that Mike had been staring at me for the last few minutes, but I played it cool. Calvin walked away to go get a funnel cake and some lemonade. As soon as he was gone, Mike walked up to me. Mike was the type of dude that was like a pit bull with no leash. Everybody tensed up when he came around. Because, one, he played too much. But two, he was known for having an ill one-hitter quitter and knocking niggas out.

But through association, me and Mike were on good terms. So as he approached I said, "What's good, Mike?" "What up, Malc?" he asked with a smile that I then knew meant he was up to something. Whenever he approached you too friendly, you knew it was something. He was up to his games. He was looking at me up and down, and he was like, "Hey, man, let's go smoke one." "Mike, you know I don't smoke." "I'm just saying, man, you're around us all the time. You might as well get down." And then there was a pregnant pause in the conversation as I realized that he wasn't talking about smoking when he'd said, "You might as well get down." He was saying I should become a Crip.

Before I could even respond, he said, "You're around us all the time, you might as well." And he had a point. While I knew that I had been excluded from this side of Calvin's life, that didn't feel good. I didn't have many other friends. I didn't want to be the guy left out. So

I looked Mike in the eye and said, "I'll think about it." He smiled as if he had just planted a seed and accomplished what his mission was, and walked back to where he was at.

When Calvin came back, he asked, "What y'all talk about?" I said, "Nothing."

As I jogged around the track at the NJSIAA Group Championships held at Egg Harbor Township High School, I took a big yawn and shook my head as I thought, *L is right, I'm tired.* It's the biggest meet of the year. The finalists go on to the Meet of Champions to determine the fastest runners in the state of New Jersey. Mr. Lester was our health teacher, assistant football coach, and the head track coach for the boys. But he also, to so many students in the school, was a therapist, a disciplinarian, and a father figure. Any day of the week you could go to his classroom and find kids who just needed an escape hanging in the back of his class or coming to him for advice or asking for food, which he always had.

Most of the kids called him Mr. Lester. But to the chosen few that he had handpicked to put under his wing, he was L. L was always put together, in his late forties, in shape. We never saw him lifting weights, but somehow he had muscles on muscles and that old man's strength that let you know he could whup your ass if you really wanted to pop off on him.

His son, Larry Jr., graduated the year before I got there and was a star athlete that landed a full scholarship at Boston College to play football and he was known as one of the greatest athletes to come through Piscataway High School. Much to his credit, that was L's doing. L had an entire program from philosophy to lifestyle to training that he obviously instilled in his son and then used that same program to build up other kids who wanted to be great. He would handpick those who he thought had the discipline, the grit, and the talent to be special and then groom them to be the best that they could be.

His program required some stipulations, though. You had to stay out of trouble, there was no bitch-assness allowed, with bitch-assness to him meaning complaining or making excuses about things that are hard. And last but not least, no fraternizing. When it was time to work, it was time to work, and I'm sure on the track this was important because there were girls everywhere. The finest in-shape girls you can find.

The reason I was on the track yawning right before the biggest race of the season is because I broke that last rule the night before.

Myself and three of our sprinters, Curtis Ford, Kyle Wilson, and Jeff Omoregie, were all a little bit too excited to be two hours from home on an overnight trip with the girls' track team right across the parking lot in the hotel adjacent to us. So, of course, we decided to devise a plan on how we could sneak across the parking lot and see about the honeys on the girls' track team. I suggested that we wear our track uniforms and warm-ups so that just in case we got caught in transition, we could say that as a group we were nervous about the races and doing a late-night jog to stay loose. But a couple of the guys decided, nah. Instead, they wanted to get fresh, and get themselves the best chance of getting lucky.

So as we walked through the parking lot, we were about halfway there, and the coast seemed clear. Kyle was on the left, Jeff and I were walking in the middle, and Curtis was on the other side of Jeff. And as we crept through the dark parking lot, we suddenly heard L's voice say, "Omoregie?" Immediately Kyle and Curtis ducked behind cars, leaving Jeff and me, who were in the middle, sandwiched between them, in plain sight. We kept walking like we hadn't heard him.

"Omoregie!?" I turned to Jeff and said, "Jeff, I think he's calling you." We both turned around to find L sitting in his truck in the parking lot, waiting for the move he knew we would make. L was always about preparation, discipline, and focus, so he knew what we were going to be on long before we even thought about it. "Where y'all think y'all going? Mm-hmm. Trying to be slick. Go back to the room." And we just ducked our heads without looking him in the eye, and walked past his truck and back to the room.

But there's another reason I was yawning, too. The anxiety of the upcoming race was starting to creep into my brain. See, these were the fastest kids in the state, and I knew their times coming into it. I was still running just under fifty seconds, but the guys coming into this race had been running sub-forty-eight times. So I already knew I was out of my league.

Mr. L taught me how to run the 400 in a way that would break most of my opponents. Instead of always worrying about the fastest time, I could eliminate the competition by testing their will. Instead of running the 400 in four parts, kicking in the last hundred meters, I would run it in three parts. I'd get out to a good start in the first hundred; then in the back hundred, I would try my best to conserve all my energy, opening my stride and pumping my arms as far as I could, controlling my breathing. And when we'd hit the 200 mark, instead of that being another place to cruise and maintain, I would start to pick up the pace, beginning my kick 50 to 100 meters earlier than most of my opponents wanted to. And then they'd have to make a decision. Do they stick to their own game plan and run their own race, or do they try to run mine?

The ones who would allow me to run my race had usually already decided they had lost and wouldn't even try to catch me. And those who would try to come with me found that those waters were too deep and would run out of gas long before we got to the homestretch, making most of my wins unchallenged, except for one guy, Bryant McCombs.

He was the guy who I had to see a few times a year. He played at the neighboring town of Old Bridge. I would see him during the football season, in which we dominated him and his teammates all the time. I was king in that arena. But out there on the track was his world. So he was the only one I was out there trying to compete with. I knew if I could give him a run for his money, then I'd land myself somewhere in the top four hundred runners in the state, and most likely I'd have to run a personal best to even compete.

When we got in the blocks at the starting line, I shook out my legs and arms to try to get rid of some of those last-minute nerves and thought about running my race. I wasn't going to be able to take those runners in the deep water or break anybody, so I needed to stay focused and give myself the best opportunity to perform.

The gun went off and we got out. Immediately, I knew that this was the big leagues. The pace was fast. Usually I tried to not start too fast, knowing that I had to conserve some energy for late in the race. But the first hundred felt like we were going to run full speed from start to finish. And by the time we got down the back stretch, that 200 mark that I was usually kicking at to break other runners, was the same strategy that these runners were going. Out front you had Ruben McCoy from Wilson Township and Shaquan Brown from John F. Kennedy High School in Paterson, both going neck and neck. But McCombs was still in my sight, and seeing those two go, he started to go. So I decided I was going with them.

The one thing I love about the 400 is when you come around that last turn onto the home straightaway with all the fans there, you feel their vibrations. You feel the tension in the air rising and you hear the crowd get into it as they see who has something left in the tank in that last hundred. And it was that last hundred that separated all of us. While they dug deep into a tank and pulled out reserves and muscled their way to the finish line, I was gassed out. They broke me the same way I had broken others, and when you're broken, you can't even finish strong. So not only did I not finish near McCombs or the rest, I placed sixth, falling behind a few runners who finished stronger and ran their own race and caught me at the end.

The winning time would be 46.77, and even though I had run my best time to date, 49.47, I was still over three seconds behind the winner. That's an eternity in the 400. I couldn't even look Mr. Lester in the eye when I came back because he and I both knew, before the race even started, that I was finished.

A couple days after the fair, Calvin and I posted up in the parking lot of Piscataway High School after one of our summer training sessions. At the fair, I shrugged off when Mike suggested that I become a Crip, but honestly, I had been considering it ever since. So I figured I'd ask Calvin what he thought, seeing as though I'd only be joining because of him. I chuckled when I presented it to him, just to make sure it had a soft landing, and said, "Oh, man, you know, Mike asked me if I wanted to get down. What you think?" He screwed up his face and looked at me. "Nah, family. Nah, that ain't for you. I don't want that for you. You got too much going on." He said, "Really, I don't want it for me."

I looked at him kind of confused, and he continued. "Man, you got too much going on. You about to go to college. You got hella opportunities in front of you. Nah, bro, that's too much to lose," he said, sternly this time. I didn't know what he meant, seeing as though we both were playing ball and he had every opportunity that I had.

In fact, he even had some smaller schools looking at giving him a scholarship to go play ball. But I could see in his eyes that whatever he was carrying, he couldn't get out of it, and he didn't want to put me in it. He said, "Really, I don't even want you around all of this," pointing to himself. And I'm like, "What you mean?" He's like, "You don't need this nonsense, man. You got it all lined up. Stay focused and keep doing what you doing." And there was an awkward silence as I could see his face was saying it all.

The things he was keeping me away from had begun to escalate. It went from small fights to robberies, to Calvin stabbing somebody during our senior year and eventually losing his scholarship. When he walked away from me that day, everything seemed cool, like normal. We dapped up. He said he'd holler at me later. But I knew my curiosity in his life had turned something off in him. He wasn't going to allow me to mess my life up trying to follow him. I knew our relationship was changed after that. As he drove away, I realized he had made a decision for me. I was going to focus on football and buy into this program that L had been pushing for all this time.

It was my senior year and I had taken the line at the end of the last turn as I prepared to run the anchor leg of the 4 x 100 at the county relays. I had already gotten my scholarship to Ohio State and was getting ready to graduate high school in a couple months. And a year after finishing behind him in the 400, Bryant McCombs had already beaten me in the 400 and the 200 that season. Even though I clocked in some of my best times ever at our county meet, he beat me in the 400 running a 47.27 and setting the new county record, while I placed second running my personal best, 48.56. That same day, he beat me in the 200 running 21.25 and setting another meet record. I ran 21.87. And there we were in the 4 x 100 relay and suddenly I felt like he had more arrogance. He had a pep in his step and a confidence that he hadn't had in previous years, and it was pissing me off.

Bryant McCombs was tall. He was about six one, strong build, but I hated everything about the way he looked. Old Bridge's colors are black and white. They sported a jersey that looks like a referee shirt with super-short black shorts that showed off his long ashy legs and his silver spikes that made for a hideous color palette. But he was good. And L had pissed me off because all week he'd been making slight jabs and jokes, trying to motivate me. "I know you ain't scared, MJ." He'd been saying that all week. He'd been promising me that he'd studied their relay team to a T, and he knew, based on the order that he'd put together, that by time I got the handoff, I should be a half step in front of Bryant McCombs, and that should be enough to finish the race.

He was like, "He's going to be right behind you," so I couldn't break, I couldn't panic. I just had to finish strong and keep him on my back. We stood right next to each other as we lined up on the track, shaking our legs out and getting out the last nerves. I didn't even look at him. I acted like he wasn't there and focused. We were in lane four. They were in lane five. Everybody was on their feet in anticipation because they knew when the two anchor legs got the baton that it was going down and this was really the last thing on my list to do as far as accomplishments in high school. I had already won three state championships in football, was on my way to Ohio State to play, and was getting ready to graduate. Beating Bryant was the last thing on my checklist, and since I knew I couldn't see him in the 200 or 400, this would be the only other opportunity that I got to compete.

The gun went off and my teammate Terrence Fox led us off. He's a shorter runner, so from the other side of the track I just saw his shorter legs moving a thousand miles an hour. He got it to Jonathan Francois, who then got it to Tony Logan. And as Tony came around the curve, I saw that he was exactly where L said he would be. Only about a half step in front of Old Bridge. And when he hit the tape that I laid on the track as my landmark, I turned my eyes back to the track and took off running. The first thing I heard was "Stick." I reached my left hand back and felt the baton and seamlessly grabbed it and went. The next thing I heard was Bryant McCombs's breath and footsteps right on my outside, on my right. As we came down a straightaway, the final stretch of the track, I heard the crowd stand up and the stands rattle as they got excited.

*Woo, woo, woo* is the sound they usually make at the end of races when a runner is being caught from behind. They were anticipating that the great McCombs was getting ready to walk me down and take over the race. Not fucking today. I was running so fast I didn't even feel my spikes touching the track, and all I had was L's voice in my head: "Don't panic, don't break." I maintained my form, picked my knees up, and drove with a burst I'd never had my entire life. As we approached the line, I leaned forward to a crowd's roar, and when I checked the time, the board said Old Bridge 43.0, Piscataway 42.9. I never ran for something so fast and hard in my life, but I had fully committed to L's plan and his program. The things I'd watched trip my brother up and trip Calvin up, I was able to avoid.

And I wasn't sure where I was going next, but thanks to L and his program, I'd accomplished everything that I had wanted to. That's how I always felt about life. Like trouble was always in the lane next to me, trying its best to catch up to me. I could hear its footsteps and I could feel it breathing, but thanks to a figure like L and a friend like Calvin, I was able to run my race and focus only on the finish line.

# 3

# COMPETE

*Success is not the result of spontaneous combustion.*
*You must set yourself on fire.*

**—ARNOLD GLASOW**

Unable to crack the starting lineup or jump over Randall Gay as the nickel, I was on the sideline in our week 1 matchup against the Detroit Lions. Up 28–10 after a Lions second-down play, I spot Tracy Porter limping. On the play before, he'd tweaked his ankle, so without hesitation, Gregg Williams called my name.

"Malcolm, get in."

It was now third down, and we needed a stop. Gregg called "Shake Silver," one of his premier blitz pressures where he lines up two defenders on both sides of the offensive protection, making the quarterback and the O-line figure out which defenders are blitzing and which two are dropping back into coverage. The coverage on the back end also has one side that's man-to-man coverage and the other side a trap. The purpose of this pressure is to trick the quarterback into throwing to the side of the field where the coverage is.

However, if the quarterback figures out the coverage, he then knows he has one-on-one coverage on the backside. This pressure was usually effective for younger quarterbacks like Matt Stafford, who was the first-overall draft pick that year. As I heard the call, I went through a checklist in my head. I'm on the backside. That means I'm solo. I look up to see which receiver I'm covering—and it was none other than Calvin "Megatron" Johnson, the six-foot-five, 235-pound phenom out of Georgia Tech. Johnson got the name "Megatron" because when he got on the field, he literally transformed. And this was the very first snap of my career.

As Megatron was not only the best receiver on the field, but arguably the best receiver in the game at that time, I looked back to my safety to see if he was going to adjust the coverage or change the matchup. Understanding this to be the big leagues, and nobody was here to save me, I told myself, *Fuck it, let's go. This is why you here.*

When Stafford snapped the ball, I went through the techniques my coaches told me: I looked at the quarterback to make sure that it was not a quick throw. Noticing that Megatron stemmed inside for a couple steps and then went back vertical up the field, I knew there were only a few routes that he could run off of that stem, and I guessed correctly that he was going to run the dig route—that at about twelve to fifteen yards, Megatron would make a hard right turn across the middle of the field. When I broke to cut him off, I was excited.

Stafford threw the ball. *Oh, this is going to be an interception!* Approaching the ball, I knew I was getting a pick six; I just needed to decide what my celebration would be. As I raised my hands up to catch the ball, out of my peripheral vision I saw two huge blue gloves come into my line of sight, snatching the ball out of the air. It was Megatron.

I made a last-ditch effort to dive and trip him up. But like a BB gun pellet bouncing off a tank, the man didn't even break stride. He caught it, stepped out of a tackle by Darren Sharper, and turned on the jets. With that frame, six five, 235, he ran a 4.34. Opening his stride, he separated from the entire pack, and headed for the end zone. But luckily Pierson Prioleau made him click his heels out-of-bounds on the 2-yard line. Tracy was back in the very next play.

On the drive back to New Jersey from Ohio with my parents; my two brothers, Martin and Miles; and my boy Trick, I was processing what the defensive coordinator for the Ohio State Buckeyes, Mel Tucker, told me a couple of days before.

"You might be the best corner in the country."

Understanding that their sons—Martin, Miles, and me—were one bad decision away from jeopardizing our future if we were left to spend the summer unsupervised in our neighborhood, my parents decided the best thing to do was to take us with them to Westerville, Ohio, to visit my aunt, who had just moved there. Their itinerary for us was to go to Cedar Point, the amusement park; relax; and on the last week send us to Ohio State's football camp.

Though Trick's real name is Rob, we called him "Trick" because he's from Florida—and the only thing us Jersey boys knew about Florida at the time was Trick Daddy. As someone who also dove headfirst into Mr. Lester's program, was just as motivated and competitive as I was, Trick was a good dude to have around. When my parents dropped us off at the three-day overnight camp at Ohio State, I had no idea that my life was about to change.

The first day, the coaches did normal things like drills and instructional teaching to all the campers—from middle schoolers all the way up to high school recruits. On the second day, they lined wide receivers and defensive backs up in one-on-ones. As a DB, I was determined to figure out who the best receivers were at the camp. When I started off on one end of the field, I shut down every receiver in that group. Once I realized that end wasn't where the most talented receivers were, I moved to the next line. Did the same thing. Then I moved to the next line and the next, until I saw Ohio State's head coach, Jim Tressel, and a couple of other members of the staff watching a very particular line of wide receivers and defensive backs.

While my parents drove eight hours and paid full price for us to attend this camp, these players were top recruits who were invited. When I got to that line, Mel Tucker, Jim Tressel, and the team's wide receiver coach, Darrell Hazell, led the drills. I won the first rep I participated in.

My physicality at the line of scrimmage and pushing and bullying the receivers all around the field was something they weren't used to. They had a hard time getting around my long arms and big frame. Out of fear of being embarrassed in front of the coaches, I noticed that some of the defensive backs hesitated as the best receivers lined up. Once they hesitated, I took their rep. I wanted all the work I could get. At one point, I went three reps in a row against three fresh receivers, locking them all down. The coaches noticed. Mel Tucker called me over.

"Stop looking at the quarterback, son. He's not throwing you the ball. To close the distance, look at the receiver."

After about fifteen or so reps, Mel asked me to follow him into the part of the facility where the Buckeyes and the staff worked. He pulled up my game tape on a projector and we watched it together. Because I wasn't a top recruit, I knew he didn't know who I was. At that point, I only had an offer for a scholarship to play at Rutgers University—and that was because the head coach, Greg Schiano, only had to travel down the street to watch me play. Rutgers Stadium is located in Piscataway.

According to Rivals.com and all the other recruiting services, out of a five-star rating, I was a one-star recruit. I wasn't even rated in the top sixty players in New Jersey, let alone the country. After watching a few of my games and some plays and talking me through my ability to tackle, that's when Tucker told me that I might be "the best corner in the country."

Now, because I had no dreams of playing college football and wasn't there to earn a scholarship, I wanted to look at him and say, "What are you smoking?" I just loved to compete and couldn't stand that these Ohio boys treated us Jersey boys like we couldn't ball. But by the time the camp was over, Mel and Jim assured me that I'd have a scholarship offer by the time I got back to Jersey. And when we pulled up to the house on Third Street, there was the FedEx letter sitting on the porch. I smiled ear to ear holding the envelope. I couldn't believe that I just competed myself into a full scholarship at one of the top programs in the country.

As a kid, I watched Randy Moss turn the NFL on its head. I had no idea there'd be a day where I'd line up across from him on Monday Night Football on 3rd and 1. By week 12 of my rookie year, the Saints were undefeated, 10-0. Since that season-opening win against the Lions in week 1, we'd been on a monstrous run. The only two teams who were undefeated at that point were us and the Indianapolis Colts. Even though I returned to playing special teams after that Megatron play, I was determined to make sure that my presence was felt. After that game, I responded with back-to-back weeks of forcing turnovers on special teams.

For context, a player on special teams can go their entire career without two takeaways. I did it in back-to-back weeks. This earned me a lot of respect from my teammates and coaches. That patience was rewarded when I got my first start weeks later against Tampa Bay, where I snagged my first interception—adding three turnovers to my stat sheet.

Part of the reason I was lined up against Randy was because all three starting corners—Jabari Greer, Tracy Porter, and Randall Gay—were out with injuries. We signed Green Bay Packers veteran corner Mike McKenzie and former first-round pick Chris McAlister to play against Tom Brady, Randy Moss, and Wes Welker.

Now, Mike McKenzie was an OG who most people recognized from the long dreads that hung from his helmet. With Mike being signed recently, he didn't know the defense at all. But he didn't need to. All Mike needed to know was if he was playing man or zone. But if you go back and watch that game, and see his hands stretched out to his sides, you'll now know he didn't know what the call was.

For this game, my matchups varied. On certain downs, I played the nickel. On others, I played corner. Gregg and the defensive staff developed a plan to stop Brady: chaos and confusion. To prevent Tom from figuring out the defense, we mixed a combination of zone, man-to-man, three- and four-man rushes, double teams, and singles the entire game.

On this third down, Tom's read told me that he was probably thinking to throw to the rookie who was lined up against Randy Moss. When he snapped the ball, Randy patiently stutter-stepped to the outside of the field, planted his left foot, and crossed back across my face toward the inside of the field. Randy was seemingly open, but I learned to play to my leverage. With help on the inside from safety Darren Sharper, Moss, feeling Sharper drawing near, dropped the ball from Brady—but paid the price anyway. Sharper shot right around Randy's kneecaps, flipping him, and sending a message: no free rides today.

The other matchup I had was Wes Welker—the short, unassuming receiver who would max out the capabilities of his body, outdoing himself with effort and savvy. If you saw him outside of the game, you wouldn't think he was a bona fide NFL receiver. To make reading if he was running short or deep difficult, he ran every route at full speed—and his ability to quickly get in and out of his breaks created the separation he needed to survive in a bigger man's game. My whole plan, which was easier said than done, was to get my hands on him as quickly as possible—while also making him believe that I was covering him one-on-one. There were times I made it seem as though he had beat me to the inside, only for the help to be there, stopping him multiple times on third down.

The plan worked to a T: the defensive line pestered Brady; the coverages and disguises frustrated him, and even when he figured out what we were doing, we won our one-on-one matchups. Mike McKenzie played out of his mind. Barely knowing the playbook, he ended the game with multiple pass deflections, an interception, and a bunch of tackles. I finished the game with eight tackles and one pass deflection in a 38–17 victory over the Patriots.

Walking off that field with that kind of win, we knew not only that this team was legitimate, but that I was also legit.

In an auditorium filled with college football's best players, I was seated next to my parents as a finalist for the Jim Thorpe Award at the 2009 NCAA award ceremony. The Thorpe is awarded to college football's best defensive back—and I was in contention with the hazel-eyed warrior out of the University of Tennessee, Eric Berry, and the hard-hitting safety out of USC, Taylor Mays.

After my junior season, another All-American season—my second in a row—and because I was projected to be a top-fifteen draft pick, I had the chance to go to the NFL, but I opted to stay at Ohio State because I wanted to finish what I had started: I wanted to win a national title; I wanted to graduate; and I wanted to be the best defensive back in college football.

After receiving All-Conference honors my sophomore season and having a good year after my first year as a starter, I felt good about my chances to win the Thorpe. In the quiet moments of the summer, I worked on my craft, running into Mike "Killer" Doss, the legendary safety from the 2002 National Championship team. He was their defensive captain and a well-known legend in the Buckeye community. At that time, he played for the Colts and was back in town to train. After my workout, he approached me.

"What's up, Killer?"

Because he and I both wore #2 he replied, "What up, Deuce?"

Then he asked me a question that sounded almost rhetorical.

"Hey, man, how good do you want to be?"

"I want to be the best."

"All right, follow me."

He took me into the same meeting room that Mel had taken me to, and popped a tape into the projector that wasn't game film; it was practice film from the nineties. The nineties was an era where the Buckeyes had a string of legendary defensive backs like Shawn Springs, Ahmed Plummer, and most notably Antoine Winfield, all of whom made it to the NFL and had dominated in their position as DBs at Ohio State.

Ohio State was known for putting out high-caliber defensive backs on a yearly basis. If I wanted to consider myself one of the greats, I needed to perform at their level. But he didn't show me highlights of their games. He wanted to show me their practice habits. I watched Antoine Winfield, who was shorter than me and weighed less than me, dominate opponents bigger than him. Putting his body on the line and locking down anybody he played against, Winfield treated every rep like it was the game. Watching the tape made me feel like I hadn't accomplished anything.

"Why are you letting Brian Hartline or any of these other receivers on this team catch a ball on you in practice? Why is that acceptable to you? If you want to be great like Antoine Winfield, you've got to do that daily. This is a way of life."

And then Mike asked another question.

"Who's the only player to ever win the Jim Thorpe Award in an Ohio State jersey?"

In all my travels up and down the Buckeyes practice facility, I saw these awards, but never stopped to pay attention to what they meant, or to who won them. But Mike gave me a history lesson then: only one. Antoine Winfield.

"If you want to be the best, this is what it takes."

Since that encounter with Mike, I approached every practice rep and game rep with the Thorpe in mind. And then I got to see the results of those efforts.

"On behalf of the Jim Thorpe family and the Jim Thorpe Association," a voice came through on the microphone, "it is my honor to present this year's Jim Thorpe Award to Malcolm Jenkins, defensive back, the Ohio State University."

Filing into the defensive meeting room on Monday morning to begin week 13, the mood was celebratory. After an overtime victory against the Washington Commanders (who were the Redskins then), we were 12-0. Though we'd won, I'll admit I didn't have the best game. That was my third start and, as I got comfortable, I got more aggressive—which allowed the Washington offense to attack like they'd attacked Jason David months before, with double moves.

Their receivers would give me one move, get me to commit, counter with another, and create the necessary distance for Jason Campbell to throw the ball deep for huge gains. On multiple occasions this happened—and it became clear that it was part of their game plan. But in a late rally and with some great luck, after Drew

Brees threw an interception to one of the Washington defenders, Saints receiver Robert Meachem stripped the defender of the ball and ran it in for a touchdown, tying the game to take us into OT.

Before Gregg Williams began the meeting, defensive captains Jonathan Vilma and Scott Fujita interrupted.

"Gregg, can the coaches step out for a second?"

A man's man, JV commanded the respect of every player, coach, and opponent. Without hesitation, Gregg closed his notebook.

"Coaches, get the fuck out!"

As soon as the door closed behind them, JV snapped.

"Malcolm, you can't play like no fuckin' rookie."

I knew I didn't have a good game, but damn. We were undefeated, on a roll, beating everybody, and now JV was upset because of one close game? But they were dead serious. Linebacker Scott Fujita chimed in.

"We got guys that are injured and you're going to play a significant amount of time for us. We're not dropping our standard just because you're a rookie."

In the league, there's something called the rookie wall. Including a bowl game, the most college games you'll play in the NCAA is twelve. With the transition to the NFL, where even before a season begins you've already played four games, by week 13, the monotony of the process—healing from a game, prepping, playing, and repeating—wears on your wandering mind and fatigued body. But this is no excuse. The defensive captains knew we were only as good as our weakest link. They understood that our secondary was riddled with injuries and, if we wanted the first Super Bowl win in franchise history for this city, everyone else needed to realize that we were our biggest opponent. I wasn't the only one who was put on notice. Two of our defensive linemen, DeMario Pressley and Remi Ayodele, who happened to be the last two to file into the defensive meeting room, and a little too giddy, felt JV's wrath as well.

"And y'all two walk in here like y'all fuckin' own the place. Everybody is here to do what they got to do to contribute for us to win." Then he flipped a chair.

When the meeting was over, I was shook. I lost all the respect I had gained throughout the season with one bad game. They made their point loud and clear: the true measure of a competitor is not by the number of opponents they defeat, but by what they do to surpass what they have already accomplished. With four games left in my first season, I had a lot of work to do.

Here's a quick history lesson: in the United States, two states fought over a strip of land in the middle of the country. Just across the Indiana state border, Michigan and Ohio wanted to claim the same stretch of land that lay at the border of the two states. With the territory being granted to the state of Ohio, and Michigan being granted control of the remainder of the peninsula, the conflict was resolved. But the rivalry between the states persisted.

Winning twelve of his first eighteen games against Michigan, legendary college football coach Woody Hayes turned Ohio State's football program around. When reporters asked Hayes why he went for a two-point conversion late in a 50–14 rout against Michigan in the 1968 National Championship game, Hayes answered, "Because I couldn't go for three."

Michigan responded to this humiliation by hiring the Ohio native and one-time assistant to Woody Hayes, Bo Schembechler, as their head coach the following year. In that '69 season, Hayes brought his same undefeated team back to Ann Arbor, Michigan, sure that they would win, but instead they lost to Schembechler and the Wolverines 24–12. This loss would ignite a legendary decade-long rivalry between Michigan and Ohio State, dubbed "the Ten-Year War."

The week we played Michigan was different. There were three clocks in the Buckeyes facility: one to tell the regular time, the second to tell us how much time we had till kickoff for the next game, and the third counted down the days, hours, minutes, and seconds to the kickoff of the next game we played against Michigan.

This was all a surprise to me the first year. They brought in former Buckeyes coach Earle Bruce, who in his senility ranted for thirty minutes about how we needed to beat "the team up north." Right before kickoff the year before, when we played them in Ann Arbor, NFL running back Eddie George kicked the locker room door with tears in his eyes.

"This is not a game," Eddie said. "This is war."

That year we went into the game the number one team in the country and Michigan was number two—the first time ever in the history of the game. The winner of that game was going to the National Championship. The losers would play the Rose Bowl. This game was also Senior Day for our quarterback, Troy Smith. Not to mention that, the night before, Bo Schembechler had passed away.

I wasn't even from Ohio and hated everything about Michigan. Compared to the raucous Buckeyes fans, their players and fan base struck me as bougie. I imagined Michigan drinking cabernet while our fans pounded Natty Lights. With all the history, hate, and hype that existed between us and them, the only thing left to do was play.

As I scanned the Michigan offense as they lined up in their formation in the first quarter, with the game tied at 7–7, I took a deep breath. I was across from Michigan's star wide receiver, Mario Manningham, who was known for his smooth stride and flawless double moves. At quarterback was the veteran game manager with the no-nonsense face, Chad Henne. And their best player was the baby-faced bowling ball, Mike Hart, their running back who had an equal combination of power and quickness.

When Henne snapped the ball, Manningham bolted to my right and I followed him, only to see Mike Hart, running with the ball, coming back to my left. As the last line of defense, I understood that if I didn't make the tackle, it would be a big gain. To change directions, I planted my foot in the ground, but slipped on the newly sodded turf. Usually when something like the grass comes up from under you, there's an opportunity to beg for the ref to give you a call. But all I heard was Mr. Lester in my head: *No bitch-assness, no excuses, this is the game.*

Regaining my balance, I beelined to the sideline, meeting Hart four yards down the field and throwing everything I had at him, taking him and me well into the sideline. When I got up, I was in a zone. I knew nothing was going to stop me from playing my best game. I also knew Michigan wasn't handing this W to us.

By the end of the third quarter, we were up 35–24. It was third down with one yard to go, with Michigan on the cusp of entering the red zone. Normally on 3rd and 1, teams are conservative, opting to run the ball to get the one yard they need to extend the drive. But something about Manningham's demeanor let me know he was expecting the ball. Studying his film, I knew he loved double moves — and I imagined, against an aggressive corner like myself, they thought they were going to catch me slipping.

So I showed them what they wanted: I gave the illusion that I'm eager to jump one of the short routes. But instead, I played back, staring at Henne, able to watch him as he released the ball. Because he was hit in the motion of throwing, the ball fluttered enough to come maybe two yards back inside, toward me. I took two steps to gather myself and dove, trapping the ball between both of my hands before I hit the ground.

"First down, Buckeyes' ball."

The crowd and sideline erupted. But then, after a play review, the referees determined that, though I had both hands on the ball, too much of the football had hit the ground and they overturned the play.

In a game that will surely go down as the greatest in the history of the rivalry, we found ourselves victorious, 42–39. Even though Mike Hart ran 142 yards for three touchdowns, it wasn't enough to overcome Troy Smith's 316 yards passing for four touchdowns, capping off Troy's Heisman-winning season, and taking us to the National Championship.

In anticipation of students rushing the field, state police swarmed the goalposts when the game clock struck zero. They weren't wrong. Thousands of people rushed the field, making it hard to determine who was who. After we fought our way to the locker room and celebrated, I snuck back out to the field. The state police thought protecting the goalposts prevented fans from taking something with them. Here, they were wrong. As fans drunkenly cheered our second trip to the National Championship game in four years, hundreds departed with big slabs of grass draped over their shoulders like championship belts.

After JV and Fujita called me out, I started two more games before Tracy Porter, Jabari Greer, and Randall Gay all recovered from their injuries. Yet again, I was back on special teams. Although we lost the last three games of the season, finishing with a record of 13-3, we secured the top seed for the playoffs, which meant home field advantage.

But after losing three games straight, followed by a first-round bye in the playoffs, the media wanted to know if we had peaked too early. We put those inquiries to rest when we beat the shit out of Kurt Warner and the Arizona Cardinals in the divisional round, 45–14. We pummeled Kurt all game. He retired following the season.

A week later, we were set to play against Brett Favre and the Minnesota Vikings. When we were younger, Brett Favre was Martin's favorite quarterback, back when Favre still played for the Packers. All these years later, gray hair and all, he was still a gunslinger. But because I strained my hamstring in the Cardinals game the week before, I was forced to sit this one out.

If you would've told me then that the Vikings had 200 more yards than we did, possessed the ball for ten minutes longer, and got twice as many first downs, with Adrian Peterson running for 122 yards and three touchdowns, and that we'd still win, I'd tell you to shut the hell up. But here we were, with two minutes and thirty-seven seconds left in the fourth quarter, tied 28–28, and Brett Favre had the football.

All game they'd marched the ball up and down the field. This drive seemed to be no different. They meticulously drove down the field, arriving at our 33-yard line. If the ball is on the 35, that's about a 52-yard kick for the kicker, which is just within the majority of NFL kickers' range. Anything beyond that is a prayer. With only nineteen seconds left in the game, them in field goal position, us with little time to respond, the game looked like it was all but over. On 3rd and 10, the Vikings came out of a time-out and got a penalty for having twelve men on the field, costing them five yards, and effectively taking them out of field goal range. Now they had to pass.

On 3rd and 15 with nineteen seconds left in the game, Brett Favre threw across his body toward the middle of the field, intended for Sidney Rice. Tracy Porter intercepted the ball instead. The game was going to overtime.

In overtime, we won the toss, and with the game still being sudden death at that point, the first team that scored would win. In a twelve-play drive, Drew marched the ball into field goal territory, setting up our kicker, Garrett Hartley, with an opportunity to win the game. Knowing what we had worked for, all we had done to get here, players on the sideline took knees, held hands, and prayed. Standing a little bit farther away from everyone, my mind drifted to a peculiar place. Well into my rookie wall and exhausted by that point in the season, I thought to myself, *If he misses it, we lose. . . . But our season will be over, and I can get some rest.*

By that point in my life, I had won three state championships in high school, played in two national championships in college, and in my first year in the NFL, we were forty yards from the Super Bowl. I figured championships were easy when you were a winner. I had no idea at that time that reaching another Super Bowl would take me nine years. That guys like Mark Brunell, who played in the NFL for almost thirteen years, had this be the first time he had ever made the playoffs. The thought was a selfish one, and admittedly an ignorant one as well.

Once Hartley's foot contacted the ball, that we were going to the first Super Bowl in Saints franchise history was clear. The stadium erupted. Looking around, you saw people from all races and backgrounds hugging and crying.

But we hadn't just come there to compete in a Super Bowl. We came to win. So, with a deep exhale, I adjusted my perspective.

"Two more weeks it is."

On the opening kickoff of the 2007 BCS National Championship Game against the Florida Gators at the University of Phoenix Stadium (now the State Farm Stadium) in Glendale, Arizona, I was confident we came to handle business and bring the chip back to the city. This close to winning a National Championship, I couldn't help but imagine what the celebration would look like when we arrived back on campus—the banners they'd raise in our honor, our names cemented in history. When our star receiver, Ted Ginn Jr., fielded the opening kickoff, he headed down the middle of the field, jump-cut out of one tackle to his right, and then showed why he was a former star athlete in track by returning the opening kickoff of the game for a touchdown.

During the celebration, our overzealous six-foot-three, 228-pound wide receiver, Roy Hall, jumped on Ted's back in excitement. The weight and angle of Roy's landing torqued Ted's body in an awkward way, breaking his ankle. Our fastest, most electric player was out for the game. What transpired after that was the equivalent to a pack of wolves attacking a fawn.

The Gators' offense opened up the game with twenty-one straight points, scoring on all three of their first three drives. By the time we got to halftime, the score was 34–14. We had fully prepared ourselves to dominate the Florida offense, but something was off in our calculations. Florida's quarterback, Chris Leak, was a pretty boy. The only thing prettier was the way he threw the football. Never taking chances down the field, he dink-and-dunked his way up and down the field, putting up points, and being efficient.

His backup quarterback, Tim Tebow, came in and moved more like a running back than anything else, and changed the pace. Thinking that I was tougher than the quarterback, I threw my 205-pound frame into his. But Tebow was covered in the blood of Jesus. Contact with him felt like running into a bronze statue.

Heading into the locker room at halftime, I scanned my teammates' faces for any signs of hope. There was none to be found. Famously known for his sweater-vest, Jim Tressel was pragmatic. In the locker room he was confident and collected. "If we continue to play one snap at a time," he told us, "we could claw ourselves back in this game."

For me, my motivation came from Troy Smith, our senior captain. From scrapping himself out of the hood in Cleveland to grabbing the Heisman Trophy, Troy was somebody who never backed down from competition. And even though he tried to hide it, I saw in his eyes that he was shell-shocked.

The determining factor that everyone knew would show up in the championship game was the speed of the SEC. But it didn't show up in the receivers; it showed up in their defensive line against our O-line. For a quarterback to effectively scan the field and find open receivers, they need at least three seconds. Even with Troy snapping the ball in the shotgun, by the time the ball reached his hand, the defensive line was on him. Florida sacked Troy five times in the first half.

All this said, we had come too far to quit. But the notoriously cutthroat Urban Meyer ensured that his Gators stayed just as hungry in the second half as they were in the first. For the rest of the game, our offense punted on every drive. By the end of the game, our offense finished with 82 total yards, and three turnovers—and our Heisman-winning quarterback, Troy Smith, who had thrown for over 2,500 yards, thirty touchdowns on the season, finished with four passes for a total of 35 yards. While I had made some big tackles, I gave up a touchdown in a coverage that I thought should've been a double team.

When the clock hit zero, the Gators done whupping our ass, I walked off the field covered in the blue and orange confetti that fell from the top of the stadium.

In a normal NFL game, halftime is about twelve minutes. You take the first three minutes to get some water, take a shit, or see a trainer.

At around the ninth minute, you're listening to the coaches' last-minute adjustments before it's time to return to the field. But in the Super Bowl, halftime is thirty minutes—and it feels like forever. So did the weeks leading up to the Super Bowl.

After the NFC Championship, my hamstring healed up just enough for me to return to special teams. Knowing I'd play in one of the biggest games in the world, my anxiety grew with each passing minute.

Whenever you reach somewhere you've never been, people say, "Act like you've been there before." But besides Randall Gay, who played in Super Bowl XLII with the Patriots the year they lost to the Giants, nobody—from the coaching staff down to the bottom of the roster—had been here before, which meant we weren't taking the conservative route when it came to the game. We were going to shoot all our shots and leave it all on the field. We were the wild bunch from New Orleans who had overachieved all year, a stark contrast to Jim Caldwell and Peyton Manning, who had "been here before" two years prior.

By halftime, we found ourselves down 6–10. Like a cyborg from the future, Peyton Manning called every play at the line of scrimmage. Usually, a coach radios the quarterback what the play is, and the quarterback conveys it to the rest of the team, and they run that play. In Manning's case, *he* was the offensive coordinator—and so far, he'd been killing us.

We went into the game understanding that beating Peyton Manning and the Colts meant taking at least one possession away from him to give to Drew. During that extended halftime, Sean Payton came into the room.

"We're going to start this half kicking off, all right? *Ambush*."

Because we all knew "ambush" was the onside kick play we practiced for two weeks leading up to the game, the locker room erupted.

Our punter and kickoff man, Thomas Morstead, had a special kick that rolled ten yards just beyond the restriction line. If we caught the Colts receiving team off guard, we'd be able to recover the ball before they reacted. If we didn't recover the ball, we'd leave Peyton Manning on a short field, which would likely end in another Colts touchdown, or at the very least a field goal. It was a gutsy play, but hey: no time to be conservative; we'd never been here before.

When we returned to the field, we made sure our body language didn't betray our plan. We lined up like usual, and when the whistle blew, Morstead approached the ball, kicked it on his right side, and it spun like a top right where we knew it would go. This was when two of our special teams players, Chris Reis and Jonathan Casillas, jumped on the football.

We scored after that play, shifting the momentum back to our side. But Manning and the Colts offense were rolling. Going into that game, Gregg had a plan. Knowing that Manning was the most prepared quarterback in the game, Gregg understood we'd have to show Peyton multiple defensive looks early in the game. That changed in the third quarter, ultimately setting up the true defensive schemes that emerged in the fourth quarter.

Manning wasn't the only cerebral player out there. Our middle linebacker, JV, was to our defense what Manning was to his offense. So essentially it went like this: when the teams lined up, Manning would scan the field and see that the defense was better to run against, and he'd tell his team to rearrange their formation, pivoting it to a run play. Manning's audibles worked for a couple drives. Until JV picked up on it.

Once Manning caught on to JV catching on to him, Manning would do what's called a "dummy check." He'd come to the line of scrimmage and yell out some arbitrary words that, to us, signaled he had switched his play. Eventually, JV caught on to that as well—and when Manning would do a dummy check, JV would do his own dummy check—which meant they were both out there shouting words that meant nothing to any of players on the field. Then Manning and JV would just run the original play they had each called.

A few days before the big game, Randall Gay got walking pneumonia. While he had done everything in his power to play, going into the fourth quarter, he checked out—and I checked in. On my very first snap in the fourth quarter, I took my alignment at the nickel, noticing Manning looking directly at me. Never in my life had I been so nervous. This was when I realized that JV had been right in that locker room: there would come a time when this team would have to depend on me and being a rookie wasn't going to be an excuse for why I didn't show up.

The plan Gregg had hatched for the defense in the fourth quarter was complicated. We went from zone to man, then back to zone, then to blitz, then back to zone, switching on almost every play. The game moved so fast, on a couple plays I blitzed when I was supposed to be in zone and was in zone when I was supposed to blitz. But as I got into the groove I caught up, deflecting a pass in the flat, almost getting an interception. With three and a half minutes left in the fourth quarter, we had a 24–17 lead. But Manning looked poised for a comeback.

In the week leading up to the game, I scoured every game that the Colts had played that season to learn their tendencies and favorite plays. So when I saw Reggie Wayne in front of me in the slot and the rookie wide receiver, Austin Collie—who was normally in the slot—lined up outside by the sideline, Tracy Porter and I shot each other a knowing glance.

The Colts had a go-to play we called "the follow." Normally out wide near the sidelines, the Colts offense would position Reggie Wayne in the slot, and then motion Austin Collie to be right behind Wayne. When Manning snapped the ball, Collie ran shallow across the formation, opening a hole in the defense that Wayne worked his way right to. Manning being Manning would then deliver a perfect throw, usually converting on third down. So of course, on third down in the biggest game of the year, this was the play.

When Collie motioned down and ran the shallow, I ran with him, switching off with Tracy. As Manning threw the ball in Wayne's direction I watched as Tracy jumped in front of the route, catching the ball and taking it the distance for a touchdown. I ran behind Tracy down the field as fast as I could. I knew this play had sealed the Super Bowl.

When the game was over and the scoreboard read 31–17, the franchise where our fan base once wore paper bags over their heads that read THE AINTS was now the best team in the world. And then came the confetti that matched the colors of the team I played for.

# 4

# THE PROCESS

*If the people knew how hard I had to work to*
*gain my mastery, it wouldn't seem wonderful at all.*

—MICHELANGELO

In the summer of 2007, three years before I won my first Super Bowl, I became a member of Omega Psi Phi Fraternity, Inc., the first international fraternal organization, founded at Howard University in 1911. After fifty-five days of pledging, I was in the living room of my dean's house, waiting for my first hit. For the uninitiated, a "hit" is a brand, a process where a symbol is permanently burned into your skin. Eager to display my allegiance to an organization that included Langston Hughes, Carter G. Woodson, and Michael Jordan, I wanted the biggest "Ω" on my arm. Knowing that these brands would likely be on the television every Saturday for the upcoming college football games, Jade, whose name in the fraternity was Prime-Time Executioner because of his showmanship and precision, wanted to make sure the hit was perfect.

"You going to have the crispiest hits in the frat."

The key to the perfect hit is making sure that the pressure is evenly applied so that when the scar keloids, it does so at the same depth. You also can't flinch or jump during the process. If you do, your brand will look fucked-up. Forever. To brace myself, I stuck our fraternity's history book under my left bicep. When the iron, which had been manipulated into the Ω, was red-hot, Jade approached me slowly.

"You ready?"

"Let's do this."

"QUE PSI PHI!"

As he methodically rolled the branding iron across my arm, I heard the crackling of my flesh. After four seconds of agony, I felt nothing. And because my line name was "Cover Two"—after the famous defensive formation because there were two of us on line, and I was the tail, doing everything twice—I'm getting two hits. After Jade hit my bicep for a second time, we went out into the parking lot, cranked up George Clinton's "Atomic Dog" on his car radio, and set out a hop.

Before I set off to Ohio State in 2005, my grandmother looked me dead in the eyes.

"Don't bring home no snow bunnies."

Though the high school I'd attended in Piscataway, New Jersey, was diverse, racially speaking, Ohio State seemed the Mecca of white people, and particularly white girls. After just a few weeks of being on campus, one was bent over in my dorm room. This was what being a Black college athlete at a predominantly white institution meant. The white women on campus were willing and eager to help with whatever you needed, whenever.

One day I was enjoying the company of one of the women my teammate had introduced me to when I heard a knock on my door. *What time is it?* Looking at my clock, I realized that it was Joel, a white evangelical campus pastor who hosted weekly Bible study sessions for the team. Because I'd raised my hand during those sessions,

Joel took my curiosity as an invitation to learn my class schedule and attempt, any moment I wasn't in class, to talk to me about Jesus.

"Shhhhhhhh."

As we lay silent, Joel's knocks faded with his departure, leaving me and my company to finish what we had started.

After Florida handed our asses to us in the National Championship, I went into a deep depression. Believing that the loss was God's wrath for me sleeping around, not listening to enough Lecrae, or not being Tim Tebow, I spent most of my time in my off-campus apartment with the lights off.

One day, my short, tomboyish Eritrean friend, Dahlak, hit me up.

"Hey. I think you should get out."

"And go where?"

"There's this probate on campus. I think you'll want to go."

"Why would I want to go to that?"

"There'll be plenty of girls there."

I obliged.

When I entered the auditorium and saw all these Black students in one place, I realized that, because my Ohio State experience up until that point was hanging out with my teammates and the girls who were fans, I knew nothing about the Black student life on campus. Once I encountered it, I felt like Jack the Pumpkin King when he discovered Christmas Town. Not only did Black students pack both levels of the auditorium, but the Black Greek Letter Organizations, also known as the "Divine Nine," lined the room.

Though each organization has a distinct personality and identity, they were created at a time when Black college students wanted social organizations that reflected their experiences and addressed their concerns, and they all share a common goal to educate and uplift members of the Black community: Alpha Phi Alpha (ΑΦΑ) fraternity was started in 1906 at Cornell University; Alpha Kappa Alpha (AKA) sorority was founded in 1908 at Howard University; Kappa Alpha Psi (ΚΑΨ) fraternity was founded in 1911 at Indiana University; Omega Psi Phi (ΩΨΦ) fraternity was founded in 1911 at Howard University; Delta Sigma Theta (ΔΣΘ) sorority was founded in 1913 at Howard University; Phi Beta Sigma (ΦΒΣ) fraternity was founded in 1914 at Howard University; Zeta Phi Beta (ZΦB) sorority was founded in 1920 at Howard University; Sigma Gamma Rho (ΣΓΡ) sorority was founded in 1922 at Butler University; and finally, in 1963, Iota Phi Theta (ΙΦΘ) fraternity was founded at Morgan State College.

At the time, I didn't know any of this shit. All I saw were the dudes with purple shirts and gold boots at the front of the room. They shielded their secret handshake with a brotherly embrace, a huge golden snake draped around the neck of one dude, which complemented his purple shirt. As all the organizations did their distinct chants, a group of Omegas led five men chained at the neck, clad in masks, interlocked in a single-file line, to the stage from the back of the auditorium.

Once the line made it onstage, they proceeded to recite, with precision and unity, Omega Psi Phi's history—which then led into steps and marches, and skits the new inductees created to acknowledge each of the other organizations on campus. The climax of every probate is when the pledges, who spent the past few months sequestered away from the public, are unmasked. When I saw that Devin Walker, a tall, quiet guy with glasses, was an Omega, I thought to myself, *If he can do it, I can, too.* Dahlak sensed my excitement.

"I told you you should come."

A few days after the probate, my grandmother called.

"Have you ever thought about pledging?"

"Well, actually, lately I've been thinking about becoming an Omega."

"Yeah! I was going to suggest pledging Omega because then we could be brother and sister."

"What you mean?"

"You ain't know I'm a Delta?!"

The entire time I knew my grandmother, I never connected that her affinity for elephants was informed by her being a member of Delta Sigma Theta. Her call was the confirmation I needed to pledge Omega Psi Phi.

A year following that fateful call with my grandmother, and two months after I had received my first two hits in the fall of 2007, I, along with all the other Ques, conducted an interest meeting for students who wanted to join the fraternity. An interest meeting provided the opportunity for potential prospects of the fraternity to express intentions. Every interest who attended was asked the same question: "Why do you want to join Omega?"

———

After weeks of Joel's unrelenting effort to talk to me about Christianity, I finally began meeting him in my dorm lobby for forty-five-minute Bible sessions. Though I was skeptical of him at first, he served as a guide to help me make sense of this new world I was looking to understand. When I'd first arrived on campus, I had no idea how intertwined the culture of football was with the Christian faith. Bible study was every Wednesday. A chaplain led us in the Lord's Prayer before and after the game. Whenever a player received an award, the first thing he did was credit his success to God. Because of the intense exposure, I began to correlate my success on the field with the intensity of my faith, leading me to tattoo the only verse I knew by heart on my arm, Psalms 91:4:

"He shall cover thee with his feathers, and under his wings thou shall trust. His truth shall be thy shield and buckler."

Playing a dangerous game in a strange land, the idea that I would always be protected by the truth of our Creator provided me with some solace as a Black man from New Jersey on a football team in a predominantly white school. As weeks passed, and I devoted more time to my meetings with Joel, he asked if I wanted to speak to a congregation about my journey.

"Nah," I responded, thinking about my fear of public speaking and my unease with the proposition. "I'm good."

A week after we asked the fifteen interests why they wanted to join Omega, we selected thirteen from the group who we believed were a good fit. A few weeks after, that thirteen shrunk to seven. In my experience, I learned that our process had one of three effects: it made you quit, turned you into one of those people whose whole identity becomes the letters on their shirt, or it activated your latent potential to show you that the person you wanted to be was already who you were.

When I was on line, we began as five and crossed with two. Though there's not much I'm willing to share about the process itself, I will say I only faced what other men had met.

A few weeks after I told Joel I was good on speaking in front a congregation, I was sitting in the front row of a church, going over what I wanted to say. When I told him I didn't know enough Bible verses to speak, he assured me that I didn't need to be a pastor.

"Just go up there and share your testimony of how you came to Christ."

Standing in front of the podium I realized that, apart from the few Black folks peppered in the audience, the congregation was entirely white. And even from a distance, I could also tell that the Black folks present were the kind that were comfortable in white spaces, something that eludes me to this day.

To reflect on my relationship with religion in general, and Christianity in particular, I didn't grow up in a practicing Christian household. Besides the occasional visit to Sunday services, we were Christians by culture. In my freshman year of high school, I remember filling out some form. When I reached the part of the questionnaire that asked for my religious affiliation, I leaned over to my friend Tiffany.

"Hey, what do I put here?"

She looked at me like I was stupid.

"Christian, duh."

That was my introduction to Christianity. With my relationship to this religion shaky at best, here I was in Columbus, Ohio, about to tell this congregation how Jesus changed my life. When they introduced that a member of the Ohio State Buckeyes was there to share a word, a standing ovation ensued. With the eyes of the congregation locked in, I cleared my throat and repeated a story I all but knew the people in this church were going to call bullshit on. But when I finished, people cheered and clapped, and praises to Jesus rang out.

Once the service ended, a line of people formed to greet me, thanking me for my testimony, telling me how my words changed their life, and how my words prompted them to give their lives to Jesus that day. I looked over to Joel, who smiled approvingly.

"You did good."

A probate signifies the end of the process and presents the newest members to the student body, their friends, and family members. New members are showered with gifts and paraphernalia, but because I pledged in the summer, I didn't have a probate.

Not yet a member of Omega when I was shown to campus, I was considered a "lamp" seeking the Shekinah light of Omega. I didn't have gold boots, purple shirts, and wasn't yet allowed to throw up the hooks. Still, my line brother and I were able to participate in the other parts of the pageantry—reciting our information, our poetry and, lastly, the steps and strolls.

The night of my lamp show, in 2007, Jim Tressel scheduled a team bowling event that was mandatory for everyone to attend. When I arrived at the team facility for workouts the next day, I was greeted by my defensive back coach, Taver Johnson, who intercepted me in the hallway with an angry whisper.

"Why didn't you tell me you were joining a frat?!"

Uncertain about Tressel's stance on football players joining fraternities, I figured I'd rather ask for forgiveness than permission.

"Well, Tressel wants to talk to you in his office."

When I got to Tressel's office, he told me to come in and sit down.

"Q Dog, huh?"

Expecting him to say the proper name of the fraternity, that he knew the frat's vernacular both shocked and impressed me.

"Hmm, I'm a fraternity man myself."

Tressel's sweater-vests and buttoned-up demeanor made it difficult for me to envision him as a frat boy. Sharing that joining Alpha Tau Omega (ATΩ) was one of the best decisions of his life, he confided that he'd learned more from his fraternity than he had from any class he'd taken. While I'm sure he said some great things about his experiences, my mind was preoccupied with whether I was in trouble or not; and I wasn't.

When I joined my teammates at workout, our team captain and fullback, Dionte Johnson, pulled me to the side.

"Man, why you ain't telling me you were joining?"

Remembering he was at the same probate I was when I decided to become a Que, I answered in the form of an invitation.

"I didn't know you were interested, but you can still get down."

---

Months after I delivered my testimony to that all-white congregation, Joel shared that, due to a mission, he and his wife were moving. I couldn't tell you where he said he was moving to; what I could tell you was the wave of relief that washed over me when I heard the news. In the last few months, I had spoken at four more churches, and even though my ability to speak about my faith in front of crowds improved, being paraded in white spaces took its toll.

"Well," I began, not wanting anything that I might say to change his mind, "you got to follow God where God takes you."

Before I walked away, Joel informed me that the team chaplain, Tom, would keep in touch to make sure my walk with God continued. I almost took the Lord's name in vain. Tom was part of Athletes in Action, a global sports ministry organization that used sports as a platform to spread the Gospel of Jesus Christ. Just as patient and persistent as Joel was, because Tom wore hearing aids in both ears, I sometimes suspected he pretended not to hear me when he'd asked me to speak at churches and I told him no.

Over the next few years, Tom organized me and a handful of my teammates, like James Laurinaitis and Marcus Freeman, to speak at almost a dozen different churches; all of them with white congregations. While I believed in the work that I was doing, I wanted to worship with people who looked like me.

This prayer would be answered when a good friend of mine, Ashley, invited me to her church one Sunday. Pulling in to the parking lot of New Birth Christian Ministries, I immediately noticed the difference. At the white churches I spoke at, no one wore their Sunday best. Everyone's attire was casual—sundresses, plaid button-ups, and, when they knew we'd be there, Ohio State jerseys. New Birth was full of folks dressed to the nines, and unlike the other churches, no one cared I was there. That alone made me want to break out into a praise dance.

When we stepped into the house of worship, the hum of the instruments and the rhythm of the choir moved me to tears. Besides joining Omega, discovering Black student life in the process, this was the first time I felt safe from the white world I was thrust into. Another key difference between New Birth and the white churches I attended was the length of the services. A service at every white church I visited lasted an hour fifteen tops. An hour into this service and they had only finished the church announcements.

Then the church's pastor, Kenneth E. Moore, a short, brown-skinned brother in a sharp three-piece suit and with an even sharper message, took the podium. He had a gift for breaking down passages that were hard for me to decipher and made them simple. In a congregation of what was at least three hundred, I felt like Pastor Moore preached directly to me. After two and a half hours, drained from worship but refreshed from the word, Ashley turned to me.

"I told you my pastor was good."

In March 2008, two months after the interest meeting where the fifteen men showed up, we crossed our line of seven men into the ranks of Omega. With this being the largest pledge line we'd had since before I arrived as a freshman, we ran the yard.

To fundraise for breast cancer awareness, we organized a powder-puff football tournament where players from the women's basketball team, track team, and the sororities from the Divine Nine paid to compete against one another. Every year we held an event called

"Sex, the Bruhs and You," where we educated students on campus about sexual safety. One of the brothers, who was a principal at Beechcroft High School in Columbus, brought us to his campus to mentor the young men who showed promising characteristics. And just as hard as we went in the community, we went hard for our parties. At our peak, we charged guys $40 to get in, and because it was worth it, they paid. Women always got in for free.

We always put a bruh at the door who was big enough to control the crowds of men who thought they could get in without paying, and who had no problem telling people no. The "neophytes," brothers who just crossed the fraternity, were assigned to greet visiting brothers and give them VIP treatment.

Because the kitchen is the place where everyone usually congregates at house parties, bruhs were stationed there to keep the traffic flowing by preparing plates of food and pouring cups of "Omega Oil," our version of jungle juice.

Then there were the bruhs who made sure everyone had a good time. That meant diffusing any tensions, de-escalating fights, ensuring the women enjoyed themselves, particularly the women who held sway over the other women in their friend group. If they didn't enjoy themselves and were ready to go, then every woman with them followed. Those women who had that power were our priority. Alternating between the role of kitchen and floater, I would often identify who those women were and give them the lustiest lap dance I could summon. It would be on this same night that I received my next and last two hits. This time on my chest. Honoring my line number, which was also my jersey number at OSU, and my line name, "Cover Two," I got a 2, housed by the symbol that helped me find my family in my home away from home.

## 5

# FINISH

*Sometimes things can go right only*
*by first going very wrong.*
**—EDWARD TENNER**

I t's May 2010, only a few months after the Super Bowl, and the off-season program has already begun. As I get up to walk out of the final defensive meeting of the day, defensive back coach Dennis Allen tells me, "Hey, Sean wants to holler at you in his office real quick."

The coaches' offices were located on the top floor of the building, away from all the areas the players frequented. Up until now, I'd never been upstairs in the Saints facility. It felt like I was going to the principal's office. Unless you were Drew Brees, if Sean wanted to talk to you, it normally wasn't good. I racked my brain trying to figure out what it could be about.

I had an up-and-down rookie season. I was productive in the small roll I had, but I wasn't able to consistently crack the starting lineup. And in my mind, as a first-round draft pick, I was beginning to feel like a bust. I knew the expectations for me were high, but nobody had expectations as high as I had for myself, and I definitely hadn't met them.

I walked through the locker room, up the steps, and the very first office on the second floor of the facility was Sean's office. I went in and took a seat. Sean, not one to tiptoe around feelings, got right to it.

"I wanted to let you know we're going to move you to safety. Look, Sharper is starting the season on PUP, and won't be ready until, the earliest, week six, and we're looking for a way to get you on the field. You played some safety in college, and the reason we drafted you was for your versatility."

In that moment, I had to be real with myself. Jabari Greer was playing great. He had better technique and was quicker than I was.

Tracy Porter was superproductive and single-handedly vaulted us to and through a championship. I likely wasn't going to jump in front of all those guys in an offseason. So if I wanted to play, I needed to embrace the new role.

Though I was mainly a corner in college, there were times during my senior year when I was placed at safety to help the defense. I was productive at the position, snagging two interceptions from the spot, but I hated it. Safeties are the quarterbacks of the defense, in charge of making all the communications to the other defenders on the field. They tell everyone where to align and what to play. Meaning, safeties usually need to be good leaders and quick thinkers.

The cornerback position is one that relies heavily on athleticism, technique, and speed, having to stay step for step with the offense's best athlete, while sometimes moving backward. While it helped to be intelligent, it wasn't a prerequisite for success. Coming out of Ohio State as highly decorated as I was, a Jim Thorpe Award winner, I absolutely loved the challenge of being one-on-one with the other teams' best wideout. It was more valuable to be confident than intelligent, and I was both!

There was a ton of debate on whether I was fast enough to play corner at the next level. Or if I'd be better suited for the safety position. I always pushed back against that, because frankly, corners got paid more.

For instance, in 2009, Nnamdi Asomugha became the highest-paid corner in the league when he landed a contract that paid out about $15 million a year. Antrel Rolle became the highest-paid safety in the league's history at that time, making $7.5 million per year.

Having a corner that can take out the opposition's top wideout is a premium for any defense. The GOAT, Deion Sanders, aka Prime-time, or Prime for short, one of the best overall athletes to ever put on an NFL uniform, was the gold standard of the position. Many questioned my athletic ability and it didn't bother me one bit. I blocked it out. But Deion's voice jumped over my wall of defense and burrowed in my brain. After running a 4.51 at the NFL Scouting Combine, a bit slow for your ideal corner, who should be running anywhere between 4.4 seconds and 4.3 seconds, Deion made a comment saying that I would likely be a safety in the NFL. I was crushed.

I didn't care what a scout with a clipboard had to say about me. But coming from someone who has done it at the highest level and was arguably the best to ever do it, that carried real weight. I tried to brush it off. I figured he was just hating because I declined to attend his pre-Combine training sessions for defensive backs. He called it Prime U, a school for the defensive backs looking to vault themselves into the NFL.

I didn't decline for any other reason, than I had promised my mother that I would graduate college. So I trained at Ohio State while I finished up my final quarter of school. I sat back and listened to him hype up the guys he trained that I knew weren't better than me. And his words in particular haunted me my entire rookie season as I struggled to crack the lineup. I knew that I had what it takes to play corner in the NFL, but I couldn't let my ego blow an opportunity to get on the field.

The safety position didn't offer any guarantees, either. Darren

Sharper was one of the best and most productive safeties to ever play the game and was coming off an All-Pro season with nine interceptions. He was our best defensive back by far, even though he was heading into his fourteenth season. If he returned at even half of himself, he'd likely be the starter, and I'd be back to playing a small role as a backup. I was stuck between a rock and a hard place, and chose the hard place.

I nodded and said, "Okay. Whatever it takes to get on the field. I just want to play." Even if that meant that Deion and everyone else who called it would be right. I was encouraged that Sean was still excited about me as a player and didn't consider me a bust just yet.

I got up, shook his hand, and headed out of his office with my pride in my throat.

It was a few weeks before my birthday in early December of my rookie season when my phone rang in the middle of the day. It was my grandmother. I was at the Saints training facility watching film and killing time between meetings. She'd been calling me every week since the beginning of the season to ask how I was doing and to tell me that "the Saints are going to win the Super Bowl."

I figured this was just one of those calls. I always met her faithful optimism with superstitious caution. I didn't want her to jinx it. Plus, I knew that there were a lot of games we needed to win first before we ever made it to the Super Bowl, let alone won it, and I wanted to focus on one game at a time. Her words had become kind and soft.

She was done teaching me lessons and was now my biggest fan, and our conversations felt more like that of siblings or friends than grandma and grandson. She loved telling me how proud she was of me. I answered the phone, looking forward to hearing her usual giddiness. After the week I was having, I needed it. "Hey, Grandma, how are you doing?" This time her mood felt colder. I could hear the concern in her voice.

"Not so good," she said.

"What's wrong?"

"Well, my throat has been really bothering me lately, so I went to the doctor to get it checked out and they did a scan to see what was wrong and they found cancer on my pancreas."

I wanted to throw my phone across the room. It was the last thing I wanted to hear and something I surely wasn't expecting.

"Noooooo," I responded, hoping my rejection of the news would make it not real. I had no clue where the pancreas was or what it did, but I knew it wasn't near the throat. The word "cancer" alone scared me enough. My parents once thought that I had cancer. During my freshman year of high school, after injuring my arm in a practice, I suddenly, over the course of a few days, began to lose the range of motion in my right arm. I couldn't straighten it fully. I continued to play ball with it stuck in a bent position, but eventually figured that it wasn't a normal injury.

My parents took me to a local clinic to get X-rays. The X-rays showed a mass about the size of a silver dollar growing inside my forearm up near my elbow. They didn't know what it was. They said we needed to see a specialist, so my parents took me to the Children's Hospital of Philadelphia. I thought nothing of it as we drove down the New Jersey Turnpike to Philly. I was only concerned about how much time I might have to miss during the season. "Myositis ossificans," the doctor said as we sat in his office. I felt like he was speaking another language. It's a very unique condition, when there's enough trauma to the soft tissue that the blood pools and begins to calcify, creating a bone-like structure in the middle of your muscle. That's what was happening, and he said I needed to get it surgically removed. I had never broken a bone and was concerned about having to get surgery, but my parents seemed oddly relieved. When we got in the car after the diagnosis and headed back to New Jersey, my mom called Barbra over the car's speakerphone.

"Hello?"

"It's not cancer!"

My grandmother praised the Lord.

"Thank you, Jesus!"

"Cancer?!"

The original doctor from the clinic had told my parents that it was likely cancer, but nobody had told me a thing. I just thought we were going to the CHOP to see what was wrong with my arm. My grandmother had been praying for me incessantly. When we went back for my follow-up to do the surgery, my doctor was amazed that the condition had corrected itself. The bone that was growing in my forearm had dissolved and was no longer there and my arm was back to normal like nothing had happened. Apparently it is a rare occurrence for such a condition to correct itself, and the doctor from CHOP wanted to do a study on it, but my parents, only caring that it wasn't cancer, never brought me back.

As I racked my brain for ways I could help my grandmother, I figured the cure for cancer or any ailments would be to pray it away, and that's exactly what I was going to do!

Barbra wouldn't let me feel pity for her; she, not surprisingly, was going to fight this. She didn't seem too discouraged or worried. I assured her that if there was anything that she needed, I had her back.

"I got you. You've always had my back, so now I've got yours."

"I know, sweetheart."

We talked for a few more minutes before I had to run to my next meeting. Before I got off the phone, she informed me that she wasn't going to start her treatments until after February. "Wait, what? Why are you going to wait so long?" Her last line of the conversation was

"Because. Y'all are going to win the Super Bowl and I'm going to be there."

I was glad at that moment that I didn't know much about pancreatic cancer, because had I known that pancreatic cancer is one of the deadliest forms of cancer with only 10 percent of those diagnosed surviving five or more years past the diagnosis, who knows how I would've taken that news. But instead I went back to the meetings, scared for Barbra, but optimistic that it wasn't her time just yet.

It was week 6 of the season after that meeting with Sean. We were playing against the Buccaneers with just over thirty seconds left in the third quarter. As I ran toward Kellen Winslow, the star tight end for the Buccaneers, who had just caught a pass and was now turning to run up the field, Jabari Greer tackled him for a seven-yard gain. But Jabari didn't get up right away. He'd injured his shoulder.

It was official. I was now a safety. My ego took another blow a month later when the Saints drafted my replacement with the first-round pick, cornerback Patrick Robinson out of Florida State. He had everything you'd want in a corner. Fast, instinctual, and could accelerate out of a break faster than anyone I'd ever seen. His addition to the roster essentially cemented my move to safety.

Sean Payton had a saying, "The more you can do." Meaning the more that you can do, the more valuable you are to the organization, and the harder it is for them to get rid of you. The injury rate is a hundred percent in the NFL, meaning every single player who plays will get hurt at some point in their career. It's an inevitable part of the game. So if you're a guy who can play multiple positions and contribute on special teams, and stay relatively healthy, you are like gold. They'd have to sign three guys in order to replace you. And because

I was the only one in the secondary that had reps at safety, corner, and nickel, I was always the first to change positions when injuries happened.

All offseason in training camp, I studied my ass off and trained my body for the new role. The position brings with it more collisions, usually from farther distances, meaning more damage to the body. I had to bulk up a bit to make sure I would withstand the demands, putting on about five pounds of muscle.

Playing safety felt like someone inverted the controls on my joystick. Everything was different. The angles of the game were all wrong. Playing on the edges of the field as a corner meant you always attacked the football from the outside in, but playing safety from the middle of the field meant attacking the ball from the inside out, the emphasis being on your ability to tackle and less about your ability to cover. I was used to playing a game that was just me against the receiver, and now I was twenty yards deep, seeing the whole formation and having to operate in wide-open spaces. Mistakes at the safety position are devastating for the defense.

The safety is the last line of defense. My natural tendency to gamble didn't fit the position. Early in camp and in the first few games of the season, I gave up a handful of plays trying to make something happen. It was boring to me. Playing so far away from the ball meant I rarely saw action, and if I did, it was in a dire situation.

But as the weeks went on, I got the hang of it, and I was getting better every week. It was week 6, and Darren Sharper was due to return the following week. I was feeling pressure to have a breakout game. I'd yet to get an interception on the stat sheet, and in my mind, that was the only measure of a DB's impact on the game.

I almost picked off Brett Favre in week 1, leaping up into the air and plucking the ball out of the sky, but wasn't able to get both feet inbounds when I landed, and I hadn't been close since. I'd been trying to fill Sharper's shoes, a tall task seeing how he had five interceptions and two touchdowns by this time last season.

We're beating the Buccaneers 24–0, and now due to Jabari's injury I'd be playing both safety and nickel, depending on the defensive package Gregg decided to put on the field. The score dictated that the Buccaneers needed to pass the ball in order to move it quickly down the field to score and they put in more wideouts, which we matched with more defensive backs. As soon as I moved to the nickel, I was immediately more productive. The game had been pretty slow, but right out of the gate, I was making plays.

In Gregg's simple but effective Cover 2 defense, the nickel was a player with very little responsibility. All I needed to do was follow whatever the quarterback did. When he dropped back, I dropped back. When he set up to throw, I set my feet to break. And wherever his intentions were, that's where I went. I mirrored the quarterback's intentions.

Josh Freeman liked to stare at his throws, making him easy to read. And as he dropped back I saw him staring at the wideout to the right of me. I broke, getting to the receiver right as the ball did. He caught it, but before he could hit the ground after our collision, I ripped it from his grasp. It fell to the ground and I immediately scooped it up. The refs on the field called it a fumble, but upon further review, they reversed the call to an incomplete pass.

The next drive, Cover 2 was called again. Josh Freeman dropped back and I backpedaled a couple of steps. When he set his feet to throw, I planted my feet to break. My cue to go was when he took his hand off the football, indicating that he was about to throw. I saw the hand and I triggered, and now it became a race between me and the football. I got there faster than I'd intended, sticking my left arm out to knock the ball down, and instead of hitting it with my hand, I knocked it down with my forearm. I clapped my hands in frustration, knowing that had been an opportunity to grab an interception. I wasn't used to being that close to the ball, and underestimated my own abilities, but nonetheless it was a stop, and we got off the field.

On 3rd and 10, the call was Cover 2 once again. I dropped back in my zone. As I tracked Freeman's eyes, I could tell that there were no wideouts open, and he began to run around the left side of our defense. I took off at full speed, in hot pursuit. Like a heat-seeking missile, I'd made up my mind as I approached. If he tried to get even an extra inch on the sideline, I was going to make him "pay the toll," as Gregg put it.

We had been brainwashed to defend every blade of grass, and like a monkey freshly sprayed with cold water, I was enthusiastically compliant. He took two extra toe taps up the field, forfeiting his opportunity to safely step out-of-bounds, and I launched myself at his legs. By the time he'd thought he'd sidestepped out-of-bounds to safety, I'd already left my feet, striking him in his knees as he stepped onto the white paint.

Flags flew everywhere. Josh immediately sprinted right at me and confronted me. I knew that if someone did that to Drew on our sideline, there was no way they'd make it back to theirs in one piece. So, in the same way I stood waiting for shit to pop off at the park with Hakeem, I walked away from the sideline, ready to swing on the first person that touched me. That person was Freeman, who grabbed my shoulder to have a few words. I didn't wait to hear what he had to say before hitting him with a quick openhanded jab to his face mask.

I knew it was a bit cheap. I hadn't hoped to hurt him, but I had intended to send him a message. A message to him and to anyone else who would see the film, that those extra yards that you try to get come at a cost, so tread lightly. The refs penalized me with two personal fouls on the same play, totaling in thirty yards for the Buccaneers, and a fat $10,000 fine for me the next week.

A few plays later, now with our backs against the goal line, Gregg sent me on a blitz off the left edge of the defense, hitting running back Cadillac Williams in the backfield and stopping him for a loss, on a crucial 3rd and goal.

But the Bucs went for it on fourth down and scored. I was pissed, because my overaggressiveness cost us the shutout we were aiming so hard to get. It's extremely hard to hold an NFL offense scoreless in a game and I had just blown our chance. Gregg, while encouraging us to play with tenacity and violence, always cautioned us.

"Live on the edge, play on the edge, but never hurt the team."

Even if it had no effects on the outcome of the game, thirty yards of penalties in one play hurt the team. It hurt my pockets more than anything. That would be the last bit of fight the Bucs had.

Late in the game, up 31–6, I still hadn't gotten my interception. The Bucs replaced Josh Freeman with the backup quarterback, trying to preserve Freeman's health, and Gregg moved me back to corner. I guess they wanted to get me more reps in case I also needed to move back to the corner spot with any other injuries. On 3rd and 21, with only a few seconds left in the game, I wanted to take advantage of the young quarterback.

The call was Cover 2 again, but as the corner that put me as the farthermost outside underneath player, with no deep responsibility. I saw the wideout running about twenty-one yards deep, sitting right on the sideline. I purposely left just a little bit of space between us to bait the QB, giving the illusion that the wideout was open. When he threw the ball, I sank back two more steps and launched myself into the air.

*Here it is! My first pick of the season!* I thought to myself as I watched the ball come in my direction. The quarterback, knowing that he was trying to fit the ball into a tight window, threw it as hard as he could, and the inertia of the ball blasted right through the grips of both my hands, right in front of our bench. As the ball hit the ground, I heard the entire sideline groan in disappointment.

After the game, my teammates had a good laugh about it on the plane ride home, as Gregg Williams's reaction was caught by one of the sound booms on the sideline meant to grab the sounds of the game for the TV viewers at home.

"You no-catching motherfucker!"

While the jokes were funny, and I had a good laugh at it, I didn't think it was a game. Still trying to find my way and my footing in the NFL, my confidence was fragile, and another week went by without an interception. As I loved playing the nickel, and believed it just might be the best spot for me, not all was lost.

Time was running low in our week 12 matchup against the Dallas Cowboys, and I could feel the frustrations beginning to build in the veteran players. With every minute that melted off the clock, the opportunities to win this game faded. After the game in Tampa, Sharper came back, but his injured knee wasn't all the way ready to take over a full workload. I continued to play well, so the coaches decided to keep me as the starter and bring Sharper in only in 3rd down situations. The next two weeks, I'd have eleven tackles and three pass breakups, until I was sidelined with a hamstring injury week 9 against the Panthers. That put me out for two weeks. But luckily, one of those weeks was a bye week and so I missed only one home game, against the Seattle Seahawks. But with me out, that meant Darren Sharper's role was elevated and he had to come back before his knee was truly ready, and once again he went out, needing to rest his swelling knee.

We were the defending Super Bowl champions with a record of 7-3, and we'd got the Dallas Cowboys on Thanksgiving. For as long as I can remember Thanksgiving is meant for food, family, and football.

The Dallas Cowboys and the Detroit Lions were a staple at the dinner table. Since 1978, the Cowboys and the Lions have always hosted games on Thanksgiving Day, and there was another rotating prime-time game that started in 2006. I can remember watching the legendary running backs Barry Sanders, for the Lions, and Emmitt Smith, for the Cowboys, on the television as the adults in my family cheered loudly.

Even in high school, we'd have an annual Thanksgiving Day matchup against our town rivals, the Franklin Warriors. Those games felt special knowing everyone in the town was in the stadium watching you play on a holiday. This stage was a thousand times greater than my small township games; the whole nation was watching. At halftime, we were up 20–6 on the Cowboys in front of a packed stadium. Our offense had no problem putting up points, and our defense was holding strong. I don't know what Jerry Jones said to them at halftime, but when they came back out, their defense was on fire and shut our offense out in the third quarter, while their offense got it going. We collapsed in the third quarter and the Cowboys took the lead with just six minutes left in the game, 27–23.

As the clock melted away, you could hear the tension in the crowd beginning to rise, knowing that the Cowboys were getting closer and closer to a Thanksgiving Day victory. With 3:18 left in the game, the Cowboys had the ball, trying to close it out, when their quarterback, Jon Kitna, threw a short slant to wide receiver Roy Williams, who was being covered by rookie Patrick Robinson. P Rob got turned around and fell, leaving Williams, in full stride, running right down the middle of the defense. Right where I was supposed to be. But, still getting used to the angles and still feeling like my controllers were inverted, I took a horrible angle and had to slam on the brakes and change direction as Williams crossed my face with the football. I accelerated and began to chase Williams as he crossed midfield, closing in on the end zone. I ran faster and faster. If they scored, it would likely seal the game. Tracy was also in hot pursuit, on Williams's right, and even though he was blocked by another Cowboy, he held Williams's attention. Williams didn't feel me as I quickly ran up on his left side, where he held the ball. I cruised up next to him and I threw my left hand onto the ball and ripped it backward toward my body, separating it from his grasp and pinning it to my stomach. While the play started off about as bad as it could be, I had just turned bad to outstanding. Saints ball! With three minutes left from the minus-11-yard line, and down four points. It was time for Drew and our offense to bring it home.

Even though they hadn't scored a point so far in the second half, we all knew that if Drew had the ball in his hands with time on the clock, he was as good as anybody in the history of the game at finishing. And like clockwork, Drew marched the ball down the field with precision passes, finishing the drive with a pass over two defenders to wide receiver Lance Moore, who hit his routine, preplanned touchdown dance. The smoothest heel-toe I've seen since the early 2000s. The drive took only about a minute off the clock, and the Cowboys would have more than enough time for a last-minute drive.

Kitna marched the ball down the field with the drive stalling out at around the 41-yard line, and the Cowboys opted to kick a 59-yard field goal. Right before the snap, Sean Payton called a time-out at the last second, trying to ice the kicker, but cut it too close and the refs didn't stop the play. A blessing in disguise because the ball, originally on track, started to slowly drift wide left, giving us the win, and shocking the home crowd.

In the locker room, I was given a game ball and credited with being the cause of what would be called the Thanksgiving Day Miracle for years to come. For the first time, I saw that I could affect the outcome of the game without intercepting the ball. The play would be a textbook example of the age-old cliché: it's not how you start, but how you finish. Effort and finish had become my most consistent attributes. Sitting in my locker for the first time, I felt like I had earned the trust and respect of my draft status.

My promising 2010 season came to a disappointing end in the last regular-season game against the Tampa Bay Buccaneers when I was forced out of the game with a knee injury. About a month later, I stood in front of the mirror in the bathroom of my two-bedroom condo on Tchoupitoulas Street, hyping myself up. *Let's go. Let's do this shit!* as if it were game time. But I wasn't getting ready to play, I was preparing to propose to Morrisa.

I met Morrisa on Facebook my senior year at Ohio State. When I got to New Orleans she was a short drive up the road at the University of Southern Mississippi. At that point, we'd dated for a year. She was kind, caring, and with all the demands of a professional athlete, made my life easier. Also, with long thick legs, high cheekbones, and full lips, she was absolutely stunning and I was ready to take our relationship to the next level. I'd invited my parents, Mo's parents, and other members of her family down to New Orleans to surprise her with the question.

I'd mapped out the logistics for months. I'd reached out to Ralonda and Kelly, other friends I've known since high school, to help me shop for a ring. I'd bought the ring months ago. It had six and a half carats of diamonds embedded in it. Anchored by a three-carat, table-cut diamond of perfect quality, and split into two bands that held twenty other diamonds, totaling about another three and a half carats.

For months Mo had told me she wanted a dog, so I consulted with another friend on how to get a small Maltese Yorkie shipped to New Orleans. Picking it up earlier that day, I carefully fastened the ring to its collar. It's embarrassing thinking back on how corny this sounds now but, between focusing on football and doing things I *thought I was supposed to*, I wasn't the most creative guy at the time.

To make sure I had his blessing to take his only daughter's hand in marriage, I had already spoken to Mo's father, Eddie, a simple man who's as country as they come. As he waved to the cars that passed by every five minutes or so, we sat on his front porch drinking Bud Lights. Comfortable sitting in silence with no radio and barely any words, when he did speak I needed subtitles to translate his thick Mississippi mumbles. The only thing thicker than his accent was his mustache; Drake's dad level.

"Y'all want to get married, huh?"

His only concern was that he wanted Mo to finish school. I had moved Mo to New Orleans and was helping her go through the steps to become a prosthetist.

Her mom, Marian, a Delta, and a retired teacher, is the spitting image of Mo; tall, beautiful, she changes her hairstyles more than a woman in witness protection. She was excited to see her only daughter be married off.

My father, not one to give much advice, only asked if I was sure, and when I said I was, his only warning was "It takes work, but if you're sure, and you love her, that's all that matters."

My mother, on the other hand, was a lot more cautious. Having met Mo on more than one occasion, when I expressed to her that I was going to ask for her hand in marriage, she looked worried.

"Are you sure? That is a big commitment, Malcolm."

Telling me things like "It takes work" or "It's hard" sounded more like challenges than warnings, and I embrace challenges. I've had to defy people telling me what I couldn't do my whole life. With a decision this big it was probably not the best way to frame it because I was likely to do it just to prove to you that I could. If all it took was hard work, then I'd be fine. I love hard work.

My mom followed up with "I don't know. I just don't feel like I know anything about her." That was confusing to me because my mom had met her on multiple occasions, and I even made sure to set aside time for both of them to talk alone. I couldn't understand how she could say she didn't know Mo, and I chalked it up to the cautions of an overly concerned mother.

When I came out of the bathroom, the entire family was situated in the kitchen, along with Morrisa. I tapped her on the shoulder and said, "Hey, I got you something." She turned around and I presented her with the puppy. I was so nervous that I forgot to give the dog a bath. I hadn't even gotten a leash yet, but she'd gotten what she wanted. As she turned around to all the oohs and aahs to show off the dog to her family, I got down on one knee. In my haste I knelt on the knee that was injured, still swollen and sore from the game a month prior. It was too late now, so I gritted my teeth and tried to breathe through the pain. I was down there for what seemed like forever, until her mother, seeing that Mo hadn't noticed the big-ass ring on the dog's collar, moved things along.

"What's that on its neck?"

Mo noticed the ring and turned around.

"Will you marry me?"

While damn near choking the puppy, Mo broke out in Viola Davis tears, nodding her head while saying yes. Bringing relief to my knee and the dog, I stood up and kissed her. We popped bottles of champagne and toasted. With my chef there, both families broke bread, and drank wine all evening.

The first person I shared the news with was Barbra. Though almost a year out from her diagnosis, and still fighting strong, the cancer hadn't slowed down and the treatments took their toll. She couldn't travel like she wanted to. I knew this news would cheer her up.

"Grandma, she said yes!"

A screech came from the other end of the line.

"I'm so proud of you, Malcolm."

---

At 9-3 in week 13, I watched from the sidelines as James Laurinaitis shot through the offensive line and made a tackle in our backfield on the opening drive of the game. We were playing the St. Louis Rams and had the second-best record in the NFC, only behind our division rival, the Atlanta Falcons. Our offense was putting up 389 yards per game and our defense was ranked fifth in scoring, allowing only nineteen points per game. We were determined to get back to the Super Bowl.

The Rams were led by head coach Steve Spagnuolo and rookie QB Sam Bradford. Their offense was centered around the All-Pro bell cow of a running back, Steven Jackson. His six-foot-two, 240-pound frame could run you over or run away from you with his 4.4 speed. The defense was led by my old teammate from Ohio State James. James is the son of Road Warrior Animal, the professional wrestler most famous for his and his partner's face paint and spiked shoulder pads. But James was making a name for himself with a neck wider than his head and ears like Dumbo and pencil lips that he inherited from his mother. James had been texting me all week, bragging about the fact that he had more interceptions than me, the same thing he used to do as my teammate in college. He'd gotten only one in the season, but it didn't matter because I had still yet to grab one. We'd stayed close over the last few years and this was the first time I had seen him play live.

To open the game, our offense had been doing what they'd been doing all year. We put up fourteen points and held the Rams to two field goals, and in the second quarter, after their second field goal, we fumbled the ensuing kickoff return and the Rams recovered it, inside our red zone. The Rams now had an opportunity to capitalize on the mistake and possibly bring the game to within one point, right before the half.

With the ball on the 20-yard line, I lined up at safety. The call was Cover 2 and I was responsible for the deep half of the field. The Rams were desperate to score, and chances were they'd try to throw deep passes into the end zone. Sure enough, on the right side of our defense, the receiver ran a slant and go on Tracy Porter and Tracy jumped the slant. This was the same spot, in the same route, that they got Jason David on the year prior in the preseason, against the Bengals. When Bradford pump-faked, I took off from my landmark. The throw didn't have enough pace or distance, leaving it three yards too far from the sideline and well within my range, and before the ball could reach the receiver's hands, I snatched it without breaking stride. I bolted down the right sideline with nothing but space, opportunity, and Sam Bradford between me and the end zone.

The worst thing you can do when you get an interception as a DB is get tackled by the quarterback. I cut to my left to get him to stop his feet and make sure I'd still have some room on the sideline, and as soon as his feet stopped, I cut back right and hit the gas. He laid out and dove to try to trip me up, but there was too much space as I skirted down the right sideline for a touchdown. My first pick of the season and it was to the house, finally. We go up 21–6.

Later in the fourth, the Rams drove down to the 7-yard line. We were up 31–6, but still trying to keep them out of the end zone. This time, we were in a nickel package and I was playing in the slot. The vets always used to tell me that, when it came to interceptions, they come in bunches. The Rams' fast-motioned from the right side of our defense to the left, and there was a bit of confusion as I ran to the middle of the field and Sharper took over the guy who was in motion.

Not knowing who exactly to cover, I watched as Bradford

rolled to his right. I followed him, assuming he'd bring me to where I needed to be. Suddenly, one of their wideouts popped out of the ground and was wide open in the end zone. Bradford saw exactly what I saw and threw back across his body to try to get the ball to the wide-open receiver, but instead threw it right to me, for my second interception of the day. I tried taking this one to the house, too, 105 yards, but got tackled about 15 yards later. I guess they do come in bunches.

I finished the game with four tackles and two interceptions—one for a touchdown and both in the red zone. When you get a takeaway in the red zone, they essentially count for double, because not only did you give your offense an extra possession, but you took away what would've been at least three points from the other team, and if you score on that like I did, it becomes a ten-to-fourteen-point swing, meaning that the offense was looking forward to getting seven points but ended up giving seven points to the other team. At the end of the game, I found James in the middle of the field as both teams came off the sidelines. The first thing he said was "Now I gotta hear your mouth for the rest of the year." That was the last time he called me talking shit. We hugged and caught up. It felt good to know that we were both, in our short careers thus far, established among some of the best in the business.

Louis XIII, the cognac, in the spirit world is an absolute piece of art. The bottle alone is made of crystals and shaped like a decanter, and by itself is worth hundreds of dollars. But the actual cognac is aged almost up to a hundred years, and it takes four generations of cellar masters to produce a single bottle, meaning that the person who starts the process will likely never see the finished product. It's labor-intensive, but an absolute masterpiece. And though it took a hundred years to make, as we toasted in the VIP lounge set aside for the wedding party, I took a shot of it all in one second.

Morrisa and I got married July 15, 2011. We'd only been engaged for six months. I didn't want to waste any time with an elongated engagement and wanted to get married before the season started. I didn't want to have to wait till the next offseason, a whole year later, for us to have our ceremony. And I had decided that I wanted to go into our marriage with a pure heart and a clear mind, so we stopped having sex for the entirety of our engagement. I'm sure that it added a little bit of haste and pep to my step.

In the same way my grandmother did what she needed to do to get to the Super Bowl, I knew it would be a cold day in hell before she missed the wedding of her favorite grandson. I hadn't seen her in a couple months because she had moved back to Piscataway to do her treatments, and I footed the bill to make sure that she had what she needed. But I was stuck in New Orleans, participating in the off-season program and planning a wedding.

My best man was James Laurinaitis, my college teammate and the only one that I thought could afford to hold that position. My other groomsmen were my brother Martin; my homeboy Jeff, who I'd been friends with since high school; my frat brother Foday, who was a chapter brother of mine and helped bring me into the fold; Usama Young, my teammate and closest friend at the time with the Saints; and Brian Barnes, Morrisa's older brother.

As I looked over the warehouse that was converted into a beautiful reception area backlit by purple and lively with music playing from a brass band, I broke a sweat thinking about what it cost. I wanted a small ceremony, but there was no way in hell my mom was going to allow that. She'd warmed up to the idea of me marrying Morrisa and was full-force pushing me to invite every cousin and friend of the family who wanted to come to the elaborate wedding. We hosted over 350 people.

Then, of course, some people couldn't afford to come, so I had to buy flights and hotels. I got custom tuxes for myself and all my groomsmen. Every flower in the reception and the wedding was real and cost $40,000 alone. We even had an ice sculpture. But it was all worth it when I saw Morrisa walk down the aisle in her mermaid silhouette dress escorted by her father, normally a strong and stoic man. As they slowly walked down the aisle, I choked up because I noticed he was crying. We recited the traditional vows that were provided by Tom, the team chaplain from Ohio State who I had been in touch with and stayed close with this entire time. The ceremony was absolutely beautiful and everything that Morrisa and I wanted.

At the reception, I met my grandmother at the front to escort her inside. She was a woman of her word. She was there, smiling from ear to ear, happy that her favorite grandson was marrying a Black queen, a Delta at that. And she loved Morrisa. She told me this every week since the proposal: "Happy to finally have a granddaughter."

But I was shocked when I laid eyes on my grandmother. She had lost a lot of weight and was too weak to walk more than a few steps before getting tired. The skin on her arms and neck was darker and burned from the chemotherapy and radiation. She wore a silver dress to match her short silver wig.

As I rolled her in her wheelchair, I asked her how she was feeling. "I'm okay, baby," she said with a smile on her face. "My hands are a little cold." I teared up as I held her thin, shaky hands that I used to be so afraid of. She stood up and we hugged, and I fell apart. Not able to hold them in any longer, the tears ran down my face as she whispered in my ear, "I'm so proud of you."

The reception was full of live music, dancing, and partying.

Morrisa and I went on a walking tour, greeting and taking pictures with everybody who was in attendance. My favorite part of the wedding was watching the Deltas perform their tradition for any of their members who get married. Hand in hand, they all linked up in a circle around the bride and sang their Sweetheart song to her. Mustering the strength to stand up with the thirty Deltas that surrounded Morrisa, my grandmother joined in on the serenade.

In my two-bedroom condo back on Tchoupitoulas Street, I filled my Game Ready machine that we use to deal with swelling to create a cold compression on my knee with ice and water. It was Wild Card Weekend, and the Saints had a matchup against the Seattle Seahawks, but I wasn't there. In the final game of the 2010 season, we played the Tampa Bay Buccaneers. We came into the game with the fifth-overall defense, and I had established myself as the lead playmaker on the squad, playing both corner and nickel.

The Bucs, who we'd beat earlier that year, came into the game with quarterback Josh Freeman and rookie running back LeGarrette Blount, who was on pace to run for a thousand yards. The six-foot, 247-pound back had been punishing defenders all year. As we watched film from previous games to prepare, Roman Harper gassed me up when I told him, "Man, I might try him," determined that Blount wasn't going to run me over. I'd been feeling myself now. I'd established myself. I wasn't going to let some rookie come in and do me bad on tape.

On 1st and 10, on the fourth play of the game, LeGarrette got a handoff, cut to the right side of our defense, and ran full speed up the sideline. The last thing you want to see is a 245-pound guy running untouched through the secondary. Approaching him, I thought to myself, *Here's the moment, I'm going to try him.* But since I hadn't quite learned the art of striking people then, I had terrible execution and technique. LeGarrette drove his shoulder into my chest.

Falling backward, I felt my right knee buckle. He fell forward, out-of-bounds, and then like Allen Iverson stepping over Ty Lue in Game 1 of the 2001 NBA Finals, he did the same, staring at me as he walked back to his sideline. With my pride as hurt as my knee, there was nothing I could do about it. The trainers rushed over and I heard something that I'd never heard of before. "Subluxation." My kneecap was dislocated, pushing all the way to the right as far as it could go, and then snapping back into place on its own.

My night was done and so was my season. I'd have to finish watching the game from the locker room. Now I was watching the first round of the playoffs from home. Injured players don't travel with the team. They stay home in rehab, especially with lower leg injuries. The flights aren't good for swelling and you don't want to take a five-hour flight to Seattle and then a five-hour flight back. It's not good for recovery. Plus, it's harder for those players to evade someone from the playing field getting washed into the sideline and possibly reinjuring them.

So I'd turned on the two screens that I have in my living room. Started my Game Ready and kicked my feet up in my recliner to elevate my leg. I was trying to get rid of the swelling as fast as I could. In the odd event that we made it to the Super Bowl, I'd be ready. The Seahawks were 7-9 and we had beaten them earlier that season 34–19. On the first drive of the game, Jabari Greer got an interception. Things were going according to plan, but it became very apparent that the Seahawks had other things in mind. They began attacking our secondary, using our aggressiveness against us with trick plays and play-action passes, moving the ball up and down the field.

In the second quarter, the game was tied 17–17, and we would never have the lead again. Blown coverages led to more touchdowns, and going into the half we were down by four points, 24–20. I hate watching the TV copies of the games because they're different from the film that we watch as players. The angles don't capture all the players on the field, and most of the time the commentators don't know what the hell they're talking about. So on one TV I rewound the game to try to see what was going on—where the breakdowns were and what was happening on defense—while I watched the game live on the other. I couldn't figure it out. Matt Hasselbeck, the quarterback for the Seahawks, was looking like an All-Pro and we were playing out of character. For the first time all year, we were not the more physical team. Even on defense.

While we played on our heels, the Seahawks offense was on the attack. But in the fourth quarter, our offense got it going, scoring ten unanswered points, bringing us within four, 34–30. And then it happened.

Seahawks running back Marshawn Lynch received a handoff, got lost in the commotion of the linemen, then suddenly popped right through the middle of the defense, shedding Darren Sharper and Jabari Greer, with the entire defense in pursuit, and stiff-arming Tracy to the ground. Marshawn then outran Alex Brown, one of our defensive ends, jumped over Roman Harper at the 2-yard line, and vaulted himself into the end zone while holding his crotch.

I poured an extra-stiff glass of Crown Royal XR, the blue bag, into a cup with a few pieces of ice and took a sip. The game was over, and so was our season.

Just under two months after the wedding, my grandmother finished her fight with cancer. It was on a Wednesday, September 7, before the season opener, and I flew from New Orleans back to Harrisonburg, Virginia, where she'd be buried. As I walked up the hill at Newtown

Cemetery, my mind was all over the place. I was mourning as I grappled with the idea that my grandmother would no longer be there to cheer me on. Then I had family members who wanted to talk to me about sports and the upcoming season, while still trying to get my mind ready to play a game the next day.

I was pretty good at holding it together until the viewing. When I laid eyes on her, the floodgates opened and a tidal wave of tears flowed from under my dark shades. I looked over her stiff and pale body and lifeless hands. If it wasn't for the picture of her sitting right next to her casket, I may not have recognized her. She was really gone.

While I don't think I saw my father drop one tear the entire service, my uncle, his younger brother, was a wreck. As a kid I heard stories around the neighborhood about my father and uncle. Legend has it, my grandmother taught my father the same lessons that she taught me. When my uncle would get into issues in the neighborhood, whether somebody stole his jacket or beat him up, my grandmother would not let my father in the house until he handled it. Legend has it that my uncle once had a new leather jacket that he decided to take to a neighborhood that was known for beating people up and robbing you. So, of course, when he got his jacket taken, and came home, my grandmother sent my father back out to get it, and even though he had to fight a bunch of people to get it, he came back home with the jacket.

I wasn't that close with my dad's side of the family. I grew up mostly with my cousins from my mom's side, so it had been a few years since I'd seen some of them. Most of them hadn't seen me since the draft. It made me uncomfortable when family members acted like fans, especially under these circumstances. I was mourning, and they wanted to take photos and chop it up with their famous cousin, asking me about players that I had played against or played with. But eventually, I warmed up to it. The small talk about football and the upcoming season were good distractions from what I had lost. My grandmother, my biggest supporter, and the person I had leaned on most for help, advice, and encouragement, was gone.

In the aftermath of the funeral, my grandmother left everything to my uncle, everything, and left nothing to my dad. I don't know if it was because she thought my dad didn't need anything because he had a millionaire son, or if there was some gripe that I didn't know about, but it caused a rift between my uncle and my father that still hasn't been mended to this day. All I wanted from my grandmother's possessions was the diamond-laced fleur-de-lis pin I got her custom-made after we won the Super Bowl and her predictions came true. I wanted to be able to pass that down to my kids if I, one day, had some. But nope, nothing.

My uncle would not surrender a single thing, not even the photos that she had saved of her and me. I had paid for all her treatments, her stay, her travel, and then finally I paid for the funeral with the understanding that once the estate was finalized, they'd pay me back for the funeral costs. But, once the dust settled and it was clear that my uncle was in full control and my father had no say, I got a letter and a check from his lawyers saying that this was all I was going to get. It was half of the funeral costs. The other half was to be the responsibility of my father, which they knew would be the responsibility of me.

Now, I understood why my dad would've had issues with the whole fallout, but I didn't ask to be in this. I thought I was helping, and now I felt like I'd been taken advantage of. And bigger than the money, we're family, if there's a problem, you call me. But when the first response I get is a letter from a lawyer, then we are no longer operating under the rules of family. It'd be years before I talked to my uncle again. When I pledged, I was taught a saying, "Every friend ain't your brother, and every brother ain't your friend."

In the third quarter of the divisional round of the 2011 playoffs, even though I'd been thrust into action as a rookie against the great Peyton Manning in the Super Bowl, this was by far the most pressure I'd felt in a game. We were playing the San Francisco 49ers and the crowd at Candlestick Park was going absolutely insane. Future was performing his hit song "Tony Montana" live, red Solo cup in hand, after every 49ers score, and they just kicked a FG to go up 20–14. As I sat on the sideline, trying to replay the plays in my mind from the last drive, I couldn't think straight. It was too loud, and admittedly I couldn't help but be impressed with the atmosphere.

The 2011 Saints were by far the best team that Sean Payton had assembled in years. We rattled off a nine-week winning streak, finishing the season at 13-3. A mark that made us the number one seed just two years prior, but this year the Green Bay Packers almost pulled off an undefeated season, winning fifteen games and losing only one. The 49ers also finished 13-3, and because they had a tougher schedule, they won the tiebreaker, making them the number two seed. They'd also get a first-round bye and host every playoff game, except the NFC Championship against the Packers, if they made it.

Honestly, this was the best season, and the best team, that we'd had to date. Everybody in the building knew that this team was more talented than the 2009 championship team. We'd been undefeated at home. Drew Brees broke the single-season passing record with 5,476 yards. Darren Sproles, our off-season free agent acquisition, broke the single-season record for all-purpose yards with 2,696, and we still had tight end Jimmy Graham, who was going crazy and was practically unguardable this year. Because we had such a home field

advantage, and so much momentum when we played in the Superdome, we knew that we needed to somehow get those playoff games
to come back through New Orleans. Our first matchup in the Wild
Card is a home divisional, or a home playoff game, against the Detroit Lions. Now, I know we had won the Super Bowl and everything,
but technically this was my first playoff start.

In 2009, I was a rookie and I played in one playoff game, against
the Arizona Cardinals, and I only played special teams because I was
injured, so I was limited. The next week, in the NFC Championship
game, I was inactive, and the only postseason game I had played in
was the Super Bowl, which I didn't start in, and I got in at the fourth
quarter, and definitely was messing shit up. So, I was actually pretty
nervous going into this game. I understand that you always hear
about the playoffs being different, and that the game speeds up in
that you need to elevate your game to meet the moment, and that
big-time players make big-time plays in big-time situations. So naturally I felt like these games required you to do more as a player, to
give more, to do something great. These were the games, so they say,
that make the legends. The first playoff game was against the Detroit
Lions. We had played them earlier in the season and held Megatron,
who was the only real threat on that team, to a very modest day, but
in the playoffs, it was a different story.

Calvin Johnson tried to beat us by his damn self. He had twelve
catches for 211 yards, and two touchdowns in a game in which we
double-teamed him in almost every snap, and even on some plays
triple-teamed him. We had a play one time where two other defenders and I were draped all over him and he still caught the ball. He
was a man possessed that day, but even Calvin Johnson, the Great
Megatron, wasn't a match for how good our team was. We still beat
the shit out of the Lions 45–28, and moved on to the next divisional
round of the playoffs, where we'd have to leave the comforts of the

Superdome and travel to Candlestick Park out in San Francisco. San Fran was being coached by Jim Harbaugh. He ran a very old-school type of team with the great running back Frank Gore, a premier receiver in Michael Crabtree, the great tight ends Vernon Davis and Delanie Walker, and Alex Smith, a more than capable quarterback, who was mobile and could command a game. They also had a crazy defense with Patrick Willis, NaVorro Bowman, Donte Whitner, and Dashon Goldson.

The two safeties nicknamed themselves "the Lumber Company" because they always brought the wood. They were known to be physical and feared, but we were confident as hell, and we felt like we had enough offense to get past their defense. The great Mike Tyson once said, "Everyone has a plan until they get punched in the mouth." The opening drive of the game, we did what we do best. Brees marched down the field and got into scoring range, and on a simple play, where he checked it down to Pierre Thomas, over to the right flat, Donte Whitner, in the open field, hit Pierre Thomas so hard that he was knocked unconscious before he ever hit the ground, dropping the ball in the process. I remember watching from the sideline like, "Oh shit, this is not a game." The game started in a sudden-change situation, but we were built for this. We had supreme confidence in our offense and our ability as a defense to get stops, and to give our offense enough possessions to win the game, no matter what happened. On par, we got in the game and made them punt, but our offense got off to a terrible start.

In the first quarter alone, the results of our drives went like this. First drive, fumble. Second drive, punt. Third drive, interception. Fourth drive, fumble. In the second quarter, we went down 17–0. The very first 49ers score was on a play where Smith threw a pass to Vernon Davis, who caught it in front of Roman, and me being the middle-of-field safety, I needed to make a tackle to reduce the amount of yards that Vernon Davis was going to get. If there's one thing that I learned about angles in geometry, when it comes to football, speed beats angles. I initially thought I took a decent angle to make the tackle, but Vernon's speed made me slightly off target. Instead of hitting him on the front side of his body, which would put my body between him and the end zone, I hit him on the back side of his body, simultaneously tripping Roman while doing it, leaving Vernon to stroll into the end zone. Even though we had a rocky start as a team, we had resolve, and we continued to battle and play our way right back into the game. Going into halftime, we were only down three points, 17–14, even with the offense adding another turnover.

The game was full of momentum swings, mostly against us. When we talk about momentum, I've never been in a game where the momentum has swung so heavy against us in our opposition. Every time they scored, we had to watch their kickoff team and the entire crowd dance to "Tony Montana." It was the livest shit I had ever seen in a stadium. If it wasn't against us, I would've been hyped, too.

As the game went on, our players were just too good to hold down. A late score by Darren Sproles put us ahead by one point, leading 24–23, with four minutes left in the game. On the next drive, the 49ers lined up, and Gregg Williams called an all-out blitz.

We weren't going to waste time disguising it. Anybody could have seen that it was a blitz. So, with the 49ers knowing that it was a blitz, I was matched up against Vernon Davis on the right side. They split him out as a wideout, forcing me align as the corner. I played off because I knew that the blitz would make the quarterback have to throw the ball quickly. I was guessing if I was playing off, he'd throw it short, knowing that he didn't have time to wait for Davis to get open. If it was a quick throw, then I could come up, make a tackle, and get off the field. The last thing I was expecting was for them to throw a deep ball. That's exactly what they did. I lined up about seven or eight yards off. I slow-pedaled as Davis was running up on me, fully anticipating that at any point in time he was going to stop and the ball would be thrown before he got to ten yards. As we got to twelve, I realized he was running too fast for me to keep up.

I ended up a half step behind, and that's all Alex Smith needed. He put the ball right in Davis's chest for a first-down, thirty-seven-yard gain. It's plays like these that trigger a negative thought cycle. They happened on our sideline. Immediately, I thought to myself, *Fuck, I suck. I can't cover this guy. He's too fast. Everything they said about me is right.* Then I looked up and saw the disappointment on Coach Payton's face, and the entire sideline, as they knew that that was a critical play I had just given up. Then I started to think, *My teammates think I suck, too.*

After that, I began to wonder what they were saying about me on social media. I knew they were killing me on Twitter. *They think I suck, too.* A few plays later, Smith scored on an old-school quarterback sweep to our left side, taking the lead back at 29–24, after they failed the two-point conversion. There were two minutes and eleven seconds left of play. We had one time-out. That was plenty for us and Drew Brees. In fact, we used only about a minute and eight seconds of that before Jimmy Graham caught the ball in the middle of the field, split two defenders, and ran it in for a sixty-six-yard touchdown to take the lead back.

Of course it was only right that Darren Sproles scored on the two-point conversion. Now up by three, with a minute and thirty-seven seconds remaining, the 49ers had one time-out to win the game. After a few plays, Gregg went again to the blitz. This time, it wasn't an all-out blitz, but it left us in man-to-man coverage, and me back on Vernon Davis.

Now, usually in this situation, you'd want to make sure that they caught the ball inbounds, tackle them, and use up the clock, knowing that they still have to go a good eighty-something yards to win with a touchdown. We could keep them out of field goal range and win the game or, worst-case scenario, as long as we didn't allow them to score a touchdown, we'd go into overtime. So, strategically, it was probably best to play off, keep the ball in front of us, and not allow any big plays that would give them big chunks of yardage without having to use time off the clock. Because I was frazzled and Vernon Davis had been killing me all day, I wanted to do what gave me the best chance of having success. So, I went to press him.

Even though I lined up a little bit inside and got my hands on him, he was still able to use his strength and push off me. The little bit of separation that Vernon created was enough for Smith to drop a dime right in a place where I couldn't get to the ball, hitting Davis in stride.

Davis ran past a diving Roman Harper and went up the sideline. I finally got him out-of-bounds around the 20-yard line after a forty-seven-yard gain, putting the 49ers right into field goal range. My thoughts started spiraling. We were going to lose the game, and it was going to be my fault. Everybody else was balling, doing whatever they had to do to give us a chance to get back into this game. The only thing that held us back was my inability to stop Vernon Davis. Two plays later, Davis scored the winning touchdown in front of Roman Harper, and the stadium erupted.

Usually, in the playoff scenario, you go into it understanding that this could be the last game of the season. This year, we wholeheartedly believed that we would be in the Superdome playing the Giants the next week on our way to another Super Bowl championship. But instead, we were on a plane heading back home to New Orleans. As I've said before, when you watch the tape, it's never as bad as you thought it was, and it's never as good. But that was one of those times when it was exactly as bad as I had thought. My negative thought cycle became a self-fulfilling prophecy. Then, when I went onto social media and read what fans said, it seemed like everybody thought I sucked. Myself included.

# 6

# SUDDEN CHANGE

*Being defeated is often a temporary condition.*
*Giving up is what makes it permanent.*
—MARILYN VOS SAVANT

After the loss to the 49ers, shit hit the fan. The night before the playoff game, a videographer had secretly recorded our defensive meeting.

"Kill the head and the body will die," you could hear Gregg Williams clearly say over the tape. "Make sure we kill Frank Gore's head."

The NFL launched an investigation into what would be coined "Bountygate," where they accused our organization of incentivizing our players to hurt our opponents. Claiming to have thousands of documents of evidence spanning the years 2009 to 2011, the NFL and Roger Goodell suspended head coach Sean Payton for the entire season, GM Mickey Loomis for eight games, and assistant head coach Joe Vitt for six games. Gregg Williams, whose contract was up with the Saints and had signed with Jeff Fisher and the St. Louis Rams, was suspended indefinitely. But it didn't stop there. They went after our defensive captains as well, suspending Jonathan Vilma, Scott Fujita, Will Smith, and defensive lineman Anthony Hargrove.

Quite frankly, we all felt like this was bullshit and that the league had made an example of us because of the recent heat they were under for their cover-up of the knowledge of the long-term effects of playing football on the brains of the players and they were trying to clean up their public image. That audio was damning, but it was also a reflection of a widespread practice among many teams in the NFL. While they characterized it as incentivizing players to hurt opponents, a bounty, defined in the collective bargaining agreement, is essentially just a noncontractual bonus. Meaning, if I give you $20 because you made an interception, that was considered by definition a bounty. By that definition, yes, we paid out players in cash for sacks, fumbles, interceptions, touchdowns, and big hits. We also fined players for penalties, missed opportunities, and dropped interceptions. But that was common at every level of football, from Pop Warner all the way through probably every NFL team and every NFL locker room.

But to characterize it as if we were intentionally going out to try to injure our opponents was false. As a defender, we wanted you to think more about protecting your body than protecting the football. So we'd hit you as hard as possible. Though I saw plenty of money get dished out, it was never for taking somebody out of a game. We were crazy, not stupid.

Steve Spagnuolo had replaced Gregg in the 2012 season, and now that the season was over and Sean Payton had returned, Spagnuolo had been fired. Word on the street was that, in the first staff meeting when Sean returned, he asked all the coaches what went wrong and what they thought of the players. He was fully intending to keep Spags as the defensive coordinator, but, according to some of the coaches who were in the meeting, he was shocked when Spagnuolo declared that almost all the leaders who were Pro Bowl–caliber or promising players weren't that good.

Upon hearing those things, Sean decided to fire Spagnuolo and quickly replaced him with the infamous Rob Ryan. The Santa

Claus–looking character who's the brother of Rex Ryan, the former head coach of the Jets, and the son of the legendary defensive coordinator and former head coach Buddy Ryan, the same mastermind that groomed Gregg Williams and led the legendary Eagles defenses back in the day.

Rob had a reputation for having a big mouth and an even bigger playbook. He had just come from Dallas, and after their defense fell apart late in the season, he took most of the blame and was fired at the end of the year. He then went on the record, saying, "Well, I won't have a job for what, five minutes?" This was the guy that was now our D coordinator. But it was an important year for me, the last year of my contract. And after one terrible season and a horrible playoff game, I was itching to make sure that I had the best opportunity to put the best version of me on the field.

So as I was walking out of the cafeteria this day in March, Ryan called me. "Hey, Malcolm, Rob Ryan here. Look, man, I'm excited as hell to coach you. I think you're a hell of a player. I got a lot of respect for what you do. I just want you to know we're going to have a lot of fun playing football." I said, "Yeah, yeah, Coach. Nah, that's going to be great. Hey, who's playing the nickel?" I just wanted the opportunity to be able to play nickel in the defense. He hesitated, then said, "Yeah, I mean, I've watched it, but sometimes you got a tendency to just let routes run away from you." I said, "Look, Rob, I'm not asking you to hand me anything. I'm asking for you to let me compete. All I want to do is be able to, when camp comes, to be able to compete for the nickel spot." After about ten minutes of me being persistent and pulling on his arm, he conceded. "You have my word, I'll let you compete for it. But no guarantees." I said, "Bet. Look forward to working with you, Rob," and we ended the call.

It was March 2012, and I was driving down St. Charles Avenue. Sometimes after Mardi Gras, even after the celebration is done and over, the beads that are thrown from the floats hang from the rows of beautiful oak trees that line the entirety of the avenue. My pride and ego still hurt from the playoff game, and I was agitated and annoyed by everything, like the fact that New Orleanians don't signal when they drive, nor do they care for red lights. Then all these tourists that walk the streets, daiquiris in hand, stumbling and bumbling about as if my S-Class Mercedes wouldn't win the matchup if we were to collide. And now I was especially annoyed as traffic was being held up by a couple riding beach cruisers dangerously wide from the bike lane.

At the end of the season, Gregg's contract was up, and they wouldn't be renewing it. Two days after the playoff game, it was announced that Gregg was signing as the defensive coordinator for the Rams. His good buddy Jeff Fisher had become the head coach and immediately snatched up Gregg. I can't say it was a surprise, as the last year had become very contentious between Gregg and head coach Sean Payton, with them openly arguing in front of players throughout the season. It was clear to me that Sean had almost no say on what the defensive side of the ball did, with Gregg having a shit ton of power. And once the defense fell apart in that last game, Sean had had enough. And that was when he hired Steve Spagnuolo, who was the head coach of the St. Louis Rams in the previous three seasons.

Spags was most famous for his time as the defensive coordinator for the New York Giants, as he was the mastermind behind the strategy that bested the Patriots offense, one of the best offenses the league had seen at that time, in Super Bowl XLII. But as the head coach of the Rams, his record was pitiful, his first year going 1-15, the next 7-9, and then falling back to a 2-14 season, which led to him being fired. We essentially swapped defensive coordinators with

St. Louis. It had been a few weeks since he was hired, and I hadn't heard from him yet.

So I gave James Laurinaitis a call to ask him about the defense. I knew James had played for Spags in the last couple years and wanted to get a heads-up to what I would face. He didn't have anything bad to say about Spags, which said a lot, given the Rams' record.

James was also interested in hearing a little bit about Gregg, but I knew James would love playing for Gregg. I know I did. He was the type of coach that you'd gladly run through a brick wall for, and he knew how to motivate and get the best out of each and every one of his players. I knew that was right up James's alley. But all of the uncertainty of a new defense and new defensive staff, and still hurting from all of the comments I'd been reading about myself, had me on edge.

As I zoomed past the couple on their beach cruisers, I thought, *What kind of man rides the same bike as the Wicked Witch of the West from* The Wizard of Oz, *with a basket in the front and a little dog sitting inside?* I still got embarrassed when I had to walk Roxy, the small Maltese Yorkie that I had gotten for Mo, and there he was proudly parading down St. Charles Avenue, holding up traffic for all to see. That's some white people shit.

As I mean-mugged them as I drove by, the face looked familiar. I looked in my rearview, staring intently, and then I recognized him. It was Spags. Our new D coordinator was the Wicked Witch of the West. And one thing was for certain: he wouldn't be leading us with fear.

<hr>

The 2013 season opened up with two division rival games. We won the first game, beating the Atlanta Falcons 23–17, and now we were in Tampa Bay, set to play the Bucs. We jogged back onto the field, after play had been suspended after the first drive of the game, and I'd never been so excited about a weather delay. Temperatures at kickoff were 110 degrees on the field, but due to quickly approaching storms and lightning, once our offense opened up the game, driving down twelve plays and kicking a field goal, the game was suspended for a whole hour and nine minutes. And now I was jogging back on the field. It was a nice 83 degrees, and even though it was windy, it was much more manageable. But we were about to walk into a storm of our own.

This team was much different from the Saints teams I'd been a part of thus far. We'd drafted Kenny Vaccaro, a rookie safety out of the University of Texas, a natural playmaker who was tough, physical, and had great instincts in the run game but had a terrible attitude. If I had been the ideal rookie, humble and obedient, he was exactly what a rookie shouldn't be, arrogant and entitled. Even being tied to a goalpost the same as I had didn't change a thing. It didn't help that Rob Ryan and Sean Payton inserted him into the lineup immediately, replacing Roman Harper, my partner in crime and former Pro Bowl safety. But Rob kept his word and allowed me to play the nickel. And seeing that Roman still had a lot of good ball left to play, Ryan created a three-safety package that he called the hat trick, an attempt to make sure that he had all the best players on the field at the same time.

It was in training camp that I saw why Rob had the reputation that he did. His defense was complicated as hell, and he was wildly unorganized. I was used to meetings being like war room debriefs, and his meetings were more like episodes of *SNL*. There was one thing Rob and his supporting staff of coaches knew how to do well: inspire. My new position coach, Wesley McGriff, aka "Crime Dog," was a rookie defensive back coach out of Old Miss. He was also my frat brother. After coming off the worst season of my career, he convinced me that I had every tool to be the best safety in the NFL and made it my responsibility to solve all the problems on the field when it came to executing Rob's defense.

The Bucs came into the game with their new head coach, Greg

Schiano—the hard-nosed rookie head coach out of Rutgers who had recruited me back in the day when I was deciding which college I wanted to go to—and quarterback Josh Freeman. Week 1, their All-Pro star wide receiver Vincent Jackson had seven catches for 154 yards and we knew he would be the centerpiece of their offense. So on the first third down, Rob Ryan threw out the defense we'd been working on all camp, the amoeba defense. The defense featured not one single player being stationary. Everyone from the secondary players to the linebackers to even the defensive linemen were all standing up and moving around, not allowing the offensive line and the quarterback to identify protections or to know who was rushing or who was covering.

On the snap of the ball, everyone would sprint to their responsibility. Although I was showing blitz off the left side of the defense, I was responsible for covering the slot receiver, as I was the nickel. It was 3rd and 7, and when the ball snapped, I got back to my spot, covering receiver Mike Williams. He took two steps to my outside, cut back to my inside, and after another two steps, whipped back outside. But all the movement didn't fool me, and as soon as he caught the ball, I wrapped him up and wrestled him down for a two-yard gain, and we were off the field. The next drive, the Bucs defense intercepted Drew Brees, and Freeman marched them down for a touchdown, taking the lead, 7–3. The Bucs under Greg Schiano were playing a physical brand of football. We were already rivals and used to there being competitive games, but the Bucs had escalated it to a new level.

Their physicality led to ten penalties in the game, three being personal fouls for unnecessary roughness. Dashon Goldson, who had been half of the Lumber Company in San Francisco, was now a highly paid Buccaneer and was making his presence felt all over the field. They hit Drew Brees so hard one time I thought we were going to lose him. But with the emphasis now on player safety, the majority of the hits were fouls, plays we would've celebrated just two years prior. And right before the half, with our offense within the 5-yard line, trying to score, four plays in a row the Bucs defense held, having a goal line stand and keeping the game 13–7 going into halftime.

Usually we liked to fight fire with fire, meaning if the team wanted to get physical, we had no problem matching their physicality. But under Rob Ryan, we had a different philosophy. We were more about playing chess, looking for opportunities to counterpunch or take advantage of tendencies that the offense presented. As the game was going on, I'd been watching how Freeman stared down his receivers that he wanted to throw to, particularly Vincent Jackson. In the third quarter, he hit Jackson for a seventy-three-yard touchdown over Kenny Vaccaro. But the touchdown was called back because the Bucs aligned in an illegal formation. Two plays later, while I was playing the deep safety, I watched Freeman drop back to pass and stare at Vincent Jackson, who was running deep from the left side of the defense over to the right.

Before Freeman could let go of the ball, I was already dropping out of the sky, cutting off the route. I intercepted the ball as I came forward without breaking stride and broke left to the open field and returned it all the way into Buccaneers territory, stepping out-of-bounds at the 40-yard line. Check. I had begun to believe what Crime Dog told me. How I was the best, how nobody had the gifts that I had. The intelligence, the long arms, the speed, the physicality, the ability to play multiple positions in a game. And I started to embrace that role. On another third down, 3rd and 7, with a minute and thirty-one left in the third quarter, I found myself at the nickel, one-on-one against the All-Pro Vincent Jackson. He had a bigger body, easier for me to get my hands on at the line of scrimmage, and liked to be physical with his route running and that played right into my hands.

When the ball was snapped, I was right in his face. He jab-stepped to my right and tried to counter back to my left, but my long arms were able to jam him, throwing him off-balance. So by the time he went to make his break, back toward the middle of the field, the timing between Josh Freeman and him was off and he wasn't at the spot that he needed to be when the ball got there. Incomplete pass. Check. Tampa Bay's defense was playing out of control. They intercepted Drew another time, returning it for a touchdown, making the game 14–13 Bucs. And with five minutes left in the game, Freeman and the Bucs were driving. On 2nd and 9, an obvious passing down, they put Vincent Jackson in motion. He'd lined up against Kenny Vaccaro in the slot, and when the ball snapped, Freeman was staring at him again, not paying attention to where I was on the field.

When he let the ball go, throwing it across the middle for Jackson, again I was coming out of the sky. This time, he completed the pass, but at the expense of his receiver. As I broke, I thought, *He's going to get him killed*. And I threw everything I had right into the quads of Jackson, somersaulting him into the air. Him being the All-Pro that he was, he held on to the football, got up, and celebrated, but he couldn't hide the effect of that hit. He went to the sideline, wincing. After driving a little bit farther, the Bucs missed a field goal.

And Drew, doing what Drew does, with a minute left on the clock and no time-outs, executed a beautiful last-minute drive that ended with a walk-off, game-winning field goal with five seconds left on the clock. Walking into that locker room, I felt like myself again. And the first person I saw when I got there was Sean Payton. Sean was a coach who rarely hid what he was feeling about you, and the look on his face told me that he was proud.

It was the 2012 season opener against the Washington Commanders. As I lined up to blitz off the right side of the defense, the blind side of the quarterback, former Heisman winner and rookie quarterback Robert Griffin III snapped the ball and executed a play fake, turning his back to me. The play fake stopped my feet just enough to allow RGIII enough time to set his feet and throw the ball, as I was unblocked to the quarterback.

All week, we had planned on taking advantage of the rookie, who had come into the league with a ton of hype and a ton of confidence. I couldn't stand the way that he would stick his tongue out after he threw the ball, like he was Jordan shooting a jumper. So even though he threw the ball, I hit him with everything I had, knocking him to the ground. Yeah, rookie.

But the pass was still completed to Pierre Garcon, who leaped, snatched the ball out of the air across the middle of the field without breaking stride, as two of our defenders collided, and took it eighty-eight yards for a touchdown.

For the first time I was a defensive captain. Not the ideal situation to take over the title. A month after they'd hired Spags, the Bountygate investigation broke open, and with so many coaches suspended, Aaron Kromer, the tall coach with a deep voice and worried-looking eyes, became the interim head coach. And Spags had an elevated role, being the only coach on the staff with any experience, as a former head coach, and he changed the culture tremendously.

But I didn't think I was ready to be a captain. That September, Hurricane Isaac, a Category 1 storm, hit New Orleans, causing damage and flooding. After our fourth preseason game in Tennessee, the airport was still closed, so we had to stay in Tennessee for an evening before returning to our city. So we all went out on the town, starting at the hotel at the resort that we stayed in.

After ordering a few shots, I didn't remember much. But I woke up to pounding on my hotel room door. It was our assistant strength coach, Charles Byrd, who frantically attempted to wake me up, as the buses were getting ready to leave for the airport. My bed was untouched, and I still had on the clothes from the night before. My bag was still by the door where I had dropped it off before heading to the bar. I grabbed my bag and rolled out.

As I got on the bus, I realized that I was still drunk. When we got to the airport and walked through the terminal to board the plane, like the scene from *The Shining*, the long hall seemed to get longer. It was clear I wasn't going to make it to the plane.

To make it worse, as I was throwing up, team owner Tom Benson and his wife, Mrs. Benson, were walking by. When I got back to New Orleans, I called Mo to pick me up and drive me home. The next day I was voted captain.

Even though we were missing some of our key players and head coach, we were still optimistic about the season. We still had Drew and all the offensive weapons we figured we needed to make do.

The new defensive scheme changed us from a single high defense that was predicated on pressure from blitzes and elaborate rush plans to a split safety defense with two safeties sitting high and relying on disguises and the only pressure coming from the defensive linemen rushing. Also, there was a new tackling style. Spags called it "arrows through snow," where you would run full speed at your target, never slowing down, never breaking down, with the goal being to attack the defender with so much speed that they stopped their feet.

He'd say there was no such thing as a mis-tackle. If you made the ballcarrier stop their feet, the other defenders that were running to the ball should be able to tackle him. And he'd never give you a minus for missing a tackle that was full speed.

In this first game, it was clear that the new philosophy fit the players like oil and water. Every play, I felt out of position and out of control. I didn't feel like I could tackle a soul. I missed three tackles, and RGIII looked unstoppable.

We played from behind the entire game, and late in the fourth quarter, we brought it into a one-possession game, thinking, *That's okay, Drew can bail us out of it*, but an interception that got returned to the 3-yard line only set up another score by the Commanders. And the Superdome crowd that is normally our biggest advantage was as quiet as it had ever been.

We lost the game 40–32 to start the season. When I got to the family area after the game, the first person I saw was my dad. He shook my hand.

"Man, how y'all let RGIII do y'all like that?"

---

Four weeks after beating the Bucs in Tampa Bay, I had warmed up for the first time in Gillette Stadium in Foxborough, Massachusetts, when all of a sudden Jay-Z's public service announcement played over the loudspeakers.

"Allow me to reintroduce myself. My name is HOV."

On cue, Tom Brady came running down the sideline toward where we were warming up. He was met by a roaring crowd. As a Jay-Z fan, I ain't going to lie, that shit was hard.

Brady was coming off a poor performance, where he had just been held for less than two hundred yards passing and zero touchdowns. It was the first time he had been held to no touchdown passes in some years. Meanwhile, we were looking like the Saints of old, winning three more games after beating the Bucs, and came into Gillette Stadium 5-0. Our defense was night and day from what it was the year before, giving up only 14.6 points a game. And I was coming off of one of my more productive performances, against the Bears, a game in which I had a sack and a forced fumble.

Only problem was, my bad habit of tackling exclusively with my right shoulder had caused a chronic pinch in my C4 and C5 vertebrae, causing constant stingers. A stinger is when the nerve endings get pinched and it causes a burning sensation that shoots from the top of your trap, or your shoulder, all the way to your fingertips, while also making your arm go numb and limp. It's a temporary sensation that lasts anywhere from a few seconds to a minute or so.

But back in 2010, I had one so bad that my entire scapular muscle was temporarily paralyzed and I couldn't raise my arm over my chest. It came back in a few days, but there was nothing that doctors or trainers could do to rehab it. I simply had to wait for the nerve to calm down enough, and the paralysis to subside. But season after season of having stingers repeatedly, it got to the point where it was chronic. Every single tackle was extremely painful. Even the routine tackles would cause a burning sensation. And with eleven games still to go, I didn't know how I was going to make it through the season.

The last two weeks, I needed to get an epidural injection into my neck. I thought epidurals were only for women giving birth, but under the ultrasound scanners, they stuck a needle that was four or five inches long into my neck to get right up next to the nerve ending without damaging it. I'd had two in the last two weeks, but the doctor told me you're allowed to get only three in an entire year.

The trainer suggested that I wear a cowboy collar, a large pad that sticks out of the back of the shoulder pads up toward the top of the helmet that restricts your neck from bowing backward. Sometimes you'll see linebackers, who are routinely in big collisions, wear them. Hell no. One, they're ugly as hell. Two, they make you very stiff.

And I couldn't play the ball if I couldn't move my neck. And three, we were getting ready to play Tom Brady. If I went out there with a cowboy collar on my pads and tried to cover Julian Edelman or Danny Amendola, I was going to be a target all day.

So the trainers and I, after much debate back and forth, settled on a small neck roll, which is a tube they stick on the inside collar of the pads, and I got them to make it as small as possible, to make it less obvious to Brady that I didn't have all of the mobility that I was used to. I couldn't even run full speed, not because my legs were affected in any way, but swinging my arms, with maximum effort and maximum range of motion, irritated the nerve. But I still found a way to manage around it and got ready to play. The very first drive, I lined up in the slot. My matchups that week were Amendola and Edelman, two very small receivers with very quick feet and high motors. They were the same prototypes as the legendary Wes Welker, who I faced just a couple seasons before.

Down to the releases, everything was the same, except this time my technique was a little better. And I knew if I was to survive in the slot, I'd have to get hands on them early in the down to control the smaller bodies. It was 3rd and 4, and Julian Edelman, when the ball snapped, released to my inside and I got hands on him. Controlling him, I took a look at the quarterback. As soon as I saw Brady, Edelman ducked under my arms and back out to the outside, with Brady putting the ball right on him.

I set chase and dove on the back of Edelman's legs. And Kenny Vaccaro, making a tackle from in front of Edelman, collided with me face-to-face, what we call friendly fire. Immediately, the burn went from my neck down to my fingertips and I lost the feeling in and control over my right arm. Standing up, holding one hand with the other, trying to make sure that Brady didn't see that my arm was limp, I went and tried to shake it back. And shortly after, it did come back.

As the game went on, I settled in and was able to make a few tackles without hurting myself.

I even racked up a tackle for a loss when Rob Ryan sent me on a blitz on the outside and I chased down the runner from behind. We went into the halftime, down 17–7. Once I settled into the game and could stop worrying about my neck, I started focusing on the chess match between myself and Brady. Brady's one of those cerebral quarterbacks, similar to Peyton Manning, that reads the entire defense at the line of scrimmage and changes the play to put them in the most advantageous situation.

Less concerned about changing runs to passes and passes to runs, he looks more at matchups, trying to figure out who has the most advantageous matchup out of all his receivers and getting them the ball as quickly as possible. Identifying who the blitzers are and manipulating his protection to give him extra time in the pocket. After our offense kicked a field goal and then came back with another drive, scoring a touchdown, the game was tied 17–17, with about six minutes left in the third quarter. I was back, twenty yards away from the ball, playing free safety, when Tom Brady executed a hard play action.

But I was learning to train my eyes not to look at the quarterback in the first few steps of the play, because often the quarterback will fool you, make you think it's a run when it's a pass, or make you think it's a pass when it's really a run. I'd learned to key the offensive line, particularly the offensive lineman who does not have a defensive lineman in front of him. If he fires off the ball, it's a run. But if he's soft or floats backward, you know it's a pass. It's easier to read and more consistent, so that you don't get caught on a play-action pass when you're supposed to be the deep defender.

I saw the center snap it, and ignored Brady's hard play action. As soon as he executed the fake, he snapped his eyes up right to his receiver that's on my right, who just made a hard right turn toward the middle of the field. I put my foot in the ground and broke on the ball, arriving a fraction of a second right after the football. I threw my entire self, shoulder first, into the wideout, jarring the ball loose. The receiver began to flail his arms, trying to entice the referees to throw a flag for helmet-to-helmet contact, which they did.

After the game, I was fined $15,750 for doing my job. My job is not to allow this guy to catch the ball. And if he gets hit in the middle of the field between defenders, it is my belief that the quarterback is the one who should get fined for even putting his teammate in that situation. But they got fifteen yards after the penalty, and even though we were able to rally later in the drive, they got three points off of it, going up 20–7.

The very next drive, I used one of Brady's tools against him. Coach Bill Belichick and Brady loved to use motion to identify who was covering and who was not. So they would do what we call a yo-yo motion. Take a wideout and start him in one spot, jog him a few yards in one direction, and then send him back to the original spot that he aligned. If anyone on the defense moves with the receiver, they know that it's man coverage. If no one moves, they know it's zone. And knowing this, I used that against them. They sent the slot receiver in motion to the outside and then back in, and I followed with him. But I wasn't covering man-to-man. I was a blitzer. And even if I didn't fool Brady, I fooled his protection.

When the ball snapped, I blitzed from the left side of their defense through a gap in the offensive line. The running back, who was supposed to block me, and had already canceled me out of his vision because I went with the motion, got out into his route, leaving me scot-free to Brady. And I brought him down with a sack. Pain-free. That was until Akiem Hicks, our largest defensive lineman, in celebration of the big sack, pushed me, jarring my neck back. And now my stinger reminded me that it was still there, but we had forced the Patriots to punt.

What then ensued was a back-and-forth between two great quarterbacks. Drew Brees got intercepted, which the Patriots turned into another field goal opportunity, taking the lead 23–17. Then Brees, over two defenders on 3rd and 20, threw a bomb to rookie Kenny Stills for a touchdown, and we took the lead by one point, 24–23. On defense, we got a fourth-down stop and the Patriots turned the ball over on downs, while Brees took another drive down the field and got a field goal. We upped the lead, 27–23.

Brady took the field with just under two minutes and thirty seconds on the clock. And on the very first play, he threw an interception to corner Keenan Lewis. With back-to-back stops, the Patriots turned the ball over late in the game. We just knew the game was over. And on the sideline, Crime Dog, who had been convincing us all week that we were ready for the challenge, took the football that Lewis had just intercepted, brought us all into a huddle, where we all touched the ball, and we broke it down on the sideline in celebration, thinking the game was over. And we weren't the only ones. Even the Patriots faithful began to file out of the stadium.

But the Patriots defense held, making our offense punt, and taking only about a minute off the clock. Tom got the ball back with a minute and thirteen seconds left and no time-outs. The game wasn't over yet. And if we wanted to win the defense, we needed to stop Tom Brady in a two-minute drill. Tom completed a few passes to his wideouts, driving the ball all the way down to the 26-yard line. And on 4th and 4, with twenty-four seconds left, the call was two-man, meaning we'd have two high safeties to protect for the deep throws, and everyone else would play man coverage underneath with inside leverage. The reason we played inside leverage is because the inside breaking routes are the easier routes to throw for the quarterback.

We wanted to force him to throw out toward the sideline, which are the farther throws and the hardest to be accurate on.

Austin Collie, their receiver in the slot, lined up against me. I funneled him to the outside like I was supposed to and broke underneath the route. But Brady, letting it go before either of us had even got out of our breaks, put the ball right on him, and I tackled him inbounds. They sprinted to the line of scrimmage and spiked the ball with ten seconds left. The very next play, Brady threw over the head of the right corner, Jabari Greer, for a touchdown. The air in our sails had just been sucked away. All of us sat there dumbfounded, having felt assured that we were going to be leaving this place with a victory. We left the loser, confused by how quickly our fate had changed. We should have known better than to take our foot off the pedal against the great Tom Brady.

After losing the 2012 home opener against the Washington Commanders, we started off the season 0-4. To understand what that does to a team, when you start off 0-4, there's a 2.7 percent chance that you make the playoffs. Almost an impossible feat to climb back from.

But in the last four weeks, we'd won three out of the four games. Now in week 11 against the Oakland Raiders, we had a chance to get back to 5-5 and get out of having a losing season. Part of that turnaround had been the insertion of Jonathan Vilma back into the lineup. He hadn't been gone because of suspension. He'd actually been fighting his suspension with appeals. He'd been out due to injury. But now that he was back, our defense had gotten a spark of life.

But the meetings had been growing more frustrating as the weeks went on. I knew that Spags couldn't stand me. Every time they installed a defense, I would raise my hand, questioning the holes and gray areas, and the answer every time was "The rush will take care of it." "Coach, but who's going to cover this guy if they run this route?" "The rush will take care of it." "Yeah, but we don't have a support here or an edge to our defense." "The rush will take care of it."

He was still using a defense that was built off of having a historically good defensive line, one that had Justin Tuck, Michael Strahan, and Osi Umenyiora on it, all of whom were Pro Bowlers and superstars in their own right. Our defensive line was good, but not built like that. He inherited a defensive line that was under Gregg Williams's design, that was better against the run, and pressure came from blitzes, not from the defensive line.

I was tired of doing things that didn't make sense. His arrows through snow technique had made me miss more tackles than at any point in my career. And I was tired of hearing the analogy. Arrows through snow sounds good, but snow doesn't move, and when we played the Philadelphia Eagles a few weeks earlier and lined up against Michael Vick, Shady McCoy, and DeSean Jackson, the most elusive trio in the history of the game, that philosophy seemed psychotic and it proved as such when they rushed for 221 yards on us. Adding insult to injury, after every game when you looked at the grades, you got graded poorly for making a slow tackle, but got a plus if you made a fast miss. It was just ass-backward. That idea that if you can just get the ballcarrier to stop his feet, then that's a win, makes no sense when Michael Vick has no problem stopping and starting and still making everyone miss.

But I noticed that in the meetings every day, I would get all worked up because I felt like, as a captain, I'd be letting my teammates down if I didn't at least try to challenge the status quo. But the guys who were my leaders, JV and Roman, were always quiet. One day, I asked JV why he didn't say anything in the meetings, when he knew none of this made sense.

"It's simple," he said. "He ain't going to listen, bro. Keep quiet, nod your head, but come Sunday, play how you need to play. It's your name on the back of the jersey, not his."

I took that advice, and for the last three weeks, I started playing better. We went from 0-4 to 4-5. In the first quarter of the week 11 matchup against the Oakland Raiders, on 2nd and 10, I listened to quarterback Carson Palmer's cadence, attempting to determine when I needed to stop disguising and get into position to cover the tight end, who I was assigned in man coverage, before the ball is snapped. Ken Flajole, the DB coach and right-hand man to Spags, wanted us to hold our disguise as long as possible. But fuck that. I wasn't compromising my technique anymore.

When the ball was snapped and the tight end released, I could see Palmer through the tight end, and he was waiting for him, staring right at him, which meant he was waiting for him to stop running so he could throw the ball. Anticipating to break, I planted my feet and as soon as the tight end dropped his weight to change his direction, I broke to the ball, snatching it before the tight end could get there. Stumbling, I put my left hand on the ground to stop myself from falling. When I looked up, I saw an offensive lineman coming straight for me. I threw my left foot in the ground, slamming on the brakes, and hesitated as three-hundred-plus pounds went flying by, unable to stop. I stumbled some more when his flailing hands grabbed my face mask, but I kept my balance and accelerated down the left sideline, with JV and defensive lineman Tom Johnson as a personal convoy getting key blocks, getting me all the way to the end zone.

The first person to celebrate with me was JV. Later in the game, he recorded a sack and Roman caught an interception. After Roman's interception, he and I were flagged for excessive celebration. We didn't give two shits. We won the game 38–17, in convincing fashion. We were back to playing how we knew how to play.

With Sean Payton's offense and Rob Ryan's new defense, we won six out of the last ten games, finishing 11-5 and solidifying ourselves as the number six seed in the playoffs.

We had already gone to Philly, and for the first time in franchise history won a playoff game on the road. Sean, having cut his teeth in the Philadelphia Eagles organization, couldn't think of a better way to celebrate the win than to take a lap around the stadium, knowing how pissed off it would make the fans. On the way into the game, they threw eggs at our bus, but left with egg on their faces as we won in a dramatic fashion, 26–24.

Now we were in the windy, wet, and cold conditions of Seattle in January, a place we knew all too well after losing the Wild Card game here a few years back. And even earlier in the season, the number one seed embarrassed us on Monday Night Football 34–7, in week 13.

But we were a different team at this point. Rob had just pulled off the best turnaround, statistically, in NFL history, with the Saints going from having the worst defense in the history of football to finishing the season as the number two pass defense, the number four defense overall in yards given up, and the number four scoring defense. Rob's schemes were working and he was listening. Each week he and I collaborated on how we should implement the defense. I would advise him on what plays were too complicated and what plays were manageable enough for us to execute.

His ability to connect with players made us play harder. Morrisa and I had just had our first child, Elle, on December 10 of that season. That week Rob installed a blitz named "ELLE-0," an all-out pressure, because when you have a kid life comes at you fast.

We were determined in that game. Although we might not have

been as talented as Seattle, we weren't going to get bullied around like we had the first time. So in the second play of the game, when Percy Harvin, their elusive receiver who had been out all year due to injury, came onto the field and lined up in the slot, I knew the plan was to get him the ball early and often.

Film study showed me that there was a high-percentage chance that they'd throw a quick bubble screen to him, a high-completion pass that would get him involved in space. So as soon as the ball was snapped and Russell Wilson, the quarterback, looked at Harvin, I broke. Doug Baldwin, also in the slot, was responsible for blocking me. I took my left hand and put it in the V of his neck, knocking him back and out of the way, leaving me free to wrap up Harvin three yards in the backfield as Roman helped me wrestle him down.

The next play, Wilson threw a deep pass to Harvin down the right side of our defense, and he was absolutely obliterated by our safety Rafael Bush, whose shoulder collided directly with Harvin's head, bouncing it off the turf violently, his mouthpiece flying out of his mouth. Harvin would stay on all fours, panting and contemplating his whole life, until the trainers came.

In the opening drive, we held them to just three points. Like I said, they might beat us with talent, but they were not going to beat us with physicality; but the Legion of Boom, a legendary defense that consisted of Earl Thomas, Kam Chancellor, and Richard Sherman, was in their element. They would hold our offense on the first five drives to a punt, a missed field goal, a fumble, a punt, and then a turnover on downs, going into halftime down 16–0.

Seattle also had another advantage, the "12th man," the name of their crowd. Their stadium at CenturyLink is the loudest venue in the NFL, designed to hold in crowd noise and reflect it directly onto the field. They fed off of the Legion of Boom. And with the defense playing as lights out as they were, the 12th man was in a frenzy.

Their other weapon, Marshawn Lynch, we knew all too well, and coming into the game, we knew we would have to keep him bottled up if we had any chance of winning. When we played on Monday night, I remember me and Roman both hitting him simultaneously in the hole as hard as we could, knocking him back and falling on top of him under a big pile, thinking that we had done something. I was confused when I heard him laughing hysterically as if Roman and I had just tickled him to death.

That was when I knew he was built different and was by far the hardest back in my career to get on the ground. Instead of running linear in a straight line, he ran with great balance and a wide stance that made him always catch himself, and it was harder to wrap his legs up because they were so far apart. His size and pure strength allowed him to shake off defensive linemen and we knew that there was going to be no such thing as a solo tackle, that we needed as many defenders to the football as possible to get him down.

So far, we had done a decent job, and right before the half, the Seahawks had the ball in our red zone and it was a run play to our left, the side where I was at. Lynch had the ball, and as all of the blockers engaged with the defenders, I saw the hole and he saw the hole. I tried my best to beat him to it, meeting him face-to-face, one-on-one, and he stuttered his feet to shake me, but I didn't go for it and threw my body at his.

This would normally knock a running back backward, dropping him, but he didn't fall. Lucky for me, my teammates jumped on him. The next play, I was covering the slot receiver, who when the ball was snapped, ran from the right side of the defense all the way across the field to the left. This was the other hard part about playing the Seahawks. Russell Wilson rarely threw the ball on time. His plays normally went like this: ball snap, the receivers run the routes that the play calls for, and then when no one is open, he scrambles for another four or five seconds in the backfield while his receivers run around like they are in the backyard getting open. It's already hard to cover receivers in the National Football League for more than three seconds, but to cover one for six, seven, and eight seconds is damn near impossible. And you would have to do that the whole game with Russell Wilson. And this play was no different.

After making it across the field, Russell started to scramble, and the receiver I was covering whipped back around to follow the eyes of Wilson. As we ran back to the original side of the field that we had come from, I saw Wilson throw the ball. He wasn't throwing it to my guy, so I just ran to where the ball was. He was throwing it to Percy Harvin, who was now wide open in the end zone because the defender who was guarding him slipped.

As the ball hung in the air, I tried my best to close the distance, and I was only a few steps away. When Harvin leaped and extended for the football, I had only one option. Assuming he was going to catch it, I had to punish him. Somehow after the mean hit he took against Rafael Bush on the first drive of the game, he was back in a series later.

And now, right before the half, I hit him hard enough to dislodge the ball, put my right shoulder on the back of his head, and then landing, he slammed face-first into the cold turf with all 215 pounds of me on top of him.

Again, his mouthpiece went flying. As his teammates tried to help him up, he was essentially deadweight, drunk from what was surely a concussion, likely his second of the day. Plays like these always present an internal conflict. I hate to see players hurt, especially knowing what we know about the effects of brain trauma.

But if I'm honest, if you put me in that same position a hundred times over, playoff game or not, I would do the same thing. It's the cost of doing business. We got a stop on third down and held them to a field goal going into the halftime down 16–0. When we came back, our defense found our footing and held firm, causing the Seahawks to punt five drives in a row.

Our offense missed another field goal, but managed to put a touchdown on the board, putting us down 16–8. Down eight points with only three minutes and fifty-one seconds left in the game, we knew that this drive would likely be our last attempt to get a stop and get our offense the ball back with enough time and field position to do something with it.

But after Russell Wilson completed a big pass to Doug Baldwin, who made an acrobatic catch over his head, tapping both feet in-bounds before falling out-of-bounds and still maintaining control, we all knew who was getting the ball next. As the Seahawks looked to close the game out, they lined up with three tight ends on the field, with Marshawn Lynch aligned deep in the backfield, a sure sign that this was going to be a run. And when they handed it to him, he wound all the way back to the left side of the defense, right where I was.

But before I could make the tackle, I got pinned into my gap by the wideout who was collapsed down to block me on my outside shoulder, leaving our corner, Keenan Lewis, to tackle Lynch one-on-one with about twelve yards of space. And thirty-one yards later, Marshawn was in the end zone as the 12th man rained down Skittles, his snack of choice, into the end zone.

There was still time left on the clock, but as I sat down on the bench, I knew it was over. We had put up a good fight, but we finally buckled.

The day after the 2012 season ended, we filed into the defensive back room for the last time that season, happy that it was over, laughing and making jokes. We finally settled down so that Ken Flajole could say what he needed to say and we could get out of there. No one was really paying attention, and all I heard was "All right, men, that's all I have. Enjoy your offseason."

After the Raiders, we went on to lose four of the last six, finishing with a 7-9 record. For the first time, I wasn't in the playoffs. In the year that I wanted to bounce back from the debacle in San Fran, I finished the year as a captain of the worst defense in the history of the game, and was ranked by Pro Football Focus as the worst safety in the NFL out of all thirty-two starters. Making it worse, I tore my hamstring off the bone in the week 13 matchup against the Giants and finished the last three weeks of the season on injured reserve.

I wished I could forget that whole year. We went from being a team to be feared with players that were known for being resilient fighters, never out of it, to just a group of guys counting down the days till the season ended.

When the season's done, everyone must come in the very next day to go through exit meetings and a few housekeeping issues. First, every player must get a physical. This is to make sure that you are physically able to play before they let you out for the offseason. If you are not, then you must stay in town and rehab until you are healthy. And just having torn my hamstring, that meant I couldn't pass the physical and I'd be stuck still coming to the facility every day for treatment.

Next, you pack your locker. But they don't give you boxes, they give you construction-grade garbage bags to pack whatever things you may need for the offseason, and to throw away any cleats or old gloves that might be tucked into crevices. Once you're done with that, there's a team meeting that then breaks down into an offensive or defensive meeting that then breaks down into a position meeting, and then you're free.

Still not having a head coach, the team meeting was brief as Joe Vitt, our assistant head coach, addressed the team, thanked us for our fight and our resiliency, and broke it down. I couldn't tell you what Spags said in the defensive meeting because I didn't really pay attention. And now that Ken Flajole was done with our defensive back meeting, there was one more thing left to do. Jabari Greer, being a phenomenal storyteller and a funny prankster, came up with an idea. Emeril's has a string of restaurants throughout the city of New Orleans, and we thought we'd play a joke on Coach Flajole, as none of us really liked him. So we got one of the team interns to laminate a fake gift card that we had printed up. It was in red, white, and green colors, made to look like an Italian restaurant named Lacondi's.

When Coach Flajole finished his meeting and dismissed us, I said, "Hey, Coach, one last thing, we know how tough this season has been. And it's not easy to come to work every day when you're not winning, and we appreciate you. We just wanted to let you know that your effort didn't go unnoticed, and we got you this gift card. It's a new restaurant downtown that Emeril's just opened up. It's called Lacondi's. Have you heard of it? But anyway, it's two hundred dollars. It's a gift card. Take your wife out to go get something to eat. It's on us." He was like, "Oh, thank you." I said, "Yeah, it is one of those new spots." And he looked at the card and said, "Lacondi?" I said, "Yeah, Lacondi's," as the whole room in unison said, "Lick on these nuts." And as we erupted in laughter, we got up and left, just like that.

Later, the intern told me that, as they walked back upstairs to where the coaches' offices were, Flajole, halfway up the steps with the laminated gift card in his hand, turned to the intern and asked, "So is this real?"

---

When the 2013 season came to an end, we had our exit meetings. And although the season didn't end the way we had wanted it to, we all felt good about the strides that we had made in Rob Ryan's defense, how we all had fun and were looking forward to what we could do the following season as a team.

But my contract was up. And now it was March, just a few days before free agency was supposed to start. I was sitting in an apartment I was renting in Columbus, Ohio, while my nerves were beginning to rise.

Since those exit meetings, there'd been radio silence on behalf of the Saints. I hadn't gotten an offer, not even a call to say, "Hey, we're moving in another direction." So I wasn't sure where I'd be the next season, or if they were even planning on bringing me back.

I wanted to start training, but not knowing where I stood with the Saints I decided to go back to Columbus to train at Ohio State while I waited for free agency to sort itself out. So myself, Mo, and Elle, only four months old at the time, moved into a two-bedroom apartment for a few weeks.

Free agency opened up on March 11, but three days before the negotiating period, where agents talk to GMs about moving players, I was nervous not knowing where my future would take me.

When I was getting ready for the draft, I didn't care which team I was going to. I just knew that I would be playing in the NFL, and that was good enough for me. But now with a family, and being part of a winning organization I had given everything to, I couldn't imagine starting over. Especially at an organization that might not prioritize winning like the Saints did.

Ben Dogra, my agent, worked at the CAA talent agency. He was an Indian American man, a sharp negotiator, and almost was never on the scene. And I liked that. I didn't want my agent to be my best friend or be trying to go to parties with me or hanging out. I wanted it to be all about business.

And Ben did a great job of educating me along the way on how the business of the game worked. I'd always thought it funny that he loved to try to pander to my Christian beliefs, always talking about the church and Jesus, when I'm sure he didn't care anything about it.

The first call was from the Rams. Gregg Williams had finally been reinstated into the NFL and was taking over the defensive coordinator job at the Rams and wanted me to lead his defense. He needed a signal caller that could get everybody lined up and help him instill the culture. The same culture that he had instilled in New Orleans and in St. Louis.

He wanted me to be his JV. The problem was, he wanted me to play the free safety spot, to be back where I started, playing deep twenty yards away from the football. Roaming the backfield, trying to re-create what he'd had in the legendary safety Sean Taylor with Washington, and what he'd had in Darren Sharper with the Saints.

When I asked him about the nickel position, he said that they already had a player, Cortland Finnegan, who they liked in the slot, and he wanted me to play exclusively free safety.

The next call was from the Raiders. After seeing me up close the previous season, they were looking for a strong leader to help them build up a losing team. Still being coached by my former defensive back coach, Dennis Allen, Oakland felt like a distant place and I didn't want to be that far away from family and friends. Although Oakland was known for dropping a big bag, that was the last resort.

The third call was from the Eagles. We had just beat them in a playoff game, and they were looking for a safety who was a leader and versatile. And they had some decent money to spend. I figured it was an opportunity for me to go back home and be closer to my family and friends and get back to what I knew. And I liked the fact that they valued my versatility and ability to play multiple positions.

I needed to get my feet under me and reestablish myself as a legitimate player. So after talking it over with Ben and weighing the options, I told Gregg that I couldn't join his team because I wanted a different role. We declined the offer from the Raiders and went with Chip Kelly and the Eagles.

I hung up the phone and told Morrisa that we were going to Philly. In my excitement, I picked up on a small cue. Morrisa's smile said that she was happy for me and excited that I'd have another job. But her eyes told me that she wasn't looking forward to leaving what she called home.

# 7

# SELF-SCOUT

*If you know the enemy and know yourself you need not fear the result of 100 battles. If you know yourself and not your enemy for every victory gained you will also suffer defeat. If you know not yourself nor your enemy you will succumb in every battle.*

**—SUN TZU**

About four months after the Eagles signed me, I was in training camp. I was in the hallway of the NovaCare Complex, staring at the walls. Two long hallways connect the locker room, weight room, and training room area to the rest of the main building. From end to end, it's decked out with large photos of players that have made the Pro Bowl in an Eagles jersey, from former players like the legendary giant of a wideout Harold Carmichael to current players like DeSean Jackson and Shady McCoy. And I'd yet to make a Pro Bowl, an honor voted on by fans, players, and coaches that says, "You are one of the few elite at your position." We had to walk down those halls fifteen to twenty times a day, and every single time that I walked past the empty spot at the end of the hallway, I knocked on it twice because I had made up my mind that I was going to get on that wall.

It was the beginning of the day, and there was a checklist of things that we needed to do before we made it to team meetings to start the day. Chip Kelly, freshly arrived from Oregon University, is a believer in analytics and sports science. It's his secret sauce and what he thinks makes the difference of elite athletes, and he is not wrong. There's evidence to support that football, although it has some of the best athletes in the world, is decades behind when it comes to maximizing the performance of athletes. Everything from diet to sleep to hydration to training schedules is archaic.

To start the day, when you got into the locker room, there was an empty cup waiting for you. A cup not meant for you to take a drug test, but for you to piss in for them to test your hydration, to see if you were hydrated enough not to be compromised in training. Next, you weighed in to make sure that you hadn't lost or gained too much weight from the day before. Next, you had to lie on the ground for two to three minutes with a heart rate monitor that tested your stress levels and your nervous system to see if your body had recovered enough to train hard.

In the weight rooms, they have trackers on every single platform that track your bar speed and power outputs and save them into a running form so that you can see and compare your performances over time. After every practice, there is a slot where players can get a ten-minute massage to flush the lactic acid buildup from hard days of training. There are smoothies custom-made for each player based on their dietary needs. And if you were to skip one of these steps, if you don't weigh in, if you don't piss, or you don't get your heart rate monitored, they will pull you out of meetings until you do.

Even in practice, we wore shirts that had GPS trackers in them, not because they wanted to see everywhere you went, but they wanted to track your acceleration, deceleration, and your high-speeds yardage to know what types of workload they were putting on you on a daily basis. If you worked too hard, they may give you a day off, or if you worked too little, they'd push you to go harder in practice, and it varied depending on your position group.

After I signed, I helped the GM, Howie Roseman, convince Darren Sproles that the Eagles were the place he wanted to come, and they traded for him. He and I laughed every day as the players who were not used to being in this environment complained about the long list of things that Chip made us do before we started our day and how they had nothing to do with football.

It was definitely tedious, but training camp was extremely easy. I was used to spending the first four to five weeks of training camp stuck in a hotel, going to and from practice every day, not able to leave until after the third preseason game. But with Chip, we only had to stay in the hotel for the first week before we ever even played a preseason game. That alone was a piece of cake.

Chip also doesn't believe in long meetings because science says that the human brain can only focus for about forty-five minutes in a given meeting. So our meetings were no longer than those forty-five minutes. Sean Payton would have us in meetings until ten o'clock at night with only enough time to go to your room, sleep, and be on the field at eight thirty in the morning. But with Chip, we'd be home by 5:00 p.m. I'd trade in the checklist of things we needed to do in the morning any day for the time and rest that Chip gave us.

I'd shown up here with something to prove. They didn't know me, but they were going to find out. I was determined to push myself every day. I wanted to get back to being the shit-talking bully that was uber competitive and extra confident, traits that in the last two seasons I'd forgotten and I'd gotten away from, things that had gotten me here. I had made it to Ohio State not by what I did in games, but how I competed in a drill. I won the Thorpe not through what I did on Saturdays, but through my daily habits of using every single rep as a chance to improve. I knew I had everything that I needed to be the best, the size, the speed, the intelligence, the length, but it was up to me to learn how to develop it and use it. So I treated every day like a game. Teammates or not, I wanted to win, and if you weren't on the same page as I was, you'd better strap in.

I'm intense in everything that I do. The Eagles signed me to a three-year contract for $15.5 million. Essentially, it was a prove-it deal, meaning I'd have two years to determine whether I was going to stay in the league or be out of it. If I didn't perform, I'd never make it to that third deal that third year. After the first two seasons, they'd know whether they wanted to extend my contract or simply cut me. And if I got cut after a second contract, the likelihood was that I wouldn't be signed again, and if this was my last contract, I was going to go out being myself.

I'd stopped comparing myself to other players. I'd stopped watching tape of the legends like Ed Reed and Troy Polamalu, the guys whose games I couldn't replicate. I wasn't above stealing a tip or two, but I stopped trying to compare my stats and my abilities to the others that were out there. I'd had to because the comparisons were killing me.

The Saints signed Jairus Byrd, the top safety in free agency at the time. They made him the highest paid safety in the history of the game after not offering me anything; and to make matters worse, Pro Football Focus put out a graphic showcasing and comparing both our stats side by side. Touchdowns allowed, I had twelve. Jairus, only three. Interceptions, I had three. Jairus had twelve. Missed tackles, I had forty-five. Jairus had fifteen. I had the most missed tackles among safeties. Jairus had the most interceptions among safeties.

I took this graphic, printed it out, and put it in my locker. But I wasn't mad at Jairus. He balled. I was happy he got paid. In fact, later that year, I would have him host my foundation's fundraiser in New Orleans during the bye week to make sure I could keep my programs lively in New Orleans. I put it in my locker to remind myself of what happens when I tried to compare myself to other players, when I didn't embrace who I was and what I already had and use it to the best of my abilities, and wanted to remind myself daily that I wasn't going to be this player. Every single day that I walked into the Nova-Care facility, I wore this chip on my shoulder, having something to prove, looking for every opportunity to get better.

As I walked through the locker room later that day, Darren Sproles came up to me. "Ey." "What's up, bro?" I said from under my hoodie that I wore every single day. "Man, what you do to these people?" "What you mean?" He said, "Man, you got these folks scared." He said that Howie Roseman asked him to talk to me. They were wondering if I was happy with my decision to come to the Eagles because I walked around like I was upset or mad. I chuckled and said, "Nah, man, I'm just focused."

Back in March while I was waiting to find out which team I would go to in free agency, I thought it was a good idea and a good time to check with my financial advisor over at Merrill Lynch, whose offices were in Columbus. I was sitting at the head of a long conference table with Morrisa on my right. Steve, my financial advisor, a former Buckeye turned moneyman, and his team of financial planners ran down my portfolio and its performance. I didn't know much of anything when it came to money. No one in the Saints locker room really talked about it except for Will Smith and Charles Grant, our highly paid defensive linemen who loved to show off their money and talk about the lavish lifestyles they lived. Other than that, I only heard rumors about a player who was no longer on the team who convinced a lot of guys in the locker room to invest in a business venture that went south and lost a bunch of money for everyone involved, including the likes of Sean Payton, Drew Brees, and a few others.

So in the Saints locker room, business and money were taboo. My only lesson in financial education was work, save, and spend. My grandmother used to give us AriZona iced tea bottles, once our parents let us start drinking them, as piggy banks. We would do chores and things around the house to earn coins, and once you saved up enough coins, you could spend those coins at the bodega at the end of the block. I had millions in the bank, and that was my understanding of money. Work, save, spend.

I always thought NFL money, the millions of dollars we would make, would mean I'd never have to work again, and my family would be set for generations. Until I saw that episode of the *30 for 30* series titled "Broke" that came out in 2012. It showcased a statistic that said 80 percent of all athletes will end up bankrupt, divorced, or depressed within five years of their career ending. It featured athletes from multiple sports, outlining how they had squandered millions in every which way imaginable. Lavish spending, scams, being drained by family, risky investments, and people these athletes trusted flat-out stealing their money. The doc scared the shit out of me. Not only was I wrong about how this money would impact my life and my family, but I didn't know enough to protect what I was working so hard to earn.

So I asked my advisors to put together a projection to see how long my money would last if I never got another contract. I was a free agent at the time and technically unemployed. There was no guarantee I'd be signed. After playing out my entire contract, I earned $16,482,000 but had only $5 million in cash in the bank. After giving half to Uncle Sam and my agent and living a little bit of life, suddenly

I didn't feel as comfortable as I thought I was. Steve explained that I was spending about $750,000 a year and, at that rate, if indeed this was my last contract, my bank account would be at zero in about ten years. I was only twenty-six years old and Steve was telling me that I'd be broke at thirty-six. I rubbed my face nervously as I didn't know it was possible to be broke with $5 million in the bank. I was in shock. What the hell was I spending this money on? Realistically, the majority of the money I was spending was barely on me. I wasn't into expensive jewelry or the latest clothes or even cars. My biggest expenditures were tithes, giving to my foundation and other charities, and surprisingly, my parents. I was spending significant amounts of money getting them out of debt and flying them to and from games. But the biggest expenditure came in my rookie season when my mother was fired from her job, for not returning from leave when she was supposed to. I had asked her to come to New Orleans so I didn't have to spend Christmas alone that first year. I didn't know it at that time, but she sacrificed work to do so and lost her job shortly thereafter.

That got worse when, about a year or two later, my father was let go from his job and couldn't keep consistent work. So I was also supporting their lifestyle as well as my own growing family. This was all becoming eerily similar to the stories I saw in that documentary. As we took the elevator back down the stairs toward the valet, Steve ensured me the whole way that I'd get another contract and would have time and a bit of leeway to correct my spending. But it was a wake-up call to a harsh reality.

It was the opening week against the Jacksonville Jaguars on a hot September day at Lincoln Financial Field. At halftime, as we made our way to the locker room, down 17–0, the Philly faithful were doing what they do best.

"Booooooooooo! Y'all suck!"

"Get your shit together!"

I thought it was the funniest thing in the world. I walked into the locker room with a full chuckle. I'd decided to take a different approach that season. I'd spent too much time being so caught up in the angst of the games that I'd missed the small details of the environment. In pregame, I didn't warm up with headphones, not wanting to go through this entire experience without ever once really paying attention to the environment. So I looked up at the banners on either side of the stadium, one representing all of the championship teams that have worn the Eagles uniform, and on the other, the legendary players that have had their jerseys retired and enshrined forever in Eagles history. You saw the Philly faithful filing in with jerseys of their favorite players, past and present.

I'd started a new routine. As the national anthem played, I'd find three open seats across the stadium. I'd close my eyes and begin to talk to my elders. I imagined my grandmother, Barbra, and both of my grandfathers, Henry and Willie Sr., all watching with the best seats in the house. I asked them for toughness, courage, and love, all of the things that I saw them pour into their own families. Today as the anthem played I wondered if they were proud of me. I felt my eyes water up and my chest fill with pride when I contemplated where I was standing. I was going into my sixth season in the NFL on a new team, and I was ready and prepared to make my name mean something.

As a scene from the movie *Rocky* played on the big screen and it was time for kickoff. They played the fight song, the fans erupted in "E-A-G-L-E-S! Eagles!" and it was time to go.

We kicked off the ball and the defense took the field. We started the game with a three and out, much to the delight of the fans, but that would be the last time that they would cheer in the first half.

Malcolm celebrates his first birthday, December 20, 1988.

Malcolm all smiles after a Pop Warner football game, 1996.

Malcolm and his grandmother Barbra Jenkins embrace, July 3, 1999.

Malcolm and his brothers, Myles (*middle*) and Martin (*right*), smile for the camera.

Barbra Jenkins reading
hieroglyphics in Egypt.

Unbothered: Malcolm in the
backyard of his childhood
home, Piscataway, NJ.

Malcolm talks with Ohio State coaches on his official recruiting visit. Left to right:
defensive coordinator Mel Tucker, Malcolm, and wideouts coach Darrel Hazell,
December 2004.

An elated Malcolm Jenkins (*left*) surrounded by family and friends after being drafted fourteenth overall in the NFL draft to the New Orleans Saints with his mother, Gwendolyn V. Jenkins (*middle*), and his younger brother Martin Jenkins (*right*). New Brunswick, NJ, April 25, 2009.

Newlywed Malcolm and Morrisa Jenkins smile as they second line out of their wedding reception, New Orleans, LA, July 15, 2011.

Malcolm and his daughters, Elle (*left*) and Selah (*right*), during a family vacation to Marrakech, Morocco, 2018.

An emotional Malcolm tours the male slave dungeons at the Cape Coast Castle in Ghana, July 2018.

Malcolm and his brothers, Myles (*left*) and Martin (*right*), stop to eat coconuts, Accra, Ghana, July 2018.

India Robinson and Malcolm share a fun moment backstage on *The Rich Eisen Show*, July 2022.

Malcolm and lifelong friend Ralonda Johnson smile after being accepted into the honors society, Piscataway High School, 2005.

The executive members of Malcolm Inc., from left to right: Gwendolyn V. Jenkins, chief philanthropic officer; India Robinson, chief marketing officer; Malcolm Jenkins, chief executive officer; Ralonda Johnson, chief financial officer; and Joe Johnson, chief operations officer.

Turf Moor stadium, Burnley, England: The Malcolm Inc. team celebrates its investment into Burnley Football Club. Left to right: Brian Hinds, India Robinson, Malcolm, Ralonda Johnson, and Joe Johnson, 2021.

Longtime teammates Malcolm and Drew Brees reunite after their first game as opponents, Lincoln Financial Field, Philadelphia, 2015.

Malcolm leaves the visitors' locker room, Lombardi Trophy in hand, after defeating the Patriots in Super Bowl LII, U.S. Bank Stadium, February 4, 2018.

Malcolm shows off his Super Bowl rings to his daughters, Selah (*left*) and Elle (*right*), December 2018. (Photograph by Christopher Horne)

Victory: Malcolm lifts the Lombardi Trophy as he speaks to thousands of onlooking Eagles fans at the conclusion of the Super Bowl celebration parade, Philadelphia, February 8, 2018.

Malcolm along with family and friends pose for a photo, May 2022.

On our first eight offensive possessions, two of the drives ended in fumbles. One ended on an interception, four ended in punts. The last possession ended as time expired for halftime. Defense wasn't doing that great, either. With all of the turnovers, we gave up seventeen points. And it could have been worse than that. We actually blocked a field goal and they missed another one.

Coming off the field, down seventeen, to the boos of the home crowd, many of my teammates were not as amused as I was. Some of them mumbled things like "That's why I hate playing here."

I was confused by their sensitivity. I even said to two of them that had found comfort in each other's complaints, "Did you see what we just did? I'd be booing us, too."

I wanted to boo at us right there in the locker room. What made it worse was that the Jaguars at that time were not a good franchise. The energy in the locker room was quiet and dejected.

But the newcomers—myself, Darren Sproles, and Super Bowl champion special teams guru Chris Maragos—all looked at one another with confusion. We had come from championship-caliber teams that never believed that they were out of a game no matter what the score was. So to see this team on the brink of buckling to the Jaguars was infuriating. "Yo, Sproles, why these guys acting like bitches? This is the Jaguars." We began to turn to any player who would listen, who still had a little bit of fight in him, one player at a time. "Do your fucking job, and I promise you, we'll be fine. If you don't think we can beat the Jacksonville Jaguars, then our season is over before it's started. Focus on doing your job one play at a time and we'll get it done." When we came back out for that second half, we never let them score again and scored thirty-four unanswered points, much to the delight of the beloved Eagles fans.

When I told Sproles I was focused, I wasn't playing. Like a madman, I was trying to find every hole in my game and close it. I wasn't interested in anyone who wasn't on the same page. And I'd found a partner in crime. Jordan Matthews, our second-round pick from Vanderbilt, was a young talent with an old soul. His six-foot-three frame, competitive drive, and seemingly endless tank of energy made him the perfect person to spar with. Every day during practice and after practice, we'd compete, hard. He was eager to learn and I was eager to teach. If I could make him better, he could make me better. It was midway through camp and the soreness had kicked in for most players, but Jordan and I stuck to the routine, pointing out any flaws we saw in each other's technique. I was always someone who did extra work, but it wasn't always deliberate. But a conversation I'd had with Drew when I was a Saint changed that.

Having one of the greatest quarterbacks of all time in my locker room, I watched Drew like a hawk when it came to his preparation and his routine. One of my favorite things to do with Roman during practice was to make up elaborate disguises on the back end in the secondary to try to confuse Drew. Rarely, though, did we succeed.

In order to get an indicator on what the coverage is, most quarterbacks read the safeties. If there are two safeties that are deep, that means a run is favorable. If there is one safety deep, pass. In practice, Roman and I positioned ourselves deep to convince Drew to run. Then as soon as he snapped the ball, I was going to shoot into my run gap.

Drew got to the line of scrimmage, licked his hands three times as he normally did, and got ready to call for the snap, then he stopped. He looked at me and Roman, changed the play, snapped the ball, and quickly completed the pass down the seam of the defense. After practice, I went over to Drew.

"How'd you know?"

That's when Drew explained to me that while Roman and I almost had him with our positioning, the linebacker was moved over just a little bit too much, leaving the entire C gap open, which meant that it was likely my gap, and I was going to blitz.

"That probably would've confused most people, but the linebackers weren't in unison with you."

That blew my mind: the level of detail that he had at the line of scrimmage, the level of knowledge that he had of where all the defenders on the field should be, not just my position, almost as if he knew the defense better than we did.

"Okay, Drew, so how do you prepare for me?"

"Well, you're a very smart player, you're good at the line of scrimmage, you're physical, a great tackler, you know what you're doing. But you don't have good ball skills. If you're ever one-on-one in the deep part of the field, I'm going to throw it up. Worst-case scenario, it's just incomplete. You break it up or drop it, but we're not banking on you catching the ball."

That fucked me up. My teammate not only identified a weakness in my game, but he also articulated it in a way no one had ever done before. Every team in the NFL has scouts, and that was probably the same report that everyone had—and they were right. I had a problem catching the ball. I still remember Jimmy Graham leaving a pair of gloves in my locker with "Drop 'em Jenkins" written on them and his signature underneath.

It was all jokes and laughs when it happened, but those moments oftentimes stayed in my mind when I missed an opportunity to make a play, understanding that this was the narrative that was building around me, and it only made it worse when the self-fulfilling prophecy became true. But this was great insight to properly and critically evaluate the player I was. In football, we call this the self-scout. We spend a ton of time scouting our opponents, scouting the offensive coordinators, scouting the receivers and matchups that we have, but spend very little time understanding our own weaknesses and studying ourselves.

I knew the coaches in Philly wanted me to play safety and likely wouldn't give me many reps at covering receivers during practice, so I had to continue to work on that part of my game. Catching the football from a distance of over twenty yards and working on my press technique were my main two objectives for camp, and as Jordan and I walked off the field, I knew it was going to pay off. I could feel it.

———

They come in bunches! After the Jacksonville game, I'd been on a hot streak. Week 2, we went on the road to play quarterback Andrew Luck and the Indianapolis Colts. And in the fourth quarter we were down 27–20, with the Colts threatening to score again on our 22-yard line. A touchdown or even a field goal would put them up ten points with less than five minutes to play. Luck dropped back and began to stare at T. Y. Hilton, making it apparent that he was his target. When he let the ball go, I had already been driving on the route. It hit me right in my shoulder pads and I trapped it to my chest like a Nerf ball to Velcro. We won the game 30–27. That interception was crucial for us to win the game.

The very next week we came back home to Lincoln Financial Field, playing the Washington Commanders in an emotional divisional game. We found ourselves up 34–27. And with Washington desperately trying to get a score late in the game, I was in the deep part of the field. Kirk Cousins, the quarterback, was under the center. He got the snap, and as he dropped back, he was staring right at me. I held my place dead center in the middle of the field, eighteen yards deep. As soon as his eyes snapped to the receiver on my left, I began to break like I was Benny from the movie *The Sandlot*, stealing bases in my fresh PF Flyers. I took three steps before he even let the ball go. He overthrew his intended target, which gave me just enough space to run up under it and make a diving catch. My hands were on fire! We went on to win that game.

We were in San Francisco, up 3–0 against the 49ers, and Brandon Boykin, our starting nickel, was out with an injury, giving me an opportunity to play the role. I was lined up against Anquan Boldin. He was a big, physical, tough receiver who, for his size and physicality, was really quick at the line of scrimmage, making it difficult to put your hands on him and disrupt his route concepts. On 3rd and 3, with me lined up right in his face, he hopped off the ball and then gave me a mean Allen Iverson–ish crossover step, breaking toward the inside of the field, while I lunged outside. At first, he appeared to have a step on me, but that was actually the plan. I had help inside. Linebacker DeMeco Ryans took Boldin from me, and as soon as we passed that off, I put my eyes on QB Colin Kaepernick. I could see that he was getting ready to try to throw to a receiver behind me.

Because it looked like I was man coverage, Colin anticipated that I would chase Anquan and that he could throw it in the hole I would leave. So when he let the ball go, he was very surprised when I slammed on the brakes and stood right in the window as he threw the ball right to me. I spun around and all I saw was linemen. I ran around the first one and then I saw Colin coming. I cut back to my right, crossing his face and making him fall. I stepped out of the grasp of one of the linemen trying to tackle me, cut back one more time down the left sideline, my legs heavy, driving head down all the way to the end zone. Touchdown. Three weeks in a row, three picks. Now I was capping it off with a touchdown. I was going crazy. My teammates were feeling it, too. They saw the immediate difference with an injection of guys like me, Chris Maragos, and Darren Sproles on the team.

Later, Sproles returned a kick for a touchdown. Usually, the statistics say if you score on defense and you score on special teams, then you have about a 98 percent chance of winning that game, yet somehow we found a way to lose.

Understanding my strengths and weaknesses was allowing me to put myself in the best positions to win.

---

It was the offseason in 2016 and I was in high demand. Coming off a Pro Bowl season in 2015 in a major media market like Philadelphia, the requests for appearances and media gigs were rolling in. A good problem to have. Up until then, I hadn't had many endorsements, and the fee I charged for an appearance was relatively small compared to some of the deals I'd heard about other players getting.

There was an appearance for me to do a commercial for some company, I don't remember who, because my assistant, India Robinson, had already shot it down.

"Nah, the fee is too low. Ask for $10K per hour."

India had been working as my assistant for a few years by then, as a side hustle. A Delta from Spelman who never took no for an answer, she worked as a booker for a marketing agency. When brands wanted to have celebrities endorse a campaign or a product, she found the talent for it. So she knew what other athletes had been paid for similar work and, more important, she knew what the budgets of these companies were. That information was vital when negotiating. If you knew what they were willing to pay, then you knew what to ask for.

Back in 2011, I had a chance to be in my first commercial. I got a call from Foday.

"Hey, I got a homegirl who's looking for an NFL player to put in a commercial. I didn't want to pass her a number if you weren't interested. Just let me know."

"Yeah, for sure."

I hadn't been in a commercial yet, and figured it was about time. India called and explained that she was organizing talent to partici-pate in Verizon's Black History Month campaign, for which Marvin Sapp and Jill Scott were already locked in. All she had to tell me was Jill Scott and I was in. We were going to play the following week on a Monday night, so I had a couple extra bonus days off in the schedule. The date they were filming was on my birthday, so I figured I could get paid and have a birthday trip to New York sponsored by Verizon. I got paid $10,000 for that. It was the most by far I had gotten for my likeness. When India first asked what I wanted to get paid, I said I usually got around $1,500 to $2,500 an hour.

"Oooooo-kay, how about this," India said. "We're going to get you $10K for only about two hours of work. And your flight and hotel will be comped. Sound good?"

Not understanding my value, I trusted what my marketing rep told me. When she came back with deals for $2,000 an hour and said that was the most they were willing to pay, I assumed they were just as incentivized as I was to get the most money possible. Players have so much loyalty to their representation and don't understand that the reps aren't actually employed by the player. They have a responsibil-ity to the client but work for the agency. They're incentivized to do what's best for the company, not necessarily what's best for you. They don't get bonuses for saving time and energy; they get bonuses for the dollars they bring in, even if that means wholesaling you.

One time I got a call from a good friend at the NFL Players As-sociation.

"You need to take your marketing rep's name off of the NFLPA registry."

"Why?"

"Well, these companies call the PA because they want to work with players. We've already negotiated the prices, we've already negotiated what the deal is, and then we'll send it directly to the player. If you list your rep, we'll send it to the rep, and they'll take twenty percent commission on something they didn't find. These are deals that we are finding for y'all and we want to be able to go directly to you, because there's no negotiation involved, and you get to keep all of that money."

My rep never told me this. But these were small details that I began to pay attention to.

When I allowed India to look over my deals, she would ask for numbers that I thought were crazy when it came to appearance fees. I had always been told by reps that it's hard for defensive players to get deals. We already wear a helmet for a living, which makes us less marketable, and defensive players don't score touchdowns.

Then I thought India might be being a bit greedy.

"How much do you make a year, Malcolm?"

"Well, I make about eight million a year."

"Okay, well, how many weeks is that?"

"Seventeen."

"You do the math, Malcolm, at approximately forty hours a week. That's a little over $11,700 an hour that you get paid for football, and that's what you love to do. When thinking about appearances and getting paid for your time, that should be your rate, and it may be high, but at least that's the basis you have to justify to yourself why you would come down off of that rate, and you have to consider the time that you put into these events. It's not just the event, it's the journey to it. So if it takes you forty-five minutes or an hour to go to this place, and then you do an hour-long appearance and you've got to drive back, that's really three hours of your time. If they want you to fly somewhere and you have to stay overnight, that's a day rate."

Realizing that I had just learned a valuable lesson about how to value my time more than money, I made India my manager. Talent without hunger, or vice versa, can only go so far. But those who have both have no limitations. When you find people who are talented and hungry, align with them.

━━━━━

That same spring I made India my manager, I had one more move I needed to make. Back in 2010, my second year in the NFL, I was due $9 million, all in one bonus. Ralonda, who I've known since the days when she would get me in trouble with Sister Friar at the Chad School, had become my closest and most trusted friend. She was an auditor by trade, so crunching numbers and finding the holes in budgets is what she loves to do. She was afraid of me being one of those athletes that go broke. She didn't want me to be a statistic. She'd literally have nightmares about me blowing my money and would always hound me on what I was doing with my finances. Quite frankly, she and her husband, Joe, are the only people who I feel comfortable with talking about how much money I make and all of the things I do financially. When I told her about the money I was due to make that year, she called me and seemed anxious. She asked what I was going to do with the money. "Are you going to invest it? Are you looking into real estate? Are you doing franchising? What's the plan?"

"I don't know. I ain't never had nine million dollars. What am I supposed to do with it?"

She said, "You need to get into real estate."

So, I called my financial advisor, and I asked about real estate opportunities.

He said, "Oh, I didn't know that you were interested in that. Sure, I'll look into it," and within a month, I had an opportunity to buy an apartment building.

The apartment building was listed for about $1.2 million and had sixteen offers on it, and it was smack-dab in the growing hotbed of the Short North area in Columbus, Ohio.

The strategy, though, was that the sellers were desperate, and having access to the new money that I acquired, I had a larger line of credit. I was able to use that line of credit to present a cash offer of about $950,000 to the sellers, which they accepted. That building was fully occupied, meaning that it was already cash-flowing with rent from the occupants. The interest rate on that credit was very low, somewhere around 2 percent. So I was able to buy a million-dollar building at a discount with cash that was not mine. A building that was generating money that paid for itself.

I remember when we did the deal feeling like I had done something illegal or that I had gotten away with something. In fact, I had just learned a new lesson about how money works. It's not about using your labor as the sole source of all your income. It's about using your labor to acquire cash that you save that gives you an opportunity to leverage credit or assets to buy other assets that make money.

They'll tell athletes all the time that your financial advisor, your agent, your marketing rep, all these people work for you, you should be the boss, and most of us are unprepared to be a boss, and quite frankly, I had to learn that those people actually don't work for you.

There was a reason they hadn't put me in real estate already. That's because they don't collect fees off money and assets that they don't manage. My financial advisor would get zero commissions on any money I made outside of his investments. So real estate, franchising, the things that grow your money double and triple that can cash-flow and do other things outside of the stock market, a financial advisor usually won't advise on those. So it made sense why he would not suggest these other alternative investments and instead focus mainly on the stock market and bonds.

Sitting at Honey's, a small restaurant in the Northern Liberties area of Philly, I told Ralonda, "I think I want to get into franchising, and I want you and Joe to run it."

It was December 20, 2014, my birthday, a week after losing to the Cowboys. We were on the road against the Commanders. With only two games left in the regular season we needed to win them both in order to make it into the playoffs and secure a Wild Card berth. Since the first four games, the interceptions had slowed down but it didn't frustrate me like it used to. I was solely focused on finding every way possible to affect the game. Trying my best to stay in the moment.

Chip believed we needed to not only be the most physically tough team on the field, but we needed to be mentally tough, too. Especially to play in Philadelphia. If I was crushed by the Saints fans just a few years back, I would never be able to make it through multiple seasons in Philly. The fans and media surrounding the sports teams are notoriously critical and don't mind kicking you while you're down, in fact they do it for fun. I liked being back in that environment. It reminded me of my dad. But I also knew it didn't bother me, because I was now playing well and wasn't on the receiving end of all of the criticism.

During the offseason and training camp, Chip had multiple speakers come talk to the team. My favorite was sports psychologist Stephany Coakley, who had a background in working with sniper units in the military. She introduced the concept of thought cycles to the team. Most guys didn't pay attention during these talks, but I took notes intently as I sat in the large auditorium-size meeting room. She asked the room to contemplate what happens in our minds when we have a bad play, then write the thoughts down in the order that they normally come. If I gave up a touchdown or dropped an interception that I should've had, my thoughts went like this:

1. I suck!
2. My teammates probably think I suck, too.
3. The fans definitely think I suck and are probably roasting me on Twitter.
4. Maybe I should accept that I'm just an average player with an average career.

Then Stephany asked us to identify the point of no return, meaning which thought, once reached, caused us to spiral mentally. For me it was Twitter. If I thought about what people said about me on social media, during a game, it was over with. "The trick," she said, "is to stop yourself before you get to that thought and bring your mind back to the present moment. You will miss the opportunities in front of you if your mind is occupied with the past or the future that has nothing to do with the now." She told us to create a reset. Something you could routinely do that would remind you to place your mind in the present moment. My cue to refocus came from knocking on my helmet twice. I would even do it in practice, after every play, good or bad. I wanted to be focused on the next rep. What I found is that I played with a clearer mind. I was more poised in the ebbs and flows of games, and I was having the best season of my career.

At halftime we had the lead, 14–10, over the Commanders, who were not very good and were 3-11 at this point. When playing divisional rivals you can always expect a good fight. I'd been playing special teams all year. Something most of the people around here were surprised by. Most starters, especially the veterans, don't care to play special teams. They want to save their energy and time focusing on their position. I've always seen the special teams units as a vital part of the game, and they could determine the outcome of the game just as well as the offense or the defense. It's considered the dirty work, for the guys being paid league minimum and who rarely get talked about in the papers. But I loved the dirty work. As I lined up as the safety on the kickoff unit to start the second half, I knocked my helmet and said out loud, as I had grown accustomed to doing, "Plan on making the play." As the kicker approached the ball, I took off down the field. My job was to tackle the returner if he happened to break free from the rest of the coverage unit, as a last line of defense, but when it was kicked to my side, I liked to play a more aggressive style. Most times, the return units leave the safeties unblocked and choose to double-team some of the bigger, more disruptive players. So I hung back just far enough to see the play develop, and then filled where the hole in the coverage appeared, knowing that was where the returner would also go. Andre Roberts, the return man for the Commanders, cut to his left, sprinting toward a seam in our coverage unit. As I tracked him and identified exactly where he wanted to go, I accelerated to get into position to meet him there. I had him pinned in the space on the field between the numbers and the sideline, so all I had to do was make the tackle. As I approached, I saw him bring his arm up as if he'd attempt a stiff-arm. I'd been working on a counter for that move. I slapped his extended arm downward with my left hand, making his body lean forward and the ball come away from his body. With the ball exposed, I quickly followed up using my long arms with a punch to the football with my right hand. The ball, like a perfect layup on the greens on the golf course, hit the ground and gently rolled, avoiding the sideline, as my teammates pounced on it. Eagles football! This shit was getting easy.

But after the turnover, our offense was kept out of the end zone and we missed the field goal. RGIII drove the Commanders offense down the field with the help of two roughing-the-passer penalties by our defensive line, and they scored a touchdown, taking the lead, 17–14. In a huge swing of momentum, the Commanders again drove down the field with a big catch and a forced penalty by wideout

DeSean Jackson and scored again, 24–14 to close the third quarter. But with everything to play for, we rallied back and scored ten straight to tie the game 24–24. A late interception by the Commanders defense in the final two minutes of the game gave the Commanders the field position they needed to kick the game-winning field goal, crushing our playoff hopes with it. Even with a win the next week against the Giants, we finished the season 10-6, one win short of making the playoffs.

On the train ride home from DC to Philly, per usual I watched the game film. I was looking like the player I wanted to be when I started the season. I was learning to play my own style of ball and I had the best year of my career. I just needed to stay in the moment and learn to use what I had at my disposal.

# 8

# TIPS AND OVERTHROWS

*Diligence is the mother of good luck.*

—BENJAMIN FRANKLIN

I was going into my seventh season, my second with the Eagles, and had established myself as a leader on the team. Players and coaches alike came to me when they had problems with other players. One of the strength coaches pulled me and Chris Maragos to the side and asked if we could go talk to Byron Maxwell, the free agent corner, the fourth member of the Legion of Boom, who we just signed for $10 million a year to be our lockdown cornerback. He was in his locker, packing up, leaving in the middle of a voluntary workout.

When Chris and I went into the locker room, Byron was halfway dressed with a nonchalant look on his face. "What's up, bro? You coming to this workout?" I asked.

"Oh, nah, I'm about to go do some yoga and go swimming." He was dead serious.

Byron was as laid-back as they come. He was definitely not one of those ultra-hard workers who loved being in the weight room. He was a yogi, who was more into a holistic training regiment. I personally don't care what you like to do. It's supposed to be voluntary. But it would've been better to not show up at all than to show up and leave when it was time to work. Chris and I knew how a move like that would look to the team and how it would definitely cause a stir among the coaches, and convinced him to hang out for a little bit. We reiterated that it was voluntary, so he didn't need to go in and try to kill himself in the weight room, but just go make himself look busy so he didn't start a ruckus.

After the workout, we got on the field and as I waited at the line for the strength coach to start the conditioning drill, I had Tim Tebow, the additional backup quarterback we just signed, eagerly waiting behind me. The drill we were doing was called Cut 300, which means you ran fifty yards and back three times, totaling three hundred yards. Meant to build your endurance, it was not a conditioning test, there was no set time that we needed to come in under. We just needed to maintain a pace that was suitable for the coaches. And the last thing you wanted was somebody like Tim Tebow to set the pace. He loved to show off how much better shape he was in than everyone else, and would likely separate from the pack, leaving the coaches yelling at everybody else to keep up. We weren't there to be track stars and the season was months away, and again, it was voluntary. Most of us were there to work on our crafts and appease the coaches.

The whistle blew and I took off. Every time I hit one of the lines, I could feel Tim on my back, talking to me like I needed encouragement.

"Come on, OG, don't let me show you up."

Chip, who'd overthrown GM Howie Roseman and had full control over our roster, had made moves that baffled everybody. We traded quarterback Nick Foles to the Rams for their quarterback, Sam Bradford. Then we traded Shady McCoy, the Eagles' all-time leading rusher who was still in his prime, to the Buffalo Bills in a one-for-one trade for linebacker Kiko Alonso, a guy that none of us knew, but had played for Chip at the University of Oregon. He let our best receiver, Jeremy Maclin, walk in free agency, and then made

DeMarco Murray the highest-paid running back in the game a year after the Cowboys just ran him into the dirt a whopping 392 times. On paper some of these signings looked solid, they were good players coming off good years. But the issue was fit.

Then there were the rumors that Chip was racist, that he had gotten rid of all the Black players who weren't afraid to speak their minds in meetings. I never believed this to be true, but it didn't help that somehow Riley Cooper was still on the roster. He was the slow, aging wideout, who the year before I arrived was caught on camera saying he'd "fight every nigger here" at a Kenny Chesney concert. All of this created a shit ton of distractions. Distractions I could not afford. The average length of a career for a first-round draft pick was seven seasons, and this was my seventh year and I was on the second year of that three-year deal, knowing that this season would likely determine my future either to stay an Eagle or get cut at the end of the season. So while all the craziness surrounded the team, I was poised to build off the career season I had just finished a few months ago.

When we finished the conditioning and the day was done, annoyed, I went back on the field to do some extra drills. The one bright spot was that we had a new defensive back coach and I finally felt like I wasn't coaching myself. Cory Undlin, a former teacher turned football coach, had us doing the most minute drills I'd done in my career, teaching us step-by-step how to get in and out of our breaks. The same breaks that I'd been doing since I was in Pop Warner. He was teaching them as if we were remedial, like he was teaching a dance to someone with two left feet. Taking one step at a time, talking about the inches between our steps and how long our feet hung in the air. When we got to the meeting rooms, he turned on some of the full-speed drills and showed us in slow motion the efficiency of our footwork, literally measuring the distance of inches between our steps. This was the first coach who ever broke down the body mechanics of how your arms affect what your feet do.

Imagine trying to run your fastest 40 with your arms out to your sides or out in front of you. It would look pretty funny, but it would also be slow as shit. But that's exactly what many defensive backs do when they transition from moving backward to forward, flailing their arms all over the place, and I was one of them. My whole career I didn't realize I had been playing with this deficiency. These were the few inches that I was looking for to take my game to the next level. My whole career I'd heard that football was a game of inches, but no one up until that point had actually taught the inches.

The 2015 season was in full swing as I stood at my locker during the media availability before our week 5 matchup against none other than the New Orleans Saints. They were asking me if this would be a revenge game for me, since the Saints let me walk just a year earlier. I gave them the politically correct answer that I'd prepared for this game just like any other game.

But I was lying. I'd had this game circled on my calendar since they announced our schedule back in the offseason. Both teams were 1-3. Our season was going about as crazy as we had predicted. DeMarco Murray didn't fit our running scheme. When he was with the Cowboys, he ran from directly behind the quarterback. But our system was a shotgun system, which means that instead of going in a straight line toward the line of scrimmage and making one cut, which he did with the Cowboys, he had to move laterally. But he was a stiff runner and not able to do that. That's why Shady McCoy, who was more shifty and agile, had been perfect for the system. On defense, Byron Maxwell came from Seattle, which was a zone Cover 3 scheme, and we were asking him to cover, man-to-man, the best receivers in the game. He opened the season with a terrible outing against Julio Jones, the Falcons phenom with a rare combo of size, speed, and savvy route-running. He torched our defense for 141 yards and two TDs.

Chip thought his system was so good that the players in it didn't matter. But this wasn't the John Madden video game. This game is played by humans with limitations and capabilities. A good coach creates a system that amplifies what his players do well and protects them from their weaknesses. I learned a long time ago to stop trying to change the coach's mind and do what I had to do to perform.

I was playing well. Already I had a fumble recovery and two forced fumbles under my belt, and was averaging about eight tackles a game, and I was getting better at trying to learn from everything and every experience I had.

Walter Thurmond, another one of the off-season free agents that we picked up from the Giants, originally cut his teeth in Seattle, and word on the street was that he was better than Richard Sherman, but a bunch of injuries in back-to-back seasons hampered his career and made room for the ascension of Sherm.

But Walt lived up to the hype. His five-foot-eleven, 185-pound frame was not typical for a safety, but he was savvy, and knew how to hold his own. In off-season practices he would continually dislodge the football from ballcarriers. Almost every day he'd force two fumbles. No matter what the offense did, no matter who it was, whether it was a rookie or the veteran Darren Sproles. Whether they held it with one hand or firmly with two, he'd still find ways to punch it out or strip it. So much so that eventually the defensive coaches had him stand up in front of the room and present his technique to the coaches and players.

I'd been studying the Seahawks for seasons by that point, as they were the gold standard for secondary play, and so I picked Walt's brain every chance I got, and we came up with ways to trick quarterbacks and manipulate the defense to fit our skill sets. We were the perfect complement to each other, and I was constantly getting better. I kept meticulous notes of all the things I was learning, "keeping book," as Gregg Williams once put it. He said, "Always remember, you'll see these coaches and players many times in your career in the league. So always keep your notebooks and game plans to remember what worked and what didn't."

I had notes and notes and notes from practicing against the Saints and Drew Brees and Sean Payton's offense, and knew it like the back of my hand. And as I prepared that week, I contemplated if they would change their signals or some of their calls. They surely must've known that I remembered all of it!

But then again, maybe not, because in week 2, when we played the Cowboys, they surely didn't. Not only had we signed DeMarco Murray, but we signed Miles Austin, the veteran receiver who was once a Pro Bowl Cowboys receiver. In the week before the game, they both presented me with a long list of every single hand signal and audible that quarterback Tony Romo would make at the line of scrimmage.

When Miles handed me the list, he even did a presentation to the secondary. "I'm telling you, these are the calls." And sure enough, when we got to third down, Romo stood up, looked at his receivers, and signaled the famous Aaron Rodgers signal, the discount double check, where he grabs his belt, signifying the championship belt. That meant, according to Miles Austin, that they would throw a quick out route to the tight end. Seeing the signal when the ball snapped, I jumped the route, probably a little too overzealous and too fast because Romo saw me and double-clutched the ball. But it was a costly double clutch, because we were sending a blitz and linebacker Jordan Hicks hit Romo, pinning him to the ground and breaking his collarbone.

Somehow we still managed to lose the game, but the Cowboys would be without their quarterback for the rest of the season. It was an example of how important or devastating having and giving intel can be. But those weren't the only notes I had. That same day Chip Kelly and the offensive coaches brought me up to their war room. They wanted to know the ins and outs of Rob Ryan's elaborate defenses. And quite frankly, I told them not to worry about it.

"Rob creates a new defense every week. He'll come in with a new plan that'll be curated specifically for what you guys do. So I'll tell you what to focus on."

It was here! The game I'd been waiting for. As I jogged onto the field, across from Drew Brees and the Saints offense, I reminded myself to take the info they give. Sometimes we overcomplicate things. This is especially true in football, where coaches or players make the game more complicated than it really is. Sometimes there's all the information you need right in front of you, if you know how to look for it. Gregg used to say, "Every time the offense breaks a huddle, they're telling you a story. Can you read the book?" *They know how I prepare. They have to know I know these things. What if they use it as bait, a dummy call like Peyton Manning in Super Bowl XLIV?* I'd been asking myself these questions all week long while I took notes on their favorite concept from previous games.

Both teams came into the matchup 1-3, desperate to avoid a 1-4 start. We'd already lost to division rivals the Commanders and the Cowboys, placing us behind big-time in the division. I was playing well. I'd already gotten multiple pass breakups and a couple of forced fumbles in the season.

Almost every offense in the NFL uses hand signals and code words to communicate plays and adjustments. These are used usually when a team is on the road. If you know it's going to be loud, then the quarterback, who needs to communicate to a receiver, who may be twenty yards away in a hostile stadium, may simply give him a hand signal instead of trying to yell over the crowd. Obviously all of us watch film, so we can see the hand signals on tape, so the good quarterbacks will mix their hand signals with a bunch of dummy hand signals, the same way a catcher will do in baseball as he's going through the pitches for a pitcher.

Having practiced against this offense for years, I knew a few of the code words and the signals, but I was guessing that they knew that I knew them as well, so I fully anticipated them changing some of them to make sure that I didn't just tell all of my teammates exactly what they were going to run.

Drew Brees going, "Yellow 80, yellow 80." That means, when he says, "Yellow," that he wants everybody on the offensive line to wait. He's trying to figure out what the defense is in. When he is ready, he'll say, "Ready, ready."

Brees had another tell. He was not ready for the ball to be snapped unless he licked his hands three times. He had a weird thing where if he only licked it one time, it was a dummy cadence and he wasn't really ready to snap the ball. He would just make you think he was ready so that you would get out of your disguise and he could figure out what your defense was in and change his play to be more advantageous. This was pre-COVID, but looking back on Drew licking his bare fingers in the middle of a football game over and over and over makes me cringe now, but that day I was looking forward to it.

Lastly, one of their favorite plays was named "All Go Special." Four receivers going straight down the field, all streaks, all go. Drew loved this because he was really good at being able to manipulate the safeties by looking one way and making them move in that direction, only to snap back and throw to whatever vertical had been abandoned by the coverage that he had just manipulated. The way that they communicated that was usually "Special, special."

I was skeptical that they'd continue to use these coming into Lincoln Financial, so I planned to wait until after the first drive to see if I could hear any of these things show up and verify if the things I'd seen on film would actually hold up in the game.

I also had a key matchup that week, C. J. Spiller, the dynamic running back known for speed and his ability to catch the ball out of the backfield. He'd been causing havoc on third-down situations, taking advantage of being covered by bigger, slower linebackers. So Bill Davis, our defensive coordinator, was putting me at linebacker on third downs to handle that coverage.

First play of the game, I lined up in the slot. I figured that Sean and Drew were going to want to get the pass game going, to get an early completion and get some offensive rhythm. With C. J. Spiller offset to my side of the formation, I had a hunch that he was likely going to get the ball. They had two receivers in front of me, but my eyes were locked on Spiller.

As soon as the ball snapped, he swung out to the outside of the formation, in my direction. I knew this was a swing pass. Before Brees could even let go of the football, I put my head down, my foot in the ground, and ran through the attempted block of Willie Snead, meeting Spiller in the backfield and tackling him for a three-yard loss. I immediately looked at Brees. "The fuck out of here with that bullshit, Drew. Y'all know what time it is." A hell of a way to start the game right in front of the Saints sideline, too.

Coming into the game, there had been a lot of talk in the media because Sean Payton mentioned that letting me out of his Saints organization was the biggest mistake of his career. But all those kind words didn't mean shit out on the field. I'd let that sink in when the game was over. They were going to feel every bit of that mistake.

Later in the second quarter, one of the tight ends for the Saints had clearly forgotten the play and didn't immediately move when Drew tried to send him into motion. When he finally began to move, Drew said to him, "Hey, special, special."

I immediately looked to Walter Thurmond on my right, just to make sure that he'd heard what I did. Sure enough, the ball was snapped and Drew tried to move Walt out of position with his eyes to throw in the opposite direction. Knowing what was coming, I had it covered and with no one open he held the ball and got sacked by Fletcher Cox.

The game was 7–7 and the Saints were right in field goal range. They were on the 39-yard line going in and it was 3rd and 22 after the sack. So if it was an incomplete pass, at the very worst, they were kicking a forty-six-yard field goal. I knew these were the situations when Sean loved to call screens to RB Spiller. As I lined up, Spiller aligned on the right side of the formation.

When the ball was snapped, Spiller did a swing route to the opposite side of the field, right where I'd anticipated. As soon as he moved, I knew it was a race. I looked to see what obstacles Sean had schemed to put in my way. I saw Ben Watson, the tight end, dragging from my left. I paused for a second, checked my feet to clear him, and noticed that there was an offensive lineman also in pursuit.

The center was tracking me, responsible for blocking me, but I moved so fast that he and Watson collided, leaving me scot-free. Only thing left to do was to finish the play. I had to make a tackle one-on-one against Spiller in open space, which was easier said than done. There were about ten yards of separation between us, but I'd played this out in my mind a thousand times and my body executed without hesitation.

When he caught the ball, before he had time to make a move, I wrapped both arms around his legs and rolled my body like a gator, bringing him to an absolute halt, five yards behind the line of scrimmage. When I stood up, Sean was standing right in front of me, as we were on the Saints sideline. I screamed at the top of my lungs, "Ahhhhhh! Get the fuck out of here."

I threw the hooks for the bruhs that I knew were watching. I can't lie, it felt great. Everybody on their sideline had the same look: *How did y'all let him go?!*

Later in the game, it was 3rd and 3, the same situation, man-to-man coverage, me and Spiller. This time, he aligned to my right, and I noticed to my left that there were three receivers all packed in very close to the rest of the formation. I knew that Spiller, again, would swing behind Brees over to that bunch, and I'd have to navigate myself through oncoming receivers and get to Spiller and get him on the ground before he could get three yards up the field. I knew I'd have to get there as fast as possible. The slower I moved, the more space he would have and the harder it would be to stop him.

The ball snapped and he did exactly what I thought he would. He swung out, and I had receivers all in my face. Somehow I slithered through a small opening and beelined right to his hip, but the ball wasn't there. Brees pump-faked and Spiller turned up the field and up the sideline, a move I was not anticipating, but I recovered. I was in a good enough position to widen him just enough and he stepped out-of-bounds, making himself ineligible to catch the football. Another third-down stop for me. I was three steps ahead of every move. I put my arms out and signified "incomplete," in case anybody was wondering.

Eventually, as the game went on, the Saints defense did exactly what I'd anticipated them to do: they imploded. Sean Payton and Rob Ryan were visibly arguing on the sideline. And our defense behind Fletcher Cox just took over. Fletcher had three sacks, six tackles, two forced fumbles, and a fumble recovery as he budded into the All-Pro that he was going to be. Walt picked off Drew late in the game after hearing "Special, special" once again.

We went on to beat the Saints 39–17, and it would've been 39–10, but on the last play of the game, the Saints and Brees threw a consolation touchdown pass to make the score look a little better. After the game, I spoke to Drew, Sean, and Mickey Loomis before heading to the locker room. Each of them told me how they missed my leadership and that they had made the wrong decision by letting me out of the building.

You realize that you don't play this game to get all the praises in the media or the accolades. To me, the most important opinions are those of my opponents and those of my teammates. It was validation that all the work that I had put in while I was there didn't go unnoticed. Everything that I had learned in New Orleans prepared me to step into Philadelphia, embracing the challenges that stood in front of me.

It was week 9 in a crucial game in Dallas against the Cowboys. A win there and our record would be 4-4; normally nothing to be excited about, but the entire NFC East was struggling, and whichever team finished above .500 would likely win the division. About midway through the second quarter, I looked up at the ginormous screen that hangs from the top of AT&T Stadium. The game was paused for a TV time-out, and while the players waited for the commercial break to end, they played Cowboy highlights from the game. I watched play after play, and then I saw Dallas wideout Cole Beasley run a nice route, sprinting toward the sideline, then changing direction and breaking back toward the middle of the field, where Matt Cassel threw him the football. The defender was just offscreen then, but came into focus as Beasley entered the end zone. It was me!

"When the fuck did that happen?!" I blurted out loud. Rodney turned and looked at me like I was crazy. Having no recollection of the play, I got up and walked away from the bench to collect myself.

As a professional athlete, especially in the National Football League, accountability and availability are the two best qualities you can have. You can have all the talent in the world, but if you are constantly injured and unable to play, then the team can't use you.

Earlier in the game, I met Cowboys running back Darren McFadden in the middle of the hole and caught his knee to the right side of my forehead. It buckled me, but I was able to recover and wrap his legs up to make the tackle. When I got up, I was in a daze that I couldn't shake off. I hadn't had a concussion that I knew of at that point in my career, so I wasn't completely sure what was up. I didn't get knocked out, so maybe I'd be fine. The fog cleared and I kept playing. But not having recollection of the play I saw on the screen scared me. But this game was significant and I knew I needed to be available for my team; my role was too important. So, I hid it. The next few drives, the game was moving a thousand times faster than I was used to, especially trying to cover Cole Beasley. Beasley's all of five eight, and as quick as a jackrabbit. For every step I took, he took two, meaning that he could change direction, make jukes, and turn faster than I could.

My strategy, as it always was against smaller players, was to get my hands on him and be able to control him. But with a concussion, it was like I was trying to cover Sonic the Hedgehog. Every time the ball was snapped, his jukes and moves literally made him look like he was a blur, and he kept catching the ball on me.

The next time I got to the sideline, I racked my damaged brain to figure out a solution. So, I stood and watched our offense on the field and tried to go through my calls and the adjustments I needed to make from the safety position. Somehow I was still sharp enough to make the calls and remember the game plan. So, I went to Cory.

"Hey, I don't like the matchup this week. I'm not feeling comfortable with my press technique. Just put me back deep so I can make all of the calls and just play strictly safety." He didn't think anything of it because I was getting my ass toasted by Beasley and he likely would have made the adjustment anyway.

I don't know how, but I managed to finish the game, surviving by avoiding as many collisions as possible, but I did have to make a couple tackles. There was one problem. The game was going into overtime. I knew that I'd been pressing my luck all day, and the thought of playing even another snap had me worried. Plus, I missed a few calls on the last drive we had. I wasn't as collected as I had foolishly thought.

We won the coin toss and our offense drove down the field with Jordan Matthews breaking free and racing into the end zone for a walk-off touchdown. I cheered in celebration, partly for the win, and partly because I didn't have to go back into the game.

I ran straight to the locker room and informed the trainers that I had a concussion. Shocked, they immediately put me into the protocols, giving me all the cognitive tests they would have given me had I said something earlier. The next day I shamefully walked into the facility and was scolded by every trainer and coach there was. Bill Davis, the defensive coordinator, caught me in a quiet moment as I was watching tape from the game in the meeting room. Bill is a good man, and is usually even-keeled, but the look in his eye let me know he was simultaneously angry and worried.

"Don't you ever do that again."

I knew that he didn't care if it was the Super Bowl and his job depended on it. If he had known I had a concussion, he would've taken me out of the game. I felt horrible. What I had done was dangerous, not only to myself but to everyone who needed me. I could have made that situation worse. It was bigger than the game. I jeopardized my career and my life. As the quote, unquote, leader of the team, I had set a horrible example. One I prayed no one followed. I was fortunate. From then on I kept in mind that if I wasn't healthy, I wasn't able to be available. If I'm not available, then I am of no use, to my team, or to my family.

———

After the Dallas game, we went on a three-game losing streak, putting us at 4-7 late in the season. Early in the year, before the bye week, our offense was really the main reason we were losing. And I know it's a team sport, but it was really easy for anyone to turn on the game and see that. Now, the defense, we had our contribution as well, but it was hard for us to put the blame on us when we were playing a hundred snaps a game. Of course we were going to give up yards and points when the opposing offenses had that many opportunities. It was simple math.

But in weeks 10 through 12, the defense really took a hit. Not only was our offense struggling as usual, but Sam Bradford got injured in a game against Miami. And so we played two games with Mark Sanchez starting. We knew defensively that we needed to step up in those games to give ourselves a chance to win, and we did not answer the call at all, instead giving up forty-five points in back-to-back weeks. Now, at some point, as a man, your pride has to kick in and something has to be done in order to change the course of where you're going. At week 12, at 4-7, it was hard for me to sit in a meeting and listen to a coach tell me that we should just stick to the plan—"Trust me, guys, just believe and it'll work"—without telling us exactly what we needed to get better at, without telling us the exact problems that were happening that we could correct.

I'm pretty sure that's the definition of insanity: doing the same thing the same exact way and expecting different results. That was Chip Kelly. I had a local radio show on WIP that I would do early in the weeks during the season. It was a nice little paid gig, and as my play rose, so did my personal profile. So it was fun to do. This was before everyone had their podcast and you used to just do a local radio show and tried not to say anything crazy to get you in trouble with the coaches or the team. Well, at this point in the season, I had already been getting all the toughest questions I could possibly get, having a losing record in Philadelphia, and now to not even have an understanding of what it was we were trying to do to get better, especially with the New England Patriots in Foxborough being our next destination. I was pissed.

They asked me, "Malcolm, what do you think needs to be done for this Eagles team to turn around?" I said, "Honestly, I have no clue." There was zero accountability in the locker room. We didn't know what it was that we needed to do to get better. We didn't know what the problem was. We didn't even know what we were going to go fix. There was just no accountability. When the show was over, I knew it was going to go viral, but I had said what I said, and it was what I had been saying in the facility already. The next day, when I was in the weight room, Bill Davis walked up to me with a look of disappointment on his face. "Come on, man, why would you go do that?" I looked confused. "What are you talking about?" He was like, "You going to go say we don't have any accountability." I looked him dead in his eyes and said, "Coach, we don't." He said, "How can you say that?"

"Because we sit in the meetings all the time and I have no clue as a leader what I'm supposed to tell younger guys to improve on. I have no idea what I'm supposed to encourage the team to do next. Because we don't know. I can see on tape that there are guys that are being put on the field that are not our best eleven, that are liabilities to what we're trying to do. Yet they keep going on the field. And it's unfair to me as a competitor and my teammates when the coach will stand in front of us and not explain to us what it is we need to do to get better or who it is that we need to help get better."

And he really didn't have an answer to that. Me and Bill Davis actually saw eye to eye on a lot of things. He was a really good dude, a great defensive coordinator, but under Chip Kelly's coaching structure, he had very little power.

He was the only one who didn't have a personal connection to Kelly. For example the D-line coach and assistant head coach, Jerry Azzinaro, had more power than Bill. Bill said, "Well, we try not to destroy anyone's psyche. It's a tough place. We don't want to cripple anybody." The face I gave him was crazy. I never thought I'd hear a football coach talking about not wanting to correct a player in front of his peers in order to avoid hurting his feelings or crushing his psyche. I came up in the Sean Payton school of thought where Sean once came to me during warm-ups before a practice, looked me in my face, and said, "A safety who can't tackle is somebody else's safety." This was after a game where I had missed two or three tackles. Just like that, and then he walked off.

I said, "Hold on, Sean. What? Hold on. What? How you going to say that and just walk off? What you mean?" He put his hands up, like, "Oh no, don't kill the messenger. Coach told me to tell you that." Of course, when he said "Coach," he was referring to his mentor, Bill Parcells, who frequently talked to Sean about the team and what he should do next. So hearing a coach talk about caring about what feelings players had at a time when we had a losing record seemed backward to me, but it's kind of an unwritten rule that you don't talk about locker room issues in the media, and this was very calculated by me. I needed to do something to spark a fire under everyone in the building. I was used to teams having captains. Leaders who were selected by their peer group, voted on by the team to stand out in front, in good times and bad times.

Payton would meet with those leaders to get a feel for the locker room, using them as the liaisons between the players and the coaches. Those captains could go to the coach and report how the players were feeling—if we needed to back down on practice or if we needed to change philosophy. In the other sense, the captains could also go into the locker room and convey the messages that the coaches were trying to get across. They could back up a coach, build a coach up, and create a following based off their own leadership. It was an important process that couldn't be skipped but was nonexistent in Chip's program.

He would rotate captains every week, meaning that being a captain only meant that you got to go out for the coin toss and get your picture taken before the game. It didn't really have anything to do with being a leader in the locker room, and so this was a chance for me to take the team by its horns, but I knew I had put myself in harm's way doing it. And with all the pressure, looking like we needed to get the win in Foxborough against Tom Brady and the Patriots, that was a tall order.

As I approached my locker before the week 13 matchup against the Patriots, there was a T-shirt hanging there that read PLAY ANGRY. The message was coming from the Eagles' owner, Jeff Lurie. He was originally a Bostonian and had tried to buy the Patriots back in the day, but the Patriots' current owner, Robert Kraft, outbid him. So Lurie purchased the Eagles in 1994. Kraft had already racked up two Super

Bowls before Lurie's Eagles could face off with them in the Super Bowl. And then the Patriots won Super Bowl XXXIX, 24–21, racking up its third franchise championship, leaving the Eagles still without a beloved Lombardi Trophy.

Normally, Mr. Lurie was quiet before the games. He'd walk around to the majority of the starters and wish them good luck or say, "Go get them," but without much conversation. He wasn't one for speeches or making the day about him. He allowed players to focus and stay in their routines, rarely even talking to the media, if at all, during the season. Even though we were 4-7, we'd yet to feel any pressure from him.

Today was clearly different. As I sat in my locker, headphones blaring "Kill Us All" by Twista, I saw him walking over to my locker. I didn't bother to pause my headphones because I knew he usually just said, "Good luck." I figured I'd read his lips, nod my head, and go back to my routine. I nodded and shook his hand, but this time he didn't let go. I slid my headphones off.

He was looking me in the eye.

"I want you to play angry. We got to make sure that guys are playing angry. Everybody, every single guy is playing angry."

Under my breath, I chuckled.

"Okay."

I always played angry. He didn't have to tell me that, but something was different and I could tell that he was looking to see who was going to waver, who wasn't going to play hard. His message, essentially, was "Don't embarrass me!"

He could endure a rough season, but he'd be damned if we were going to come to Foxborough against his archnemesis and get blown out of the water. When we got onto the field to warm up, I made sure that I took in the scene, as I had everywhere we went. Looking around the stands in Gillette Stadium, you got a feel for the history and the epic games that have happened on that field.

And just as I got lost in my thoughts . . .

"ALLOW ME TO REINTRODUCE MYSELF!" Jay-Z's voice blasted over the loudspeakers, and onto the field trotted Tom Brady to a roaring crowd. He ran down the length of the sideline, all the way to the awaiting fans, threw a punch into the air, and screamed, "Let's go!"

Tom looked motivated, to say the least. The Patriots were without Tom's best targets, Julian Edelman and Rob Gronkowski, so we felt like we had a decent chance. But this was Foxborough. This was Brady and Belichick.

During the national anthem, I gave a strong prayer to my ancestors. I knew I was going to need all the help I could get, so I prayed for toughness, poise, and love. All that I hoped they passed down onto me. I closed my conversation hoping that I had made them proud. But even some ancestorial assistance couldn't stop Tom Brady and the Patriots from jumping up 14–0 on us. And quite frankly, early in the game, it felt like it was going to be another one of those days and another one of those games where we couldn't get out of our own way. But up 14–0, the Patriots and Belichick took unnecessary risks. After their second score, they went for an onside kick, guessing that they would catch us off guard and have an opportunity to go up 21–0 and break our will early in the game and never have to worry about it again.

But instead, we recovered it, and with the short field, we converted it into points, making the game 14–7. Then, right before the half, with only seconds left, the Patriots went to punt and Chris Maragos blocked it. The ball was recovered by Najee Goode and returned for a touchdown right before the half, with us going into the locker room 14–14.

At halftime all the momentum was on our side. But the Patriots started the second half with the football and marched the ball all the way to our 5-yard line. I lined up over Danny Amendola, their most consistent receiver, in the slot.

He hopped off the ball to try to get me to stay in place, but I knew that I had help to my inside, and I stuck to my heavy outside leverage. He then broke toward the middle of the field on a shallow crossing route, right at the goal line. I reached to jam him and missed.

"Shit!"

He was open for a quick two or three steps and Brady noticed it right over the ball. The easiest throw for him to make right in front of him. But when Brady threw the football, he didn't account for Walter Thurmond breaking on the ball.

Walt got to Amendola at the same time as the football and tipped it up right in front of me, at eye height. I caught it right on the goal line and took off. Headed toward the left sideline, I jumped over the outstretched arms of an offensive lineman, who lunged to tackle me. Now the only things in front of me were space, opportunity, and Tom. No way in hell was I letting Brady tackle me in the open field.

I ran right at him, and then cut back toward the middle of the field, accelerating past him without even looking at him again. Tom dove, fell, and watched me run the entire length of the field, back into the end zone. We went up 21–14.

A few drives later, the Patriots went three and out and were forced to punt to Darren Sproles, who returned the ball down the left sideline for a touchdown. Later in the game, our offense scored again, making it 35–14. Thirty-five unanswered points against the New England Patriots in Foxborough. A punt block for a touchdown, an interception return for a touchdown, and a punt return for a touchdown, all in the same game, is like a hat trick in hockey. And yet somehow the Patriots scored twice quickly by getting the onside kick and brought themselves within one touchdown late in the fourth quarter. I was instantly reminded of the last time I came to Foxborough and Tom completed the last-second comeback. I knew better than anyone, except the Atlanta Falcons, of course, that Tom Brady never dies. But on 4th and 4, we broke up a pass thrown over the middle of the field and got the ball back to our offense to close the game.

It became clear in the locker room that, regardless of what our coaches were going to do, regardless of what they were saying, if we wanted to win, there were certain guys we needed to follow, and those leaders were going to step up to the ring. Myself on defense, Darren Sproles on offense, and Chris Maragos on special teams: we would lead the way without a *C* on our chest, without permission from the team, without being voted in. We'd just do what we needed to do and lead the team with our play and our daily actions. This was the day that I knew I had won the hearts and minds of my teammates. Sometimes you don't need to be the most talented team to win; you take advantage of the mistakes your opponent makes. Walt set me up for one of the best plays of my career.

# 9

# STEP UP

*After my spectacular failures, I could not be*
*satisfied with an ordinary success.*

**—MASON COOLEY**

On July 21, 2016, I arranged a meeting between local citizens, folks in the media, local business leaders, Ivy League alumni, grassroots organizers, and some Eagles teammates—Chris Maragos, Jordan Matthews, Jason Kelce, and Brandon Graham—to meet with the commissioner of the Philadelphia Police Department. Commissioner Richard Ross opened his office for us to be heard.

Just two weeks prior, there were back-to-back police shootings of Black men, Philando Castile and Alton Sterling. Philando Castile was shot and killed by a police officer in Minnesota on July 6 during a traffic stop. And that was immediately following the shooting of Alton Sterling, who was killed by police in Baton Rouge on July 5, after they were called to investigate a man accused of selling CDs outside of a store. Both incidents were captured on video and quickly spread on social media, leading to widespread protests and calls for police reform.

I could remember seeing the video myself, sitting in my office, teary-eyed at what I had just witnessed. And because it happened on back-to-back days, it felt like we were under attack. I could easily see myself, my brothers, my teammates, and any Black male or Black woman, for that matter, in those shoes of Philando Castile and Alton Sterling. And those lives were lost with no accountability, adding to the long list of names like Eric Garner, Michael Brown, Tamir Rice, Trayvon Martin, Freddie Gray, Rekia Boyd, Sandra Bland, Tanisha Anderson, and so many more.

I'd been doing a ton of work in both my foundation and the community, but I could do all the charity and programs I wanted and it wouldn't stop the police from killing us. I decided that I needed to do more, but I wasn't sure where to start, so I did what I knew how to do. I took the same approach that we used for the foundation: find out what the needs are and how you can play a role in addressing them.

I'd learned a lesson already trying to get involved in issues like this. In New Orleans I was invited to join an organization through a fraternity brother of mine. The organization was called Solutions Not Shootings, whose mission was to stop the rampant gun violence that had New Orleans ranked as the murder capital of the U.S. When I showed up at a community forum to hear discussions, I was caught off guard by what I encountered. There were many organizations in the room and many activists and elders. They were discussing funding grants from the city to help with the solution and arguing over who should get them. Someone asked me who I was with and when I naively said Solutions Not Shootings, he went off on me, saying that he and other community members had been doing this work for years with no support and how they should be the ones getting these grants, not us. I had no clue what I was getting into. I learned something, though. Oftentimes you've got a thousand organizations working to solve the same problem, but competing for the same dollar. My role now wouldn't be to add more organizations to the mix, but to somehow get them to collaborate and share resources.

At the table with Commissioner Ross, I asked questions and discussed some of the concerns of our community members, but also some of the challenges that the police force was having internally in trying to service the community.

As we sat with Commissioner Ross and he fielded questions and criticism, he wasn't naive to the problems of policing, and as a Black man he admitted that there needed to be reforms. But as we continued to boil down to the root of it all, I realized that the police are on the front lines of a bigger system. If we didn't attack the system, even when we got rid of some of the individuals, front lines were always replaceable and could easily be reproduced.

So after the 2015 season, Chip Kelly was out. He got fired and then the Eagles signed Doug Pederson as the next head coach. Prior to becoming a head coach, Doug was the offensive coordinator for the Kansas City Chiefs under the former Eagles legendary coach Andy Reid. And not only did Doug coach under Andy, but he played for Andy as well, as the Eagles' quarterback one year.

He was the perfect fit for Philly because he was drastically different from Chip Kelly's college-style program. Doug was a player's coach and understood what it meant to play football, specifically in the city of Philadelphia. Being a former quarterback himself, his first order of business was finding a new quarterback for the team. After a couple lackluster seasons with Nick Foles, Sam Bradford, and Mark Sanchez, the quarterback was the first position that needed to be addressed. So they looked to the draft to do so, and they set their eyes on Carson Wentz, who was a highly touted prospect out of North Dakota State. He'd had a successful college career and impressed scouts with his size, arm strength, and competitiveness.

But if we wanted to get Wentz, we'd have to move up in the draft because he was the top quarterback out there. We ended up giving up a first-round pick. We had the eighth overall pick in the 2016 draft. And so to move up to the second pick, we gave up the first-round pick in 2016, a third-round pick in 2016, another first-round pick in 2017, a second-round pick in 2018, and another conditional pick to get one player, but we got him. Second overall, we drafted Carson Wentz.

Usually when you get a new coach, they come in and clean house, firing all the coaches who were previously there, and bring in their own handpicked staff.

Defensive coordinator Bill Davis was let go and Pederson brought in Jim Schwartz, the former head coach of the Detroit Lions and the defensive coordinator of the Buffalo Bills, to lead the defense. Schwartz had a reputation for being arrogant, stiff, and a tough coach, but he turned out to be quite the opposite. He was a very emotional man who wore his heart on his sleeve, oftentimes crying or getting choked up in front of the meeting room.

But he was tough, and he'd tell you about yourself, too. He wasn't afraid to hold guys accountable, which is what I loved about him. He treated his top guys the same way he treated the bottom-of-the-roster players, and he truly wanted everyone to get paid.

"When I say your name, stand up. Fletcher Cox, Malcolm Jenkins, where y'all at?"

We both stood up.

"When you play like these two do, you get paid. And when you go earn it, you deserve to get paid. Good shit, men. Everybody give 'em three."

On cue the whole room clapped three times in unison. As a new coach, sometimes it's hard to learn who your players are. So he had come from Buffalo and brought a couple players with him, nickel back Ron Brooks and linebacker Nigel Bradham. Two guys that he knew he could trust to put into the lineup who would already know the scheme. But I already knew how this went. I had to do the same thing with Spagnuolo, Rob Ryan, and Bill Davis, and that was to convince them that I could play multiple positions, specifically the nickel spot.

I pulled Schwartz to the side and said, "Hey, I want the opportunity to compete for the nickel position. I truly believe that is my best spot, where I'm most productive. And I know training camp is where y'all evaluate all of the young corners and stuff like that. So I probably won't get reps until the end of it, but I just want the opportunity to compete for the position." He looked at me with his face kind of screwed up, and he was like, "You too heavy to play nickel. You weigh, like, two fifteen, can't run at that weight." And I said to him, "I'll be fine. I'm just letting you know I want to compete for the spot." And I'm like, "Now I got a chip on my shoulder." Because now all I heard was *I don't think you can play, I don't think you can play the slot*. So I put that in my head and kept going.

But one of the best things about Pederson and Schwartz was that they kept some of the staff that was already there, specifically defensive back coach Cory Undlin, who was with me under the Chip Kelly reign. After one season of his coaching, I had made my first Pro Bowl. His ability to teach techniques and concepts in the classroom and on the field was everything I needed.

His approach to teaching was very different from many coaches. In the evenings during training camp, some coaches wanted to hold you in meetings as late as they could, installing the plays for a third and fourth time, just the basic minute elements of the game. But he would do something different. He'd ask one or two guys every night to stand up and tell the room about who they were, where they came from, what motivated them. And that was something I had never experienced.

And he went first. So he told us about his background, starting out as an elementary school teacher and climbing his way up from there to become a coach in the NFL. He got his start as a graduate assistant at Eastern Michigan University, which was his alma mater. Then moved to the Cleveland Browns as a DB coach. Then he worked for myriad teams—the Denver Broncos, Detroit Lions, Jacksonville Jaguars, Patriots, and then, finally, in 2015, coming to the Eagles. He was a journeyman, a surfboarder, and a hunter in his spare time, but truly cared about and loved his players.

But that exercise, understanding what motivates people and who they were, made leadership very easy. And so doing that, I learned a whole bunch, not only about Cory, but about my teammates. You learn where they came from, where their motivations are, what makes them tick. And as a leader, that information was invaluable. You learn that some players play for money, some play for respect, and some are motivated by a past life that they never want to go back to.

But then they had to learn about me as well. I'm normally a guarded person and don't talk much about my personal life in the facility, and I'm sure they assumed that because I was the decorated vet—Super Bowl champion, first-round draft pick out of Ohio State, and fresh off a Pro Bowl season—that I had an easy path to my success. But I got a chance to let them know my story and how I could have easily ended up on a different path and how my dedication to competition was what drove me. Not money, not fame, none of that moved me. But my career and my success have been meticulously and painstakingly welded together through the heat and pressure of competition and the feverish pursuit of obtaining the respect of every opponent I faced. The exercise was simple but effective in bonding us as a group. Especially for a secondary that had been subjected to a ton of criticism over the last few seasons.

As I was getting ready to play for my fourth defensive coordinator in five years, I was happy to have some consistency. I informed him, just as I had with Schwartz, that I wanted to compete for the nickel spot. But as training camp went on, I never got those opportunities and that pissed me the fuck off. I felt like they just lied to me and brushed it off. I can respect the man who tells me flat out, "We have who we want for the position and that's that." I'd still be mad, but I can't say that you lied to me or were being dishonest.

One day I asked Cory, "When am I going to get some reps at the nickel? Season's starting in less than two weeks and I need to get some practice." He was silent for a minute, and then he said, "I think Schwartz wants to go with Ron Brooks at the nickel and keep you at safety." With a steel face, I simply replied, "So y'all lied to me? Okay, got it." The line was drawn in the sand, in my mind.

The emphasis in practice that day for the defense was on spacing and off coverage. I was drafted as a press corner, meaning I'm comfortable playing close to the line of scrimmage, in the face of the receiver. And playing off meant playing with more technique, more discipline, and that was not really my game. But Schwartz, installing this new defense, wanted everyone to play six to seven yards off, mainly because it helped clog the throwing lanes for the quarterback. Even though I may be covering one wideout, my presence can provide help for the other defenders that are to my left and to the right.

But fuck it, since I wasn't getting any reps at the nickel and the emphasis was off coverage, I needed to work on my press, so I was going to press. I didn't care what they said. So during a play in practice, I aligned over the slot receiver in a press technique, and of course I hear yelling off in the distance, "Back up, no press." I didn't budge. And then I heard Jim Schwartz getting louder, but he was no longer yelling at me. He was yelling at Cory. And what made it worse was that on the very next play, the quarterback completed the pass in the window that I was supposed to be standing in.

And so, yeah, I heard Schwartz yell again.

"What the fuck are you doing?!"

And because shit rolls downhill, Cory started yelling at me.

"If you don't want to play the defense, get the fuck out."

I ignored Cory and kept playing. And he kept yelling. *There's no way I'm coming off the field. I don't care what he says. I'm not going to get replaced because I'm trying some press in practice.* I heard him yelling more.

"Ain't nobody trying to hear that. Chill the fuck out and let me practice."

A few days before the season opener, I got a text from Cory saying that he wanted to talk. I wasn't really proud of that moment because I knew that younger guys had been watching and likely didn't understand the context of my actions. My whole career, I had been listening to people telling me that I couldn't play corner.

As Cory and I sat in the DB room and had a man-to-man conversation, I started.

"I would've been okay if you just came and told me that y'all had who y'all had for the position. But that was never the case. So I felt like you were just lying to me. Or at some point when you knew that it wasn't going to happen, you could at least have given me the heads-up."

I wasn't above playing my role. I understood the importance of everybody doing their specific job on the team and not being able to do someone else's job.

"Honestly, Malcolm, I didn't know you were this serious about playing the position."

"I didn't pull you aside to tell you these things casually, I'm dead fucking serious."

It was that type of conversation between me and Cory that made us supertight. I'd never had a relationship with a coach like I'd had with Cory Undlin, mainly because we both cared a lot about what it was that we were doing, and were able to have these man-to-man conversations on and off the field, putting our egos aside, understanding that we both needed each other's help to be the best versions of ourselves.

A few weeks after that meeting, Colin Kaepernick began a silent protest during the national anthem at the third preseason game. The first two preseason games, he wasn't dressed to play, so when he sat on the bench in protest during the national anthem, no one really noticed. He didn't make any statements or give any explanations. But the third game, when he dressed and then sat on the bench, everyone noticed and began to ask why he took the stance and began to talk about how disrespectful it was to the flag. And in the last and fourth preseason game, he adjusted his stance to taking a knee after speaking with retired Army Green Beret Nate Boyer about the most respectful way to go about protesting during the national anthem. As Kaepernick stated, this was not about our military or service members, but about the contradictions of patriotism in the face of centuries of systemic oppression.

The protests started a movement. They garnered coverage from every major sports network, every major news network, from ESPN to CNN, and were even gaining international attention. Athletes from Little League to other pro sports around the world joined Colin in taking the knee, protesting in solidarity to raise awareness about the injustices in their communities. It brought the issues of police brutality and systemic oppression to America's main stage. And doing it during the anthem was perfect. It didn't disrupt the game at all or the business of football directly. He did it peacefully and silently, so it didn't do anything to anyone, yet was triggering enough people to spark the controversy that was needed for him to get the point across. It's the same effect that the Freedom Riders had when they rode in the front of buses through segregated states. It's the same effect that the sit-ins had during the civil rights movement. This was not a drill.

I started a group chat with about sixty NFL players representing all thirty-two teams, including Kaepernick, to figure out how we could all join together to support the movement. I didn't know Kaepernick that well but I was inspired by the momentum that had been created by his stance. This type of groundswell of coverage and eyeballs hadn't really been seen before, and we had an opportunity in our hands to grasp it if we could organize. I just hadn't anticipated that organizing would be so damn difficult. You had certain guys who thought that taking the knee was too controversial and didn't want to risk pissing off fans and the NFL to make a statement about police brutality. Some others were adamant that they had already been doing this kind of work and already had plans, and wanted to do protests as a team and not as an individual. Some had plans to lock arms, or not do anything at all and simply encourage their teams to donate money to a cause.

Regardless, it was a shit show and the call ended with everyone agreeing to do their own thing. But collectively, we kept one voice and came up with a list of talking points to make sure that everyone was saying the same thing, even though the demonstration might be different. We all wanted to talk about and draw attention to police brutality, to the injustices in our criminal justice system, and the disparities in education and opportunity.

I chose to raise a fist. I had grown up seeing the image of John Carlos and Tommie Smith at the 1968 Olympics standing on the podium, heads bowed, fists in the air, wearing black gloves. There was no doubt in my mind that when you see a Black man raising his fist in protest, you don't need to hear his words in order to know what he's fighting against. It can't be misconstrued and it can't be misunderstood.

When I went back to the Eagles to present to my team what other teams were doing and to potentially find out who would join me or support the movement, after a team meeting had finished, I asked the coaches and staff if they could leave and we could have a players-only meeting. Once all of the Eagles front-office folks and coaches left the room, I gave an update to my teammates on what was happening. I knew many of them had been having conversations about the protests that were going on around the league, and possibly what we could do.

And so I began to talk about the taking of a knee, the options of locking arms or raising a fist, and immediately three or four guys got up and left. To my surprise, they were all Black. As I answered questions about the flag, what we were trying to do, what the reasons were, it was quite apparent that many of my white teammates wouldn't dare do anything during the national anthem, out of fear of disrespecting or pissing off any service members. Even though I spent considerable time trying to convince them that the protest had nothing to do with the military or service members, they had seen how the media was presenting it as such. The protest was never about any of that, it was only in reference to police brutality, systemic oppression, and the false advertisement of America being the "home of the free and the land of the brave." And a lot of the Black players were either uninterested or worried about the backlash they would face if they joined the protests.

A room of fifty-three guys was whittled down to three. Myself, Steven Means, and Ron Brooks. "I'm with you, Big Dog," they each said. I could see it in their eyes. Those were guys who were on the cusp and were taking a big risk to join this movement. They didn't have the security that I had. Steven Means was just a practice squad guy and Ron Brooks was a backup player. But I knew what it meant for me to step out in front. It provided protection for anyone else who came, because what they couldn't do to me gave them a little bit of a shield.

I was warming up in Soldier Field before our week 2 Monday Night Football matchup against the Chicago Bears. I was trying my best to focus my mind on the game plan and the things I needed to do in the game, but it was almost impossible to ignore what I was getting ready to do on prime-time national television. A few days before the game, I'd had a couple conversations with some active and retired servicemen about the protests. I wanted to let them know what I was about to do and make sure they knew to ignore the rhetoric being circulated and that this wasn't about the military, but had everything to do with the flag and the contradictions it represented. Eddie, one of my air force buddies I met years back when I was rehabbing in Pensacola, Florida, was someone I really wanted to hear from. While in Pensacola he was also rehabbing after surviving an Osprey crash in a training exercise.

"Hey, Eddie, man, you see what's going on with all of these protests? I'm going to start my own protests this week, but I wanted to run it by you to see how you felt about it. I wouldn't want to do anything that was disrespectful or that I thought would piss you off."

And he reassured me, "No, bro, this is what we fight for. For you to have your right to free speech. I talk about it all the time with guys here on the base and they understand what's happening. You're good." Then he said, "Oh, but it would be pretty cool the first time you make a play, if you could give us a salute or something."

"Oh, that's easy. I got you."

Normally before games, I didn't notice the crowd. It was like white noise and vibrations mostly. But this night on prime-time football, Monday night, I felt like the world was watching. As we went through our normal game day routine and took the field, this time felt anything but normal. They rolled out a huge American flag that stretched out across the length of the field. Up until that point, most coaches, long before the protests, would direct the team to toe the white line of the sideline and stand at attention to pay homage to our service members during the national anthem. It was an actual emphasis.

So when I put my ten toes on the white line and Ron Brooks and Steven Means stood to my left and right and instead of putting our hands over our hearts, we raised our right fists high in the air as the national anthem played, I knew what we were getting into and it had just begun. I closed my eyes and talked to my ancestors, as I had grown accustomed to doing during the national anthem. Talking to my grandmother Barbra and both of my grandfathers, I normally ended our talk with "I hope that y'all are proud of me." The question, most times, was rhetorical. Of course they were proud of who I was as a player and all that I had accomplished on the field. But this time I wondered if they would be proud of the man I had become. And this day, clearer than ever, the answer they gave me was "Absolutely!" Their voices were the only ones that mattered.

The Bears received the ball first and on the second play of the game, Jim Schwartz called a safety blitz. The call came in, "Strong safety storm, single. Ready? Break." I lined up to the left of the formation and noticed that Jay Cutler, the Bears quarterback, wasn't paying attention to what I was doing. None of the Bears really were. Usually when I was blitzing, I needed to pretend that I wasn't doing so, so that the offense didn't identify me before the ball was snapped and assign someone to block me.

But because I could tell that none of them seemed to notice that I was standing right on the line of scrimmage, I got into a track stance in order to get to Cutler in the least amount of steps possible. When the ball snapped, in eight steps I'd gotten both arms wrapped around Cutler and slammed him to the ground. Completely unblocked and unimpeded, I got a sack. He had carried out a play-action pass. And as he executed the fake, he turned his back to me. So not only did he not know that I was blitzing, but he never saw it coming. When he finally turned back around, there I was and all he could do was duck for cover. Sack. I stood up, found the nearest camera, and gave a salute. Just like that, the game had begun, and all the anxiety and nervousness I had about the protests and what was to come when this game was over, for now was on pause for the next four hours.

Both defenses held their own in the first half and we went into the locker rooms at the halfway mark up 9–7. In the second half, Jim Schwartz's defense proved effective with the Bears offensive drives ending in three takeaways, a turnover on downs, and a punt. We won the game easily 29–14, with the only other Bears score being on a punt return late in the game.

After the game, when I got back to my phone, I had messages from Eddie and his buddies on base. They were geeked and appreciative of the gesture, the same way that the bruhs get hyped when I throw up the hooks.

---

Normally on my off days and bye weeks, I would fit in all the community work that I couldn't get to because of the hectic schedule of the season. But this work was different. Now I see why they gave me a bulletproof vest that I was wearing under my hoodie as we responded to a shooting in North Philly on the corner of Randolph and Venango. Two weeks after I had raised my fist in the Chicago game, and about a month and a half since we had met with Commissioner Ross and the police, I arranged a ride along with Vice Sports under Carmelo Anthony's show *Clubhouse*, trying to document an extension of the conversation that we'd had with Commissioner Ross, where we go behind the scenes with police officers in Philadelphia and talk about the issues between the community and police, hearing from both sides and seeing what some solutions may be.

Honestly, I thought they were going to give me the most polished officer that was media trained and knew exactly what to say, and I was surprised when they didn't. I was paired with Officer George Soto, a third-generation police officer. Earlier, when we had gotten into the police cruiser, I could tell that he was nervous, and I for sure was nervous. I just asked some simple questions that I thought were layups. "Do you think there's a problem with police brutality?" In my mind, I thought anybody, even police officers, would be willing to admit that there's such a thing as police brutality and that there maybe needs to be reforms and training or things of the sort. But his answer was a flat "No. I don't think there's a problem with police brutality. I think there's a problem with behavior."

With the cameras rolling, I tried my best to stay calm and hear him out, and he went on to explain why police officers couldn't allow people accused of having weapons or bombs go freely without being harassed. But I wasn't talking about people with bombs or guns, I was talking about normal traffic stops that turn deadly whether somebody has an attitude or not. It was clear to me that he didn't understand why people, especially Black people, would have a disdain for or fear of police. And I had to tell him that even I grew up with lessons from my parents teaching me how to survive encounters with the police, what to say and how to act to make sure that I made it home. I told him how the police circling my neighborhood never stopped to speak to me or say hello. They never made me feel more protected or more safe, and it was quite the opposite. I felt like I was constantly being monitored and controlled.

We stopped over at the 12th and Cambria Rec Center in North Philly and met with Philadelphia police captain Michael Cram and some community leaders and activists there, and they were a good example of what it looks like when the police and community have a good rapport. They work together to keep the neighborhood safe; they create safe places for our kids to thrive and build and dream. But that visit was interrupted with a call of a shooting that we were now responding to.

When we got to the corner of Randolph and Venango, there were about five squad cars parked in the middle of the street, with officers all in a huddle, and citizens on their front porches or at their front gates watching, but not interacting. When I asked the lead detective what happened, he explained that there was a person shooting at a green van that then took off down the crowded street with adults and kids outside playing. Two of the bullets hit parked cars and two others went through the front windows of some of the homes.

One of the women allowed us to enter her home and have a conversation without the cameras there, and I asked her what it was like living in that environment. She said that she never went outside. She'd been in that neighborhood for over two decades, and the only time she left home was to go to work and to go to the grocery store. Luckily, none of the bystanders were hurt. But when I talked to the police, they were frustrated because no one wanted to give up any information. It was a crowded street, but according to the citizens, nobody saw anything. That's what happens when people don't feel like you're there to protect them. It was ineffective; essentially a bunch of cops standing in a circle talking to one another about what just happened and the community just glad that no one got hurt and praying that it didn't happen again soon, but knowing that it likely would.

At the end of the day, on my drive home, when I was finally alone, a few things dawned on me. That this was bigger than the police. There was going to be a thousand Officer Sotos out there, and you couldn't change the hearts and minds of all of them. We think that cops stop crime from happening, but they respond to crime. The citizens didn't talk to the police because they knew that talking to the police wasn't going to prevent anything else from happening, just as they hadn't stopped this shooting from happening. So, if police can't stop murders, solve murders, but they're still brutalizing communities, what's the purpose?

In week 6, we took a quick train down to Washington, DC, to play the Commanders. We were 3-1, and they were 3-2. Playing for an early jump on a division lead, I was lined up against wideout Jamison Crowder. There were fifty-three seconds left in the first quarter. When he hopped off the ball and began to go toward the flat, I thought I knew what the play was. There were two other receivers to my right and I figured they were going to cause a traffic jam, like a pick, and get it to Crowder in the flat before I could get there. So as I navigated my way to the outside low portion of the field, Crowder wheeled back up toward the end zone and Kirk Cousins threw him the perfect pass for a touchdown.

I'd guessed wrong and gave up a score but shook it off. The Commanders took a 7–0 lead. Later in the second quarter on 3rd and 5 Schwartz called a bracket coverage that put three defenders on two wideouts. Schwartz's bracket coverage always gave the defense the advantage against pass plays, but it was complicated to execute because all three defenders would need to see the route concepts exactly the same. The goal was to double-team the deep routes and single the lower routes, but you had to wait till the routes were declared in order to know how you matched. The problem with that was, in the red zone, everything happens fast. It's a tight space and defenders need to match their routes as fast as possible. Because the five-yard gain down there, where it's inconsequential in the field of play, in the red zone can be devastating.

As Crowder hopped off the ball, he trailed behind tight end Vernon Davis, who ran the deeper route. The three defenders—myself, inside linebacker Nigel Bradham, and corner Jalen Mills—all read it differently, leaving me one-on-one with Davis with leverage to his outside. When he broke to my inside, he was wide open, and Cousins got the touchdown with an easy pass. *Here we go again*, I thought. *You suck*. And all of a sudden I felt that thought cycle coming on. Already down 14–0, I knocked on my helmet and told myself, "Control what you can control. Be patient. Make the plays that come." On a following kickoff, Wendell Smallwood returned the ball for a touchdown. That got us back into the game, 14–7. On our next drive, on 1st and 10, I had man coverage against Davis. I played off to make sure that I could tell whether it was a run or a pass. If it was a pass, I didn't want to get caught up by the traffic jam of defenders that were around.

So I played off, and behind all of them, my eyes were trained on Davis. I didn't even see the run fake by Cousins, as Davis took off on a shallow drag underneath the linebackers. When Cousins looked up after executing the play fake, he saw rookie defenseman Marcus Smith barreling down on him and quickly threw the ball to Davis without reading the defense. He never saw me closing on Davis like an eagle swooping down from the sky to snatch his prey. But before the ball reached Davis, I snatched it in stride, going back toward our end zone, with nothing in front of me but space, opportunity, and Kirk Cousins. And Marcus Smith, who not only caused the pressure, but was out in front blocking for an easy touchdown.

The game was now tied, the benefit of staying in the moment and making the plays that come. The problem was, we couldn't stop Matt Jones, the Commanders running back, who on the next drive rushed for another touchdown before the half. When we came out of halftime, our offense had scored only three points the entire game. And we never did stop Jones as he rushed for 135 yards, adding to the team's total of 230 yards rushing. We came into the game with the number two defense, holding teams to only 12.6 points a game, but went home with a loss, 27–20. On the train ride home, I realized that I, more than anybody on the defense, couldn't afford to be off my game. Even the smallest of mental errors from me had to be unacceptable, and I needed to understand the details of every defense to a T. Some jobs were harder than others. I needed to embrace that and figure it out.

Week 15, we had the New York Giants at home on a Thursday night, just two days after my birthday. Yet we had no chances of making it to the playoffs. After a short week and a loss on the road to the Baltimore Ravens, this was a chance for us to finish out the season strong against a divisional opponent, and we had yet to win a single divisional game that season. The New York Giants were trying to clinch a playoff berth with a win against us. But if we beat the Giants, we secured a playoff berth for the Dallas Cowboys, making them the number one seed.

After the loss in Washington, we'd won only two of the last eight games and were currently on a five-game losing streak. Ron Brooks was also banged up this week, so I got to play the nickel. The matchup

I had was Odell Beckham. He was a star phenom player, and already established himself as one of the more dynamic and dominant players in the league in the receiver position. His ability to win on the line of scrimmage, catch crazy passes, and evade defenders when he had the ball in his hands made him a dangerous player. And they liked to align him all around the field to get him the best possible matchup. With me starting as the nickel, I was almost guaranteeing that I'd see him in the slot exclusively, with the Giants trying to exploit that matchup.

While Schwartz and some of the staff might not have had a ton of confidence in that matchup, I knew exactly what I was doing. And I knew this was going to be a good game for me.

It was a prime-time game, in front of everybody. I knew I was going to get Beckham's best. And I had everybody, whoever had said I couldn't cover in the NFL, on my mind; they were going to learn today who the hell I was. To add insult to injury the Pro Bowl selections had been announced a few days before the game and I was not on the list, even though I'd followed up my 2015 season with another productive season.

Our game plan against Eli Manning was to disguise everything as much as possible. This would help us slow down his recognition process at the line of scrimmage and give us a little bit of time for our pass rush to get to him as he processed what our defense was after he snapped the ball. So every play, we lined up exactly the same with two safeties showing deep in the field, giving the appearance of maximum coverage, and daring Eli to change the play to a run because we were light in the box.

As much as possible, we wanted to keep a safety close or in the vicinity of Beckham to make sure that we'd get as much coverage dedicated to him as possible. Even if it wasn't a true double team, it may give the appearance of a double team to Eli and discourage him from throwing the ball to our corners. Again, this was all a disguise simply to slow down the thought process of a cerebral quarterback.

On the opening drive, the second play of the game, as designed, I lined up deep on the right half of the field in our disguise. I really had the tight end. If the tight end were to run a vertical route, meaning if he went past five to seven yards, then I was obligated to cover him, which would leave our corner one-on-one with Beckham.

When the ball was snapped, my eyes went straight to the tight end, and right at the five-yard mark, he stopped and turned around, meaning I was now free to go wherever I liked on the field. I put my eyes back to Eli and saw that he was looking directly at Beckham, who was to my right. So I took off running. I knew that my alignment was not deep enough or wide enough to go make an interception, there was just too much ground to cover. But the corner, Nolan Carroll, did a good job of funneling Beckham inside. And so when Eli tried to throw it deep to him, the ball was brought two to three yards closer to my alignment, allowing me to arrive just as the ball arrived, with a forearm right to Beckham's chest, dislodging the ball. Incomplete.

But it let me know that Eli was looking for Odell, and even if he could squeeze it in between the safety and the corner, he was going to take his chances.

The very next play, on 3rd and 3, the Giants aligned in a two-by-two formation with Beckham to our left. Now we were in our sub package, meaning I was the nickel in charge of covering Odell. So I go to what I do best, press coverage. It was obvious that we were playing man-to-man. And if I'm Eli Manning, I know exactly where I'm going to go with the ball. I'm going to go to Odell Beckham, matched up against a 215-pound safety.

The ball was snapped, and Odell skipped off the line and then broke to my left. I recognized the release. They do this to run a pick against guys who press Beckham in the slot. He will skip off the ball just to keep the defender standing right where they are, and then he'll run to the outside of the field. But what the defender who's covering him doesn't realize is that the other receiver who's aligned farther to the outside is going to create a pick to clear space for Beckham to run up the sideline. This is usually only set up if that slot receiver is patient enough to skip off the line and hold the defender and give the other receivers enough time to get in position to create the pick.

As soon as I felt the release, I knew there was a pick to my left, and I immediately went to run around it, meeting Odell right on the sideline, running step for step. When Eli threw the ball, I was in the perfect position to prevent the catch. Incomplete. Two plays in a row. Whatever advantage they thought they had against me wasn't there.

Still in the first quarter, the defense took the field again on a 3rd and 5; I was back at the nickel. This time they had Beckham on the outside being covered by one of the corners. On the inside, I had slot receiver Sterling Shepard, the shifty, five-foot-ten rookie out of Oklahoma who proved to be a great complement to Odell.

I recognized his alignment, something that I'd seen on film. They liked to run a concept called the high low, where one player ran shallow across the middle of the field, while the other ran up about ten yards deep and went across the middle of the field, giving the quarterback an option to throw it to the low receiver or the higher receiver, depending on how the defense played.

It put the defense in a bind. If they played farther back to take away the ten-yard route, then the shallow crosser was wide open and could catch the ball while in stride and continue to run in space. Or if the defense was playing the crosser too tight, he could dump the ball over the top of those defenders to that ten-yard route right behind them. It was a basic concept that every team has that the Giants loved to run.

The ball was snapped and, as anticipated, Sterling Shepard went under. I snapped my eyes right to the tight end, who I knew was going to run the ten-yard crosser. As soon as he did, I undercut it, and a bad throw by Manning put the ball right in my hands. I caught it on the 35-yard line and took off down the right sideline into the end zone. Touchdown.

A hell of a first quarter. I'd already gotten two PBUs and a pick six on a Thursday night, giving us a fourteen-point lead with eight minutes still in the first quarter. The crowd was going crazy.

But the Giants were no slouches, and they slowly climbed back into the game. Driving down into the red zone, I found myself lined up across from Shepard, who hit me with an impressive release, faking me to the outside, and using his patience and quick feet to throw me off balance. Eli delivered a strike, Shepard caught the ball, and just like that was in the end zone.

I shook it off and told myself, "He gets paid, too."

They kicked another field goal to bring the game within five points going into the fourth quarter. On another third down, 3rd and 5, an injury to Jaylen Watkins, our backup safety, who filled in for me when I went down to the nickel, was out with a concussion. So I was back to playing safety. And on 3rd and 5, I have the responsibility to play the deep half.

We lined up in our disguise, but instead of me showing it right away, one of the things I knew about Eli was that he liked to read the first few steps of the safety to see if the safety was going to go to the middle of the field, to the half on the outside, or stay straight back. I knew I could influence his read based on what I did.

When the ball was snapped, even though I knew I was responsible for the entire field, from the hash mark all the way to the sideline of the left side of the field, I went straight back as if I were going to go to the middle of the field instead. Just two steps. And in those two steps, he took his eyes off me and went back outside to Sterling Shepard.

I took off immediately and easily got to the ball, which was probably five yards from the sideline, high-pointed it, and got both feet down as I went out-of-bounds. The first person I saw was Cory Undlin, the DB coach, and nobody was more excited than he was. We immediately chest-bumped, boom, and went crazy on the sideline. That was two in one game. Happy birthday.

We went on to win the game 24–19, after Eli threw another interception to one of my teammates late in the game. Even though the win didn't mean anything for our season—it meant everything to the men in the locker room and everything to me. I had a career year and made plays all season long and didn't make the Pro Bowl, and it was cool. I know that the film doesn't lie. The actions that I took and the work I put in, whether acknowledged or not, were having an impact. When I go back and review what I did in those times when no one was watching and it gained me nothing, I'm secure in who I am.

# 10

# POISE

*The first test of a truly great man is his humility.*
*By humility I don't mean doubt of his powers or*
*hesitation in speaking his opinion, but merely*
*an understanding of the relationship of*
*what he can say and what he can do.*

**—JOHN RUSKIN**

In the opening series of a week 2 matchup against the Kansas City Chiefs, it was 2nd and 3, and I was playing man coverage on tight end Travis Kelce, the six-foot-five, 250-pound rising-star white boy with the athleticism and swagger of a brother. Off the field, I loved to see it; on the field, I hated it. I'd been looking forward to this matchup all week.

Going into the 2017 season, Doug Pederson's second year, we knew from the previous season that we were a few pieces short of competing for a championship. With the additions of veterans Alshon Jeffery, Torrey Smith, Nick Foles, Chris Long, and Patrick Robinson, we had what we needed.

For three seasons in a row, I played at a consistently high level, establishing myself as one of the best safeties in the NFL. I also established myself as captain, the heart and soul of the team. The same way a passenger looks to the flight attendant when the plane experiences turbulence, my teammates, and even some of the coaches, looked to me for that same security. If I was calm, so were they; if I freaked out, all hell broke loose.

And we were getting ready to play the Chiefs, who were coached by Andy Reid, Doug Pederson's mentor, the former Philadelphia Eagles legend, who is known for his epic mustache, Tommy Bahama shirts, and elaborate play calling. He's one of the brightest and most creative offensive minds in the NFL.

My years with Sean Payton taught me that the first fifteen plays were where a coach displayed their creativity. In those first fifteen plays, coaches plan every single play they want to run, then fill them with shifts, elaborate formations, and motions to see how the defense adjusts, in order to exploit whatever weaknesses become apparent later in the game.

The opening drive is like the first few seconds of a heavyweight bout, just kind of feeling each other out. But in this matchup with his young protégé, Andy went for the headshot. Lined up against Travis Kelce, I expected the first play of the opening drive to be a quick throw to get an easy completion for their quarterback, Alex Smith.

Based on Kelce's split and the formation that the offense was in, I anticipated an inside slant, and shuffled my feet to his inside. Instead, Kelce took a jab-step to the inside, and then took off straight up the field on a deep route. Not only was he smooth with his release, but for someone so big, he could run. And Alex Smith made me pay by throwing a perfect ball, completing it easily for a forty-four-yard gain. Seeing that they had just kicked the heart and soul of our team in the chest like Charlie Murphy kicked Rick James on *Chappelle's Show*, I shook off the frustration and lined up against Kelce again. A few plays later, I got a key third-down stop, holding the Chiefs to a field goal on their opening drive.

The Chiefs offense was filled with firepower—Kelce; their wide receiver and the fastest player in football, Tyreek Hill; and running back Kareem Hunt—but not enough for our defense, as we held them to six points in the first half. We took the lead, 10–6, in the third quarter, but a gashing run by Hunt through the middle of the defense for a fifty-three-yard touchdown put them back up by three points. Then in the fourth quarter, the game tied 13–13, with six minutes left, Andy had another trick up his sleeve.

As big as Kelce is, he wasn't a blocking tight end, so when he aligned in the core of the formation, I knew something was up. When Smith snapped the ball, Hill motioned across the line of scrimmage to our left. At that moment, Smith faked a handoff to Hunt on our right. With our defense split between covering Hill and pursuing Hunt, Smith pitched the ball to Kelce, who folded back behind the line of scrimmage and was now sprinting with the ball through the middle of the defense toward the goal line. The only man left to stop him was our free safety, Corey Graham. And like Michael Jordan from the free throw line, Kelce leaped from the five-yard marker over Corey and into the end zone, making the score 20–13.

With our offense unable to make a rebuttal, Kansas City scored again late when Hunt muscled his way into the end zone, increasing the score to 27–13. Just when we thought the game was out of reach, a late touchdown with only about thirteen seconds left on the clock brought us within seven. In order push the game to overtime, we needed to recover an onside kick, then make a Hail Mary pass to the end zone, within five seconds of clock. When our kicker executed the onside play, the ball bounced clean through the Chiefs front line, leaving our tight end, Trey Burton, to recover it—and putting us within the range to throw a last-minute rainbow ball that would land in the end zone. We had hope.

With five seconds left, Carson Wentz snapped the ball, heaving it toward the end zone. Watching the ball helplessly bounce to the ground wasn't nearly as inspiring as watching the ball fly through the air. Though I finished the game with a game-high five tackles, we also left with an L, splitting our early-season record to 1-1.

One thing I liked about playing away games was that we received the film immediately afterward. The quick turnaround helped me metabolize the game to create a plan for what I needed to improve the following week. Watching the game tape also enabled me to evaluate my game before the media's and fans' voices entered my head.

On days when I'd played my worst, the film was never as bad as I thought; and even when I'd played my best, the film was never as good. As we flew home from Kansas City, I was encouraged, because I knew our chance of making it to a championship was within our control.

About thirty-one miles outside of Philadelphia, at the Graterford Prison, I noticed my guide, Bill Cobb, the deputy director of the ACLU's Campaign for Smart Justice, wipe beaded sweat off his bald head.

"I hate this motherfucker," Bill said.

Even though his job was to advocate for the rights of people who were incarcerated in America's jails and prisons, because he was once an inmate at this facility, this assignment was different. In 1994, he pled guilty to robbery, kidnapping, criminal conspiracy, and violation of the Uniform Firearms Act and, after serving a six-and-a-half-year sentence, was released in 2000. This visit in July 2017 marked the first time he had come back of his own accord.

When the Players Coalition began, I focused on the issues plaguing Philadelphia and the Pennsylvania criminal justice system. More kids were sentenced to life without parole in Pennsylvania than any other state in the country. Today I went to meet with some of them.

Up until then, I had never been to a prison. The only frame of reference I realized I had were shows like *Oz*. Accompanying me on this visit was my teammate and linebacker Steven Means. After security cleared us, we met with the superintendent, Cynthia Link, a woman who couldn't have been taller than five two. Cynthia was clearly a leader and understood the challenges of the justice system. Because of some of the programs this prison offered, programs that didn't exist in most facilities, Graterford was known as one of the more progressive state correctional institutions in the country. As she told us that the men could make money, and talked about their computer lab, she beamed with pride.

"How much money do they make an hour?" I asked.

"Seventeen cents."

The bare minimum required to disqualify their work as slave labor.

B Block was the first stop on the tour of the prison. With gates slamming behind us at every checkpoint, there were cells as far as my eye could see. I didn't know what to expect on this visit, but being locked in a cell block without security and a five-foot-two warden exceeded my darkest nightmares.

We continued through the block toward the computer lab, where six desktops that resembled television sets from the 1980s sat. Thinking about the couple thousand incarcerated men who were there, learning to type and build their resume, I wondered how those six computers were enough.

In the large auditorium, we were scheduled to meet six men who were sentenced to life terms when they were minors. Though all of them were incarcerated longer than I had been alive, I was humbled by the fact that they didn't seem bitter. In fact, they were eager to tell Steven and me about their plans to protect young boys and girls from becoming victims of a system that didn't hesitate to hand out life sentences like penny candy.

Of all the six men we met, I could tell that Kempis Songster, with dreadlocks that hung all the way down to the floor from underneath his beanie hat, was different. He understood the cycle of incarceration and how he got caught up in it. He talked about his debt to society and had a well-thought-out plan on how to become a healer of the communities he once hurt. At the age of fifteen, Kempis ran away from home in New York to Philadelphia, where he joined a gang. Under the orders of the gang leaders, Songster murdered another kid runaway—and was convicted of first-degree murder, which carried a mandatory life sentence without parole, in 1987, the same year I was born.

Before this encounter, I thought all murderers deserved to be cast away from society forever. But to think about being held in a facility with grown men for a crime I'd committed when I was fifteen challenged my preconceived ideas. If Calvin hadn't discouraged me from becoming a Crip, my fate could've been like Kempis's. I also reflected on how different I was when I was fifteen compared to now, at twenty-nine. I couldn't fathom being held for life without parole for a mistake I had made when I was fifteen. It reminded me just how close I was to gang life and how easily it could've been me. Listening to these men's stories, I thought about the human potential we lock away to rot—out of sight and out of mind.

As we were leaving the prison, Bill encountered one of the men who he'd been incarcerated with nearly twenty years ago. The complex mix of guilt and relief that he had his freedom caused him to hang his head—picking it up only after we were outside, to exhale for the first time that day.

After the loss to the Chiefs in week 2, we went on a nine-game winning streak. The best part was that Doug Pederson allowed us to have fun. After an interception in our week 11 win against the Bears (31–3), the defensive backs and I celebrated by hitting the electric slide on the field. But then a hungry Seattle Seahawks team humbled us in week 13 when they won 24–10, ending our streak.

Because the 11-2 Los Angeles Rams were our opponent the week following the loss to Seattle, and flying to Philly from Seattle just to get back on a plane to LA this late in the season would limit the team's recovery time, we stayed on the West Coast in preparation for the game. Beating the Rams would allow us to win the NFC East and secure at least one home playoff game at the Linc. But when I looked up to see Nick Foles under center in the third quarter, I was scrambling for answers.

"Yo, where's Carson?" I asked safety Rodney McLeod.

"I think he might be done, bro," he whispered, "for the year."

With over three thousand yards passing, twenty-nine touchdowns, and three games left in the 2017 season, Carson Wentz was having an MVP-caliber season. But whenever things seem like they're going according to plan, God tells a joke. On our last offensive drive of the third quarter, Carson scrambled and lunged into the end zone for a go-ahead touchdown. Two defenders sandwiched him, tearing the ACL in his left leg. *What now?*

Before I allowed myself to take that route, I shifted my focus to what I could control: *What do we need to do to win this game?*

After Foles drove the offense to set up our kicker, Jake Elliott capped off the possession with a field goal. We were down 35–34 in the fourth. To walk out with a win, all our defense needed to do was get one stop for our offense.

Right on call, Chris Long stripped the ball from quarterback Jared Goff to have Rodney recover it, advancing it a few yards before being tackled. Rodney's fumble recovery put us in field goal range. We took the lead, 37–35.

In an act of desperation to score late in the game, the Rams ran a hook and lateral play on their last drive. Instead of converting on the lateral, the ball bounced right into the hands of Brandon Graham, who ran it in for a touchdown to end the game, 43–35.

Wearing hats and T-shirts that read NFC EAST CHAMPIONS in the locker room, we celebrated. Congratulating us on being the NFC East champs, while also reminding us we played for something bigger, Coach Pederson spoke first. Winning our division guaranteed us only one playoff game at home. Number one seed meant we'd get a bye week, which left two games at home between us and the Super Bowl. There were three games left in the season. To secure the number one seed, we needed to win at least two. After Coach spoke, I contemplated what I wanted to say to the team.

Earlier in the week, Coach Pederson had arranged for Kobe Bryant to speak to us. One of his favorite series as a Laker was the 2010 NBA Finals against the Boston Celtics, where the Lakers beat the Celtics in Game 7, winning Kobe his fifth and final ring. After going down 3-2 in the series, in a 92–86 loss, and at risk of losing a second title to the Celtics, Kobe's teammates watched in confusion as Kobe sat in the locker room, laughing hysterically.

"If somebody told you all you gotta do is go home and win two games and you're the NBA champions, you'd fucking take that, right?" Kobe explained about his response. "Then what the fuck is the problem? We just gotta go home and win two."

When speaking to my teammates, I wanted to fortify us against the media's desire to sow doubt in our mind about our trajectory now that Carson was injured. No matter who was or wasn't in that locker room: our goal was the same. I needed to remind them of this.

"Carson being out of this is fucking tough. But dig this, the people in this room is who we ride with. We all we got; we all we need!

Believe that! We've got bigger goals at the end of the day: a championship. Nothing short of that. We just need two wins. They ain't got to
be pretty. Let's go! Family on three."

*ONE.*

*TWO.*

*THREE!*

One of the biggest questions the media, team owners, and fans all
had heading into the 2017 season was "Will the players protest again
this year?" With Steven Means and Ron Brooks no longer on the roster, I'd made up my mind that I would—even if I was alone in doing
so. But Rodney McLeod joined me in raising a fist, and Chris Long
made a powerful gesture of solidarity by placing his arm around me,
becoming the first white player to publicly endorse the protests.

With the protests putting the league on notice, we invited Roger
Goodell and some of the officers from the league office to come on a
tour to show them the inner workings of the justice system and why
we were so motivated to mobilize our momentum. Though the NFL
designated Tuesdays as the day off, the Eagles made Monday the
mandatory day off, using Tuesday as a day to review game tape, get
a workout in, and go home early. One Tuesday, in early September,
while our teammates cleared the cafeteria to head to the 9:00 a.m.
team meeting, Chris Long, Torrey Smith, Rodney McLeod, and
I hung back. Today we were going to host the NFL commissioner,
Roger Goodell; the Eagles' owner, Jeffrey Lurie; and the NFL executive vice president of football operations, Troy Vincent, on a "Listen and Learn Tour" around Philadelphia. The purpose of the tour
was to show why so many other NFL players like us protested and
advocated for the concerns of our communities. When they arrived,

we provided them with the day's itinerary and then packed into a Sprinter van.

As players, we were used to being on the league's time, but now: they were on ours. We walked around like we had a huge organization with a large staff and support, but really in the beginning there were two women who did it all for us. Kristi Roehm, my PR director, and Angela LaChica, Anquan's PR director, served as the Coalition's comanagers in its infancy. They helped us organize conference calls, connect with subject-matter experts, arrange messaging opportunities in the media, and even provide talking points for everyone who wanted to participate under the Players Coalition. They started out as our personal PR reps but had become full-time managers of our social justice work. Kristi and I worked hand in hand to make sure that the "Listen and Learn Tour" was as impactful as possible. We knew we had only one shot to grab the league's attention in a real way and they needed to see just how organized we were. There were four stops on the agenda: the first was a meeting with the commissioner of the Philadelphia Police Department, Richard Ross, to discuss what role we could play in repairing the relationship between the community and those who'd taken an oath to protect it. Next was a trip to Germantown for a meeting with community-based organizations. Even with tight budgets, grassroots organizations fight to prevent people from going into the criminal justice system and provide the necessary support to reduce recidivism. Our third stop was the Criminal Justice Center to watch bail hearings, so that Goodell could see how the criminal justice system fed individuals into incarceration. Our final stop was a visit to the Public Defender's Office to talk with the chief defender, Keir Bradford-Grey, and other public defenders about the various needs of the clients they represent.

Because we knew Goodell would welcome any opportunity to get photos with the police, and wasn't aligning himself with any anti-police rhetoric, the meeting with Commissioner Ross would be our first stop.

The second stop allowed for Goodell to see how the justice system impacts disenfranchised communities. The ACLU had helped us bring some of the most powerful groups in Philadelphia all to one table. In attendance were J. Jondhi Harrell, the founder and executive director of the Center for Returning Citizens; Reverend Michelle Simmons, the founder and CEO of Why Not Prosper; Dorothy Johnson-Speight, the founder and executive director of Mothers in Charge; Reuben Jones, the executive director of Frontline Dads; Bill Cobb, the deputy director of the ACLU's Campaign for Smart Justice; Laura Fine, the codirector of the Youth Sentencing & Reentry Project; Russell Craig, the director of the Restorative Justice program with Mural Arts Philadelphia; and the moderator, Ann Schwartzman, the former executive director of the Pennsylvania Prison Society.

As we sat over lunch around the large rectangular table, each of these community leaders and organizers communicated what they and their organizations did, how they did it, and why they continued to do it. Introducing some of the women who stayed at Why Not Prosper's women's shelter, Reverend Simmons explained the cycle of poverty for single mothers and explained that instead of incarcerating the people from these vulnerable communities, their success with the resources they were able to secure through grants showed what could be sustained with more funding. To provide the people whose work often went unnoticed with an audience of the top figures in the NFL, and the recognition that their work mattered, was significant. The meeting was tense, as each organization eagerly awaited their turn to be heard. Most of the organizations have had to compete against each other for limited funding, but at that table I could clearly see the opportunity to have a collective impact if we could secure enough funds to have the organizations work together.

While witnessing the bail hearings through a closed-circuit television at the Criminal Justice Center, Goodell was shocked to learn that the person responsible for issuing bail amounts wasn't a judge but an elected magistrate who wasn't even required to have a law degree. This same magistrate levied a $50,000 bail for a woman who had gotten into a fight in a concert venue's bathroom. This fight was the woman's first offense. With very little conversation and not much deliberation, the magistrate handed out bail costs like an employee at a fast-food restaurant.

Arriving at our last stop at the Public Defender's Office, the chief public defender, Keir Bradford-Grey; her first assistant defender, James McHugh; and the board president of the Defender Association of Philadelphia, David Rudovsky, presented that, in 2015, Pennsylvania spent $42,727 per inmate. The same amount of money many of the community organizations we visited operated on for the year.

When we got back to the NovaCare Complex, we shook hands with Roger Goodell and his team. When they left, Torrey Smith, Chris Long, Rodney McLeod, and I knew we had the NFL's attention. The next move was to organize the best and brightest minds among the players in the league to keep this momentum alive.

Two weeks after our win against the Rams, we found ourselves in another tight game against the Oakland Raiders. Whereas the Rams game was an offensive shoot-out, where we only needed one stop to seal the game, which defense buckled first and which offense could control the line of scrimmage longer decided our fate against this Raiders team. And with this being our second-to-last game of the season, a win would lock us in the number one seed.

Like a pendulum, the momentum swung back and forth between

our defenses. Our defensive back Patrick Robinson intercepted a pass, only to have our running back Jay Ajayi give it right back to the Raiders with a fumble. Then defensive end Vinny Curry caused a fumble from running back Marshawn Lynch. By the end of the third quarter, the game was tied 10–10.

With six minutes left in the fourth, the Raiders lined up in heavy formation with three tight ends and one running back. A telltale sign that they were running it, and they'd been successfully moving the ball out of this formation all game. If we didn't make an adjustment on our corners, who were 185 pounds soaking wet, they would have to take on blocks from three-hundred-plus-pound offensive linemen. Not only would that be a matchup we'd likely lose, but we could also lose a corner to injury. As a bigger body accustomed to negotiating offensive linemen, I didn't mind doing the dirty work, so the adjustment was to put me at the corner position in these situations.

On 1st and 10, quarterback Derek Carr handed the ball to running back Jalen Richard, who punched a hole in the right side of our defensive line, cut left, and then crashed right into me. Because I wanted the ball, I remembered what Walter Thurmond had taught us about how to take the ball away from the ballcarrier. No matter how well you secure a football with two hands, there's always a weak spot behind the elbow of the bottom arm. So, I took my hands, reached up under his, and felt the point of the football. As Jalen fought for extra yards, I yanked the tip of the football down as hard as I could. The ball came out and, before anyone else jumped on it, I scooped it up. Even though our offense couldn't capitalize on the turnover, the strip prevented the Raiders from getting what could've at least been a field goal to take the lead.

Now, in what seemed like a game-winning drive by the Raiders with less than a minute to go in the fourth, our cornerback Ronald

Darby intercepted Carr's pass to the right side of the field. Nick Foles then marched the offense into field goal range, where Jake Elliott kicked a forty-eight-yard field goal, putting us up 13–10. But with seconds left, anything could happen.

With two seconds left to play, the Raiders attempted the same hook and lateral play that the Rams had attempted, with similar results. On a botched execution of the play, our defensive end Derek Barnett scooped up the ball, which was bouncing around, and took it to the house. The final score was 19–10, and we were the number one seed in the NFC. Since we played that game on Christmas Day, it was only fitting that we gifted our fans the present of home field advantage for the playoffs.

---

As part of the Players Coalition prepared to discuss the national anthem protests with the league and the possible ways they could support us, there was a debate over who should lead. At this point, the Coalition had grown beyond players who had taken a knee or raised a fist—to those who were well known for their contributions to the space of community work. Over the weeks that Anquan Boldin and I had created the Coalition, we conducted weekly calls about strategy, messaging, and how to best utilize our platforms for pushing the protests to something sustainable for the other players.

Between the players protesting and Trump's comments about how players who protested should be fired, the league was polarized—and it impacted the bottom line. With declining viewership rates, NFL owners wanted the protests to end. While Trump put pressure on the owners to do something, which was good for us, his commentary steered the focus away from the social justice issues the protests were intended to bring attention to.

Two days before the Coalition was scheduled to meet with the league, Colin Kaepernick filed a lawsuit against the NFL and didn't tell us about it. It was a year since his contract was up and it was clear, at least to me, that the team owners had blackballed him. At the meeting, there would be thirteen players, eleven owners, and a couple players union representatives. Colin was invited to the meeting, but wasn't there. It wasn't surprising, but seeing Eric Reid in his I'M WITH KAP tee made me wonder what they were up to. But I had no time to dwell on it. For the first time in history, a group of active players would be negotiating with team owners about something other than a collective bargaining agreement.

When the meeting began, it was more than awkward. We didn't sit across from one another, as expected, but among one another, every seat alternating between player and team owner. I sat next to two familiar faces, Eagles owner Jeff Lurie and Falcons owner Arthur Blank. If Jerry Jones represented the voice of the opposition, then Mr. Blank and Mr. Lurie represented the slither of hope that we may get some support.

We continued to put emphasis on the fact that we knew what it looked like when the NFL supported something, like Breast Cancer Awareness Month, and we'd all participated in their Salute to Service month. When they wanted to lift up a cause they transformed the playing fields, the uniforms, the ads during the broadcasts, and raised millions of dollars. Yet, so far, their support had only been a few empathetic team owners having private conversations behind closed doors. They were allowing our message to be hijacked and portrayed as anti-military, when they knew better than anyone that was not the truth. They were only interested in protecting the shield, not the players.

After a back-and-forth that seemed to carry on longer than it needed to, the meeting adjourned, and we agreed to continue the dialogue. When we got outside of the New York offices, the media swarmed us. To ensure our message was concise, consistent, and cohesive, the Coalition appointed me as the spokesperson.

Scanning the sea of reporters for an empathetic ear, I called on someone with an I'M WITH KAP tee to ask the first question.

"Why wasn't Kaepernick invited to the meeting?"

"He was invited."

"Well, why isn't he here?"

"I'm not sure, you'd have to ask him."

On the two-hour drive from New York back home to Philadelphia, I replayed every moment of my answers to the media in my head like game film. I called Kristi.

"How'd it go?!"

"I fucked up."

"What happened?"

Telling her about the question I received about Colin, I knew the media would spin my answer to write something negative about him. Though my answer about why Colin wasn't there was honest, I regretted my failure to have prepared myself for that question.

In the following days, I get a call from Colin's lawyers, telling me I needed to publicly retract my statement about Colin being "invited" because Colin had been "explicitly told that he was not."

As the one who had organized the meeting, I spoke with Goodell, Vincent, and DeMaurice Smith and Don Davis, the heads of the NFL and the NFLPA, and we all agreed that Colin could attend the meeting. The NFLPA even offered to cover his travel. I invited him personally. He never responded.

"If someone told you he wasn't invited, I need to know who."

They informed me that they had talked to a lawyer from the NFLPA's office.

"Well, that's who needs to make a statement."

A couple days later, Colin's lawyers sent me an email, again demanding that I retract my statement that Colin was invited to the meeting. For months prior, Colin and I had spoken on numerous occasions about how we could organize and how to get on one accord. It was contentious at times, but seeing how he had started the movement and was integral to the reason that we were all there, I made the effort to work together.

Like how my uncle handled the situation when my grandmother died, once someone brings lawyers into the situation and forgoes the simple courtesy of a call, it lets me know where I stand with them. I informed the rest of the Coalition what happened and let them know that I had removed Colin from the group chat.

---

As the Rams were one of the hottest teams in the NFC, we were sure we'd see them in the playoffs. But after they ran into a hungry Atlanta Falcons team that beat them 26–13 in the Wild Card, Matt Ryan, Julio Jones, and the Dirty Birds were coming to Philly.

This was the playoffs and I wanted to switch things up a bit. I took a page out of Tom Brady's book. Earlier in the week I asked the people in charge of stadium operations to play Jay-Z's "Public Service Announcement" when they said my name. Every starter on the defense was introduced one by one to the rowdy crowd in the Linc. As I stood in the tunnel, the last Eagle left to take the field, the hair on my arms was standing up and my stomach was in bunches. I knew that this game and the ones that followed were a chance to cement my legacy in this city, on this team, and in this league. All of those nerves melted away as I heard Jay-Z's voice blare from the speakers, "Allow me to reintroduce myself, my name is . . . ," and stormed the field like a gladiator ready for battle in front of the 69,596 fans in attendance. By far, my favorite introduction in my entire career.

This game all came down to the wire. Up 15–10, it was 4th and goal on the 2-yard line, and the Falcons had the ball. There were fifty-eight seconds left in the game, after the Falcons put together a thirteen-play drive all the way to the 2-yard line. This was it, our whole season, our hopes and dreams all coming down to this play. It was what we'd prepared for. Our red zone defense had changed from the season before. We played only one simple defense, and we were experts at it, allowing us to play fast, focus on the pre-snap tips and cues the offense might be giving away. When they lined up with Julio Jones to our left and a tight end offset, I knew exactly what play was coming. And I wasn't alone. Rodney and Nigel knew what was coming, too, and we all began to scream it out to the rest of the defense. "Sprint out! Sprint Out! Sprint Out!" We knew that quarterback Matt Ryan was going to snap the ball, roll out to the right, and target Julio in the back corner of the end zone. The play was designed to attack one side of the field, placing targets for the quarterback at the goal line and at the pylons in the end zone.

Our coverage dictated that corner Jalen Mills lined up one-on-one with Julio. I was lined up against receiver Mohamed Sanu in the slot. Knowing where Sanu wanted to go, I immediately grabbed him when Matt rolled out. Jalen did the same, even knocking Jones down to the ground. Knowing the play, Nigel beelined for Matt, who, in waiting for Julio to recover, double-clutched the ball and extended the play.

Eventually, Matt threw to Julio, who was back up. Though the game was played at breakneck speed, whenever the ball is in the air this late in a game deciding plays, everything slows down. Normally a sure catch for Julio, the ball flew right through his hands. To his credit, he might've been focused on making sure his feet were inbounds when he landed. When the ball landed out-of-bounds, the crowd went absolutely crazy. We were one game closer to the Super Bowl.

———

A few days before our week 12 matchup against the Bears, Troy Vincent called me.

"Malcolm, I'm going to send you this proposal. Look it over and make sure everything that y'all want is in there before I send it to Roger. I want to make sure everyone is good with the deal."

"Cool. I'll look it over and get back to you."

We had begun getting traction in the media not only for the protest but for doubling down on the work. There were more "Listen and Learn Tours" with other team owners, more media interviews, more impactful moments like me, Chris Long, and Torrey Smith going to Harrisburg, Pennsylvania, to lobby for a reform bill the morning after winning a game on Monday Night Football. The NFL knew that we were committed and they wanted nothing more than to get out of the crosshairs of the media. After multiple memos back and forth between the Players Coalition and the NFL, we'd seemingly come to an agreement. Over a seven-year period, $89 million would be allocated toward social justice initiatives. Thirty-three percent of those funds would go to the Coalition so that players could decide which organizations to support and which initiatives to fund. The other 67 percent would be governed by a working group of five players (of which I was not one) and five team owners. The working group kicked off the dissemination of funds by giving grants to the United Negro College Fund and Dream Corps (now known as Dream.org).

Then there was the team matching grant. If players wanted to fund a particular social initiative, every team would be obligated to match them dollar for dollar, up to $250,000. Then there was a grant of $5,000 any former or current player could apply for to create change in any city that existed outside of the NFL market. And like what the NFL did for breast cancer and Salute to Service, the Coalition also wanted the league to dedicate a month to bringing awareness to the various social justice issues we cared about.

I sent the memo to the Players Coalition group text. Eric Reid took issue, asking why Troy had only sent it to me. I simply said, "Look at it. If anything is off, say so, but it seems like this is everything we asked for on our last call." Feeling his hesitation, I called him. The last time we had spoken to the league was about a week before and Troy had asked the negotiating committee bluntly if we would end our protests if they gave us the last bits of the deal we were asking for, to which we all agreed, surprisingly.

We had created a negotiating committee consisting of myself, Anquan Boldin, Eric Reid, and Michael Thomas. We negotiated with Troy Vincent and Roger Goodell directly for a little over a month, but it felt like a year trying to fit in conference calls and meetings during the thick of an NFL season with many of us in different time zones. It was a logistical nightmare. Plus, the infighting among the players in the coalition had only grown as the stakes got higher.

The two factions of players, kneeling and "non-kneeling," truly had a difference in philosophy. Those different philosophies had turned into flat-out distrust and animosity. At one point, the idea came up that we should all meet in Dallas to talk as men face-to-face and squash our differences so we could keep from having a divided front. Eric responded by saying that he would only bring such a proposal to Kaepernick if we were agreeing beforehand that we would meet only to discuss how the Players Coalition would remove itself from the negotiations and allow the kneeling players to, in short, take it over from there. That was a hard no. But we continued to press forward and presented a united front, knowing the chasm that stood between us.

That is why it was necessary for the negotiating committee to include two players, one from each faction, making sure that the wishes of all were being, to the best of our abilities, captured in the negotiating.

I knew that I would likely need to be the first chip to fall. I was the only one left in the league raising a fist. If I stopped, the overall movement would still be focused around taking a knee. As they were the last leaders of those five or six players who were still taking a knee, I was a bit shocked when Mike and Eric also reluctantly agreed. But a few days later on the phone, Eric was talking as if we had never had that conversation. "I don't know, man, this doesn't seem like enough guaranteed." Now I was frustrated. I asked him, "What would make you feel comfortable? If there's absolutely nothing that will get you to stop, that's fine, but we should probably get up from the negotiating table. But if we want to move forward, what would make you feel better?"

We hadn't fully formed the Coalition and were still waiting on some of the paperwork for it to be a certified 501(c)(3), so technically we couldn't even take a donation if we had wanted to. So I asked if he would accept an act of good faith if we pushed them to make an immediate donation of a few million dollars to an organization of our choice as a guarantee, in case they tried to back out of the deal at the last minute. He said he'd sleep on it and get back to me. It would be the last time I talked with Eric. A day or so later, early on a Wednesday morning, as I sat in a meeting room by myself, watching tape and eating breakfast, my normal Wednesday routine, Mike Thomas called me. "I don't know, Malc. We risked it all and put it on the line and this just doesn't feel like enough."

I took a deep breath and I asked him the same thing I had asked Eric. If our stance was that there was nothing that we'd be willing to take to stop protesting, then we should probably just say that and live with it. Nowhere did the deal require us to give up our stance or our protests; it was only behind closed doors that it was being asked of us. To me, it seemed very simple, and they had given us, to some extent, everything we'd asked for. I didn't plan on protesting forever—I thought the protests were a means to an end—but if our goal was to just protest for something larger and there was no dollar amount that the NFL could give us in order to do the work, then we should just say so, and that was fine. Mike said he couldn't accept it, and I said, "Okay," needing to rush to my meetings that were about to start.

A few hours after those meetings, right before I headed out to practice, I got a notification on my phone, then another, and another. Twitter was blowing up. Eric Reid, Mike Thomas, Russell Okung, Kenny Stills, and Julius Thomas had all posted the same message on Twitter: "With much thought and consideration, I've decided to officially withdraw my involvement in the Players Coalition founded by Malcolm Jenkins and Anquan Boldin. The Players Coalition was supposed to be formed as a group that represented NFL athletes who have been silently protesting social injustice and racism. However, Malcolm and Anquan can no longer speak on our behalf as we do not believe the coalition's beliefs are in our best interests as a whole. We will continue to have dialogue with the league and find equitable solutions, but without Malcolm and Anquan as our representatives."

This threw me for a loop because they painted the picture that me and Anquan had been negotiating or speaking on behalf of the Coalition on our own, as if Eric and Mike weren't at the negotiating table with us and hadn't negotiated the entire deal that we'd accepted a couple of days earlier. Having to go straight to practice, I had no time to think about the questions that I would surely get in today's media availability. I racked my brain as I went through plays and sat on the sideline anticipating what could possibly come down the pipe.

How Eric had organized these messages and what that meant for all the things that we had negotiated for.

When practice was over and I returned to my locker, it was surrounded by at least thirty media members, all with cameras and recorders and questions. I tried to, as I normally did, answer them with poise, trying not to get rattled by the questions they threw at me or things that people said. I was complimentary to Eric and all those guys, recognizing their work and contribution to all that we had done so far. A few days later, the remaining ten board members of the Coalition voted to accept the deal from the NFL. With the kneeling player out, they could continue the protests and we could continue to expand the work. The announcement once again had media swarming my locker. Anquan had retired in the offseason to fully commit his time to fighting for social justice and no longer had the obligation to talk to the media multiple times every week. And with the other two that negotiated the deal now having removed themselves, I was seemingly left as the lone wolf, who had negotiated this deal on his own, which was far from the truth.

But the truth is who got the credit wasn't important to me. Being called a sellout wasn't a deterrent. I saw clearly the opportunity we had to have a real impact on society, and the work and time we put in paid off. The league did in fact deliver what we asked for. Besides the money they committed to donating, they provided millions of dollars in ad support during the playoffs and Super Bowl. It opened doors that led to the NFL acknowledging the issues around Black Lives Matter, justice reform, and police brutality. What we did opened the door for other sports leagues to follow, more proactively, in our footsteps. Today the Coalition has helped expand our reach to pro athletes in more than a dozen other leagues as well as constantly engaging with collegiate athletes. This is what it was all about in the first place. The people. The countless people who have their freedom back after wrongly being incarcerated, the kids in poor school districts who now have access to quality books and computers, the programs that service the most vulnerable populations in this society that have funding to continue their work. It wasn't perfect by any means, but with all of that at stake, I couldn't care less about how I was going to be labeled in the media.

"Does this mean that you'll stop protesting?"

"Yes, I feel comfortable with ending my protest."

Remembering in my rookie year, when we were told to "act like we've been here before," I told my teammates something different.

"Don't be anybody but yourself. Don't do anything different. Whoever you are, whatever it is that you do, is the reason we're here."

But on the eve of the Super Bowl, our defensive coordinator, Jim Schwartz, expressed his worry about the Patriots' tempo on offense and shifted the game plan at the last minute. From the film we studied, the Patriots showed that they lined up in multiple personnel and ran their offense quicker than our ability to respond. So, I would play linebacker. That meant I would have the responsibility that JV had had playing against Peyton Manning in the 2009 Super Bowl: operate as the on-field brains for our defense.

To simulate the conditions we'd face with the Patriots offense, Schwartz didn't give us the defensive call until the offense broke the huddle, meaning we'd have only about five to six seconds, as a defense, to line up and make our calls. This last-minute shift threw me off my game. So, to prevent allowing my frustration to undermine the larger goal, I voluntarily asked my backup to replace me.

As the offense broke the huddle, I watched from the sideline. There was one particular formation of theirs that was going to be a problem, "21 Pony." That's when the offense comes out with two receivers, two halfbacks, and one tight end. Teams normally would put three linebackers on the field to deal with the two running backs and the tight end, a base defense. But because the Patriots had a dynamic running back in James White, they liked to flex him out as a receiver.

When you put three linebackers on the field, you did so under the premise that they'll cover the two running backs and the tight end. The Patriots exploited the matchup by taking your linebackers out on the corners. Now your linebackers were functioning in a role they didn't play. Though I was pissed, I understood what Schwartz was trying to do.

"Don't call 'Base' against '21 Pony,'" I told him. "We'll have bad matchups."

That night at the hotel, the coaches asked the captains what song we wanted to come out to. The answer was unanimous. With Meek Mill's "Dreams and Nightmares" blaring from the stadium speakers, we stormed the field.

Our defense took the field first and the Patriots opened the game as we had thought: they played the speed game with different personnel every single play. In our attempt to match up against the rotating personnel along with the tempo, we got a penalty for having twelve men on the field. And just as I'd predicted, Schwartz called base defense against "21 Pony" and the result was exactly what we knew would happen: confusion.

Playing linebacker on the weak side of the field, in the second quarter, I watched Tom Brady hit a wide-open Brandin Cooks. As I ran to tackle him, he was juking my teammates, not paying any attention to his blind side. He never felt me approaching. I executed a six-inch rising blow right up under his pads, also hitting him in the chin. He left the game with a concussion. Though I would make a hit like that ten times out of ten, I never wanted to see anybody carted off the field. After the Patriots kicked a second field goal, making the score 15–6, Tom hit another gear.

In seven plays, Tom moved the ball ninety yards and scored a touchdown, but they missed the extra point. Now the score was 15–12. With the second quarter ending, our offense looked to score. On 4th and goal, on the Patriots' 1-yard line, instead of kicking a field goal, we went for the touchdown. Our backup quarterback Nate Sudfeld's eyes lit up on the sideline when he heard the call.

"Hey, what's the call?" I asked.

"The Philly special," replied Nate.

Two weeks before the Super Bowl, our offense had run this play, where the center directly snapped the ball to running back Corey Clement, who ran to the offensive left, pitched it to Trey Burton, who then found an open Nick Foles in the end zone. It worked like a charm in practice, and it worked on fourth down, at the Super Bowl, against one of the best franchises in NFL history. We went crazy. We were up 22–12.

The irony was that, a few drives earlier, the Patriots had run a similar play—pitching it to one side of the field, giving it to another person, who reversed to the opposite side of the field to throw it to their quarterback, who was open—except Tom dropped the pass. As someone who trash-talks when I know it'll amplify a player's negative thought cycle, when I saw Tom drop the ball, I sprinted across the field, slapping him on his ass.

"Come on, Tom."

Not only did he not look at me, he didn't even flinch when I slapped him. He just returned to the huddle and called the next play. That's when I knew Tom was different. He's a machine, focused only on winning, I don't even know if he knew I was there.

In the first half, locking up running back James White was my assignment, their go-to guy. For many of the matchups I was effective, so the Patriots' adjustment in the second half didn't surprise me. Their new target on offense would now be their future Hall of Fame tight end Rob Gronkowski. He was matched up against my backup, Corey Graham. A mismatch for us. In the first drive of the second half, Tom targeted Gronk four times, scoring a touchdown, moving them within three points, 22–19.

But our offense didn't slow down one bit. Alshon Jeffery made plays in the perimeter, deep in the pass game. When the Patriots adjusted to the pass, our offense pivoted to the run, giving the ball to Jay Ajayi and LeGarrette Blount, and our rookie running back, Corey Clement, caught a touchdown in triple coverage. So now the score was 29–19.

On the next drive, Tom came out in one of their favorite formations, where they spread the field by lining their faster receivers in the inside and their slower threats on the outside. That alignment caused some confusion, coverage-wise. To provide some help, I shifted to the right side of the field. Staring directly at me, Tom snapped the ball—making me think he was throwing it to my side of the field—then quickly snapped his head to the left side of the field, completing the pass to his wide receiver for a touchdown. *Damn*, I thought to myself, *he got me*. When I got to the sideline, my message was simple.

"For the next drive we're looking for one stop."

Even after tight end Zach Ertz's diving touchdown put us at 38–33, my message was the same.

"All we need is one stop."

If you would've told me at the beginning of the season that, to bring Philadelphia its first Super Bowl victory in franchise history, all we had to do was stop Tom Brady once, that's a bet I would take every time. Tom was the GOAT, but we were the Eagles.

Right before the Patriots' drive, I told Darren Sproles, "We just need that one play and somebody's about to make it. Whoever makes it goes down in history." Brandon Graham was that guy. On the second play of the drive, the Patriots ran a play where they put one receiver in the shallow part of the field near the sideline and another in the deep part of the field. With receivers over top and underneath, the purpose of the play was to put us in a coverage dilemma.

When my movement in the secondary dropped just a couple yards, Brady hesitated in the pocket, allowing Brandon to knock the ball out of his hands, causing a fumble for defensive lineman Derek Barnett to recover. It was the Patriots' first turnover of the game, and the one stop we needed. After our offense scored a field goal, increasing our lead to eight, Tom had only fifty-eight seconds to drive the ball ninety yards, score a touchdown, and convert a two-point play to tie the game.

On the last play of the game, we knew that it was going to be a Hail Mary. When defending one last heave of the ball toward the end zone, all you want to see is the ball hit the ground. Just before the ball touched the turf, corner Patrick Robinson tipped it back up into the air. My eyes opened as wide as they'd ever been as I gasped—finally exhaling when the ball hit the ground in the painted end zone.

Tears welling up in my eyes, I dropped to my knees and started laughing. I couldn't do anything else but just yell out loud.

"We were all we needed!"

# 11

# 1/11

*I am only one, but I am one. I can't do everything,
but I can do something. The something I ought to do,
I can do. And by the grace of God, I will.*

**—EDWARD EVERETT HALE**

In July 2018, six months after the Super Bowl against the Patriots, I headed to the Cape Coast region of Ghana. The stresses of negotiating the responsibilities of my family, the Eagles, and a movement had taken their toll, so this trip was a gift to myself.

Until I met defensive end Mike Bennett, I'll admit the narrative I had of the continent was one of rampant corruption and extreme poverty. He was an old-school player with a physical game, often wearing pads three sizes smaller than his torso, which didn't match his expansive mind and stature. Mike was more well read than I was and we discussed the need for athletes to push for social change. He saw a bigger picture to unify athletes all around the world to fight oppression across the globe.

Though his favorite destination in the continent was Senegal, Mike went on about the importance of visiting West Africa, the slave castles, because of its deep connection to the African American experience. His insight only watered a seed that was planted a few weeks earlier by a woman I met at a fundraising event. The event was called

444. It was a celebration for four friends, partying for all four of their birthdays, in support of four charities. The four men are some of the top Black professionals in Philadelphia and I knew everyone from the Black business world of Philly would be in attendance. I don't even remember her name. I only remember her inviting energy. While everyone else was dancing or buzzing around networking, she was patiently floating around the room, content in her own world. "Wow, you're beautiful," I said as she walked by. She wore an elegant dress and headwrap covered in elaborate print that was distinctly African and her brown skin glowed even in the dim room. She began to talk about her dress and headwrap. They were made in Ghana, where she was from. When I told her that I'd been wanting to get to the continent for some time, she assured me that Ghana was where I needed to start that journey. She talked about how beautiful it was. She said, "It's the perfect place to start your journey into Africa."

Taking these two conversations as signs, I booked a trip for my two brothers, Martin and Myles, and me to go. At the point in the trip where we headed to Cape Coast, we had been there for two days, and I already saw with my own eyes what Mike and this woman had said about how Black and beautiful the country is. Except for the images of Jesus, who was everywhere, everything else was Black. Churches in Ghana are what liquor stores are to the hood: every quarter mile there's one. All with the image of a white Jesus.

While in the van, my stomach rumbled. Because I knew that at some point we'd stop at a restaurant, I did my best to be a team player and not complain. As we stopped in traffic, our tour guide, Reddick, called out to one of the women to buy three hush puppies. As there were nine of us in the car, I was shocked when even after everyone in the van had taken a piece, a sizable portion made it to me. This is when our cameraman, Eban, explained that even though there are huge disparities in wealth, people rarely go without food or shelter because sharing is common and expected. If one of us has food, we all eat. While the individual contributes to the collective community, the collective provides for the individual.

After a two-and-a-half-hour journey, we arrived at the slave castles that had served as a hub for holding and transporting stolen Africans to the Americas. One of them, Cape Coast Castle, was built in 1555 by the Portuguese as a trading post and the British had converted it to serve in the slave trade. Now these castles serve as tourist attractions. On the tour of the castles, the air vibrated with the deaths that lingered over centuries. The guide then took us to the "Door of No Return," the last thing many of our ancestors saw before boarding the ships to a foreign world. Now harboring boats from local fishermen, the large double doors opened onto the ocean that once harbored slave ships.

Though I will never know for sure where in Africa I come from—my African ancestry DNA test says that my paternal lineage is traced to Guinea-Bissau and my maternal lineage traces to Nigeria—what occurred to me on that second day in Ghana, is that anyone who's a descendant of those who passed those Doors of No Return owe it to themselves and their ancestors to travel here, at least once.

Before that trip to Ghana, while the 2017 season was still under way, I was in my car, driving home from the team facility one night, when the thought to steer my car off the road crossed my mind. During this time, in the midst of my crumbling marriage with Morrisa while she was eight months pregnant with my second daughter, Selah, countless people sent death threats in response to my decision to protest during the national anthem; and even with the NFL coming to a deal with Players Coalition, because of the split that occurred with Eric Reid, a narrative existed that I was a sellout, like the $89 million went into my pocket; and I was one of the players entrusted to lead that 2017 Eagles team to a Super Bowl. No matter what I attempted to do right, shit just seemed to consistently go left.

I could normally compartmentalize my feelings, but in that moment, with my foot pressed down harder on the gas, the speedometer hitting 120 mph, ending my life seemed like the best solution. For weeks I struggled to sleep and my chest felt like someone or something heavy was sitting on it. I was having an anxiety attack, and the only thing I wanted to do was stop the feeling. As my car continued to accelerate, I wondered what the most efficient way to end it all would be. *Do I run the car off the road? Or run straight into the divider?* Right before my exit to enter the Northern Liberties section of Philly, I thought about Elle, who was four at the time, waiting for me to come home. It was the only motivation for me to brake and make the last-minute turn onto my exit.

After walking into the house like nothing happened, the fact that suicide was on my mind and how well I could hide it scared me. Shortly after, I reached out to the psychologist who worked with the team when Chip was the head coach about what I experienced. "Let's start with the good things," Stephanie urged from the other side of my computer screen a few weeks later in an early session.

I remember considering her question and while I want to be clear that there were many things in my life to be grateful for, the only thing that came to mind was my health, which meant that I could suit up on Sundays.

"How often do you meditate?"

"I don't."

"Well, what ways do you cope with your feelings?"

That was when I explained my various methods to cope with my anxiety. I tried drinking, but because of the effects it had on my body, I didn't like drinking too much during the season. Then I switched to smoking and edibles, but I didn't want to be high all the time. I had a prescription for Xanax, but my fear of addiction prevented me from taking too many. So, I rotated between the three.

"I want you to try something."

Stephanie shared that while she understood the responsibilities that I had and all the pressures I faced, she wanted me to understand the importance of setting time aside for myself. She wanted me to spend five minutes of my day deep breathing and meditating. Because I didn't want her to think I was a threat to myself, I didn't tell her about the suicidal thoughts in our initial sessions. Even when I was behind the wheel, I knew I didn't want to end my life; I just wanted the anxiety to die.

———

Two weeks after winning the Super Bowl I took Stephanie's words to heart about doing something for myself and bought a gold-on-gold Day-Date Oyster Perpetual Rolex watch. Because I hadn't purchased any jewelry since my rookie season, which was eight years at that point, this was a big deal for me. With me being back home in Jersey for the first time since the season ended, I was excited to celebrate my brother Martin's birthday with family. I put on my new watch and headed to dinner.

Though no one said anything to me about paying for the dinner, when the check arrived, I knew my family expected me to foot the bill, so I did. But before the bill made its way to the head of the long rectangular table at Steakhouse 85 in New Brunswick, I heard mumbles.

"What was that?"

This is when my younger cousin Aahkir, who sat next to me during the dinner, responded.

"I'm just saying you over here bragging about this new watch and you didn't even bring your own brothers to the Super Bowl."

When I heard the mm-hmms circulate around the table, I felt like Denzel Washington in *Training Day*. One of the most difficult things about being in the NFL is the assumption made by those who get to experience the perks of your career, that's always one bad play away from ending, while remaining ignorant to its costs. When players go to the Super Bowl, we receive only two comp tickets for the game. Every ticket after, we pay for out of our own pocket. In that first Super Bowl I won with the Saints, I bought twelve tickets—the max allotment per player—for family members, which went, at that time, for no less than $1,200 apiece. Because very few of them could afford the flight to Miami, I then paid for airfare, hotels, and meals for everyone who attended. Add that up with paying bills, buying vehicles, loaning money, and helping to buy houses, and the bill was bigger than the one I paid at dinner.

Being the sole financial pillar of your family is a gift and a curse. While providing for those you love and care for is one of the most empowering feelings in the world, the expectations that come with being the only one playing this position takes a toll.

After going on a quick vacation to clear my mind, I sat in the living room of the new apartment I had moved into in the Fishtown area of Philadelphia after separating from Mo, watching the water from a newly installed washer and dryer pour through my living room ceiling like a waterfall. While the neighborhood I moved into was being gentrified, many of the buildings there were being built at lightning speed to meet the growing demands of the incoming residents. That meant that there was a disparity between the outside presentation and the inside reality, a metaphor for my marriage.

When they told me that marriage was hard work, it was an understatement. When I married Mo, I was twenty-three years old, which meant then I only knew what I wanted and ran full speed at it. I didn't know who I was, who she was, nor who we would become. Over the course of four years, we went to therapists who gave us tools to communicate better and through spiritual marriage counseling to see if God could fix our marriage, and none of it worked. To put it simply I was genuinely unhappy, although it is much more nuanced than that. I didn't feel safe or understood. But I did try.

By the time we moved to Philly in 2014, small things like where the salt and pepper shakers belonged took on deeper significance. Whenever I'm anxious, one of the things that helps keep my mind at ease is organization, which when you have two kids is damn near impossible.

After sharing with Stephanie that organizing things assuages my anxiety, she suggested that if organization was what I wanted, I should do it myself. Feeling stressed one night, I went into the kitchen to clean. While putting everything in its place, I felt Mo's eyes burning through my back. When I put the salt and pepper shakers with the other spices in the cabinet, she had had enough.

"Why are you in here touching everything?"

"I'm putting everything where it belongs. What's the problem?"

"You're not the one who has to cook! I put the salt and pepper shakers next to the stove so I can access them easily when I'm cooking!"

"Mo, the cabinet for the spices is right next to the stove. Are you saying it's too much of an inconvenience to reach your arm out two feet?"

We were speaking two different languages. I was trying my best to take care of my own mental health but it was communicating to her that I thought she kept a dirty house. By then I was a shell of myself—walking on eggshells, circling the block multiple times because I knew what awaited me on the other side of the door. Once the football season ended there was nowhere for me to escape. In the final days of my time with Mo, I thought about my father who, around the same time I lost my virginity, had this way of being in the house but rarely present. With the new perspective I had how marriage, raising children, and being an adult are all hard as hell, I no longer held the resentments against my father's emotional absence as I once did, but in my own fear of being the father whose body is in one place and mind's in another with Selah and Elle, I mopped up the water in the living room of the apartment I just finished decorating in preparation for their visit that week, grateful for the peace that came at the expense of so much else.

# 12

# BUSINESS DECISIONS

*If you want to lead the orchestra you*
*must turn your back to the crowd.*

**—ISLWYN JENEINS**

During the 2019 offseason, after making the Pro Bowl again in 2018, following the Super Bowl and gearing up to go into my tenth year in the NFL, I figured I could use the time off to rest, recover, and take my mind off football before the season started. We had hopes of making it to another Super Bowl, but Carson struggled all year and our roster was riddled with injuries. Only one player played every snap: me, extending my streak to five seasons straight without missing a single game. I finished the season with ninety-seven tackles, three forced fumbles, one fumble recovery, one sack, eight pass breakups, and an interception. Even though I played well, as a team, we struggled to get wins consistently throughout the season, but stayed competitive. We were able to force our way to the divisional round of the playoffs but ended our season with a loss to the Saints.

While I was at home resting, spending time with the girls, I'd kept getting alerts on my phone about safeties in free agency who were getting paid big bucks. I still had another two years left under my contract and had very little negotiating leverage to get myself a new contract. So, I had to watch safeties Landon Collins, Tyrann Mathieu, and Earl Thomas, arguably three of the top safeties in the game, get paid upward of $14 million a year, while I was still making $8 million, barely in the top ten highest-paid safeties in the league at the time. After coming off a Super Bowl and three Pro Bowls in the last four seasons, I wanted a pay raise as well.

Honestly, I know the team didn't have to give me anything, but I wanted to see if they were willing to add value to my contract to reflect the way I was adding value to the team. I played at least five positions, I contributed to the development of younger players, my community work made them look good, and I oftentimes functioned like a coach on the field and off. I wanted to know if they felt like that was of value and something they wanted to keep around. Whether it was a couple hundred thousand or a couple million, I wanted to see if they would be open to paying me more.

The team knew I wanted a new contract, so even though I was skipping the off-season program for personal reasons, it gave the impression that I was holding out for a new contract. It was voluntary workouts and practices, where you go over the basic fundamentals of the playbook, and you train and condition with your teammates. I was very self-motivated and usually worked out on my own anyway. But because I was always a mainstay in the off-season programs, I didn't explain why I was missing those things to the organization. I allowed them to think that I wasn't showing up because I wanted to get paid.

That made the Eagles' front office very nervous. The only part of the offseason that's mandatory is the three-day minicamp that closes out the program in mid-June. When Howie Roseman called to make sure that I was planning on showing up, I told him that I wasn't sure. That seemed to add some urgency to the situation, and Howie set up a meeting between himself, Jeff Lurie, and me, in which they both assured me that my value on the team could never be higher and that I was surely going to be in the Eagles Hall of Fame one day. They said their intentions were to make sure that I finished my career in the Eagles uniform, but they wouldn't be able to give me a contract extension with two years left on my deal because it set a bad precedent.

Roseman said, "What would stop the next player from just asking for the same thing? Two years before their deal is up, they want a raise? We can't set that precedent." My reply was "With all due respect, that's not my problem," but they told me to be patient and assured me that, by the end of the season, I would surely have a deal. But they warned that if I didn't show up for mandatory camp and I made things public in the media, then they would not reward me with a contract, as they definitely did not want to set that precedent, either, that people could make noise, rock the boat, and be rewarded. So I told them I would consider the conversation and get back to them.

As I sat on the phone with Ben, I racked my brain to decide what to do. On one hand I knew I wanted to finish my career in Philly. I loved the city. I loved the team. I loved my role. But on the other hand I didn't trust what they were telling me. Something they said in the meeting made it sound too good to be true. "We know you just turned thirty and you're up there in age, but we see you every day. We know you're not getting any older, you're still looking young, and we won't hold that against you when the time comes." Even I knew that was some bullshit. When you turn thirty in the NFL, it's almost like, unless you're Tom Brady, I guess, you've got a terminal illness, like you've only got but so much time left before you expire. The shelf life is almost over, and they'll pay you according to that. I've been through this before with the Saints. I knew that they would always do what's best, in their eyes, for the team, and I have to make sure that I do what's best for me and my career. We might break the huddles on "Family," but I never forget that this is a business first.

Even though I had so little leverage, the one thing I did have was a great relationship with the team owner, Jeff Lurie. Ben had an idea. "This is a long shot, but maybe we can get Jeffrey to agree to knocking the last year off your contract, so if they don't give you a deal, at least you can hit free agency next year and test the market."

In my mind, I really wanted to stay in Philly. I never wanted to leave, but my gut was telling me that I needed to protect myself. I called Mr. Lurie and informed him that I'd agree to showing up to minicamp and everything else if he gave me his word that he would cut me or release me before free agency opened up. He agreed. The next day I reported to minicamp as focused as I had ever been.

The ball was about to be kicked off in the divisional round of the 2018 playoffs. We were set to face Drew Brees and the Saints in a rematch from earlier in the season. The last time we came here they demolished us 48–7. Coming into this game, we didn't care what our record was or what happened the last time we played them, or even who we were coming into the game with. We were just going to go compete. As we built the game plan, Schwartz and I decided we should play a simple defense and play only what we did best. We were going to play our version of three-deep coverage, because we knew it and we could execute it versus anything. All the starting defensive backs, excluding myself, were out with injuries. Playing a simple defense would give the young backups a chance to play confidently and play fast. We needed our defense to play well if our team wanted to have a shot at winning. Carson was also out with an injury sustained late in the season and Nick Foles was leading the team on a win streak.

The very first play, the Saints came out in an empty backfield. We wanted to scare Sean Payton out of elaborate formations, so our adjustment to an empty backfield was to send an all-out pressure. If they were going to use minimal players in their pass protection then we would blitz Drew with everything we had, forcing the ball out of his hands quickly. It was a ballsy call. Drew Brees quickly identified the blitz and threw the ball to his fastest receiver, Ted Ginn Jr., who was matched up with our backup nickel, Cre'Von LeBlanc.

Cre'Von located the ball, leaped into the air, and intercepted it at its highest point. We took a risk and that risk paid off with an interception on the first play of the game. Nick Foles started off just as hot as our defense. The offense marched straight down the field, going five for five on his passes, with him completing the ball to five different receivers on a drive and capping it off with a thirty-seven-yard touchdown pass.

The Saints' next two possessions ended in punts as we held them to a scoreless first quarter. Foles, however, went right back down the field and scored on a QB sneak, putting us up 14–0 going into the second quarter. On our next drive, Foles targeted tight end Zach Ertz, which was normally a great decision, but not if he's being covered by the Saints' best cornerback, Marshon Lattimore. Marshon plucked the ball out of the air with an amazing leap and catch. The interception woke up the home crowd, who'd been quiet, dramatically shifting the momentum back to the Saints. That momentum turned into ten unanswered points for the Saints before we went into the locker room for halftime.

We had the lead and started the game on fire, but the momentum was not in our favor as we started the second half ice cold. The Saints orchestrated a seventeen-play drive that ate up almost the entire third quarter, which they capped off with a touchdown, taking the lead and making the score 17–14. Our offense was stalling, continuing to punt the ball away.

The Saints added another field goal to their lead, making the score 20–14 as the fourth quarter began to dwindle. With eight minutes and forty-one seconds left in the game, defensively we knew we needed to stop them. We were running out of opportunities to give our offense the football to get just one more score to put us in the lead. Defensively, with a banged-up secondary, we were hanging on by a thread. Drew was on fire, already throwing for more than three hundred yards and two touchdowns and we had no one to stop Mike Thomas. The pressure mounted, knowing we just needed one spark to change the momentum of the game. On second down, I was in man coverage on the Saints tight end, who began to block when the ball was snapped, but suddenly turned around as if he were ready to catch a pass. It was a screen. I recognized it before the offensive linemen, who were racing to get into position to block me, could get there. I ducked under the first lineman and lunged into the legs of the tight end, wrapping him up, squeezing his knees tightly together, and rolling him to the ground for a five-yard loss. "Come on, Sean, you gotta come with some better shit than that," I said to him on the Saints sideline as if I were unimpressed by his play call. It was exactly the spark we needed! Now it was 3rd and 13, meaning there is usually less than a 20 percent chance they'd convert. Drew didn't get the memo. He identified the coverage and knew exactly where the small window of opportunity was. He dropped back and completely in rhythm threw a dart to Thomas over the middle of the field. The perfect play and the perfect throw. It was demoralizing as now they had crossed midfield and were closing in on scoring range with less than six minutes to play. I tapped my helmet twice and focused on the next play. After a few more plays it was third down again but this time there were only six yards for the Saints to gain. The ball was on the 31-yard line, well within field goal range. The Saints chose to run the ball, but Michael Bennett fired off the defensive line, pressing the offensive center five yards into the backfield like a sled on ice, tackling running back Alvin Kamara in the backfield for a loss. The Saints missed their attempted fifty-two-yard field goal wide right. Our sideline erupted! Our resolve had paid off and the stop gave us some desperately needed juice. With two minutes and fifty-eight seconds left in the game, our offense had one last opportunity to take the lead and get us the win.

The drive began, and a couple of big plays and penalties on behalf of the Saints had us all the way down to the 27-yard line. The momentum had finally swung back on to our side. We were going to score, we could feel it. The conversations on the sideline had gone from hoping we'd score to hoping we didn't score too fast and leave Drew with enough time to drive down the field and get a field goal to win it. We'd seen that movie before, and Nick Foles was going to come through in the clutch when we needed it most.

He dropped back and threw a simple pass to the left side of the field to Alshon Jeffery. Then the unexpected happened. I watched from the sideline as our hopes and dreams came to a crashing halt as the ball slipped through the sure hands of Alshon into the arms of Marshon Lattimore. On the following drive the Saints ran out the clock and the game was over. I knew the results weren't what we wanted but I walked off the field damn proud of my team. We knew we'd gotten this far off pure grit, relentless effort, and an unbreakable belief in one another no matter what we faced. We finished the season a skeleton of the team we had started with, yet somehow we felt like we were the best version of ourselves, playing a simplified game centered around execution and toughness. Schwartz engineered a defense focused around the disruptive defensive line and my versatility to handle the multiple positions in the secondary. Our offense, even with the injuries, had plenty of talent. There were still questions surrounding our quarterbacks. There was an investment in Wentz, but Foles produced results. It's not always based on merit, production, or the role you play on the team. Sometimes it's just business.

Nick opted out of his contract. He wanted to be a starter.

We finished 9-7, winning the last four games to win the division and guarantee a home playoff game. But the injury bug hit our offense the way it hit our secondary the year prior. Our premier receiver was Greg Ward, a practice squad wide receiver who shined in his elevated role. The other guys, I didn't even know their names.

We scrapped our way back into the playoffs. This was one of the most testing seasons as a leader, trying to keep the team together, encouraged, and competitive. But the impact that players like myself, Chris, and Sproles have had since we got here was clear. No one stopped believing because we were down, or injured, or because things were hard. We dug deeper, loved harder, and laid it all on the line. We came a long way, but unfortunately I thought my time as an Eagle might be coming to an end.

During the 2019 season, I watched the Eagles give four different players contract extensions throughout the season, and I was not one of them. The season came and went, and I never got that offer that Howie assured me I would get. As I stood back by the bench, behind the players on the sideline, as the national anthem played, I looked up at the banners hanging from both sides of the stadium. I knew I would forever be remembered with the Super Bowl banner hanging permanently on one side, but I was contemplating if my body of work as an Eagle was worthy to be memorialized with a banner next to the names of Reggie White, Jerome Brown, and Brian Dawkins in the ring of honor. I closed my eyes and talked to my ancestors. This year, another person joined my grandfathers and grandmother Barbra in this spiritual pregame huddle, Mr. Lester. He passed away earlier in the year after battling cancer. It was heartbreaking to lose a mentor, father figure, and friend. The man who was always strong and fit quickly withered away until he was too weak to speak. I normally avoid hospitals and don't enjoy spending time with people in their last days, but I needed to tell L personally how much he meant to me, even if he couldn't speak back. His funeral services were held at Piscataway High School's football field. I was asked to be one of the speakers during the service. I know he loved me very much. He sent me an encouraging text before every game of my collegiate and professional career. As I looked into the packed stands filled with former students, parents, family, and friends I got a firsthand glimpse of what real impact looks like. This was a man who used all his knowledge, love, and discernment to impact the lives of those he could. He wasn't a celebrity, a politician, or someone with a huge platform, yet his presence permeated the generations of youth that passed under his watch. I pray that when I die, and it's all said and done, that I'll go knowing that I used everything I could—my time, talent, and treasure—to change the world around me, as he did. L is my measuring rod, against which I take inventory of my own deeds. What I do on this field will, hopefully, be the least of what I'm remembered for and what I do on this field is damn good.

I turned my attention back to the game. We were about to play Russell Wilson and the Seattle Seahawks in the Wild Card round of the playoffs. Even if we won this game, the rest of our playoff games would be on the road. I never did get an offer from the Eagles. I could only assume that this would be my final game as an Eagle if Mr. Lurie kept his word and released me in the offseason. I didn't want a farewell. I didn't want to make it about me. I was just going to have fun and compete my ass off like I always did.

The Linc was rocking, as it always was for a playoff game. Even though we weren't that good of a team and were riddled with injuries, they, like we did, believed that magic can happen when you're the underdog. We'd played the Seahawks earlier in the year, and sacked Wilson six times in that game. Two of them were by me. Our strategy was to use me as a "spy" on him so that when he scrambled, I could use my speed and athleticism to get him on the ground before he could get the ball to one of his playmaking wideouts, Tyler Lockett and D. K. Metcalf.

Schwartz wanted to use me in the same way as the previous game, asking me to take away the tight end and rush the passer. One of the ways I would create extra opportunities to pressure Wilson was doing what we called an add rush. Essentially in any man-to-man situation, if I have a tight end and the tight end blocks, then there's no need for me to try to cover a guy who's not looking for the ball. Instead of trying to cover him, I'd add into the pressure going directly to the quarterback. Normally the mechanics of using an add rush take just a little bit of time. For quarterbacks like Aaron Rodgers and Tom Brady, they'll get rid of the football before you could ever get there. But with Russell Wilson, it was almost every play that he'd hold the ball. That's what made him special. He was never on time, always scrambling around and creating plays with his legs. So I'd always have time to get there if I added to the rush late.

In the first half I was doing a bit of everything, covering tight ends, rushing the passer, even playing on the punt team—like they said, the more you can do. If this was going to be my last game, I was going to do it all! Despite the effort we played with, the Seahawks took control of the game, injuring Carson Wentz and forcing seventeen-year veteran Josh McCown to make a playoff debut. A guy who spent the majority of his Fridays coaching high school football and then flying back to join the team on Saturdays was now forced into a game, and a playoff game at that. As a team we had become accustomed to playing without Carson, so we were not discouraged by the loss. Plus, we trusted Josh. He had an infectious attitude and was more than capable of making decisions. With the game tied 3–3 with one minute and eleven seconds left in the first half, the Seahawks had driven the ball down to the 6-yard line. Everybody in the stadium knew who was getting the ball next. Marshawn Lynch was back with the Seahawks, and after blowing the chances of a Super Bowl victory a few years prior by deciding to pass instead of giving him the ball on the 1-yard line, coach Pete Carroll wasn't going to make that mistake again. The ball was snapped and Wilson handed it to Lynch. He scooted to a wide-open hole on the left side of our defense, and then cut right back to the middle, ending up face-to-face with me.

Marshawn was by far the hardest running back for me to tackle. His wide base gave him great balance, so just running into him and throwing your body around is not going to knock him off balance, and his size and violent running nature made him hard to wrap up and gator roll, as you could never get to both of his legs. If you attempted to tackle him around his body, his stiff arm would send you flailing to the ground. We were within the 5-yard line and every yard mattered. If I wanted to knock his momentum backward, I was going to have to see him, mano a mano. As he came through the hole, he jumped over someone, and before his feet could hit the ground, I hit him with a perfect six-inch rising blow, catching him right up under his chest plate. The impact caused his body to rise and his momentum began falling backward. I thought to myself, *Finally, I got that motherfucker.*

And then suddenly, with his feet back on the ground, he began to spin and churn his legs, loosening my grip on him. A push from his own offensive lineman helped him spin off me and into the end zone. I had spoken too soon. We knew the Seahawks were going to do what they do. They were going to make plays. Marshawn Lynch was going to make runs. D. K. Metcalf and Lockett were going to make catches. All we needed to do was keep chipping away. By the time it got to the fourth quarter, the game was 17–9. Carson never came back to the game, and Josh McCown had been playing like he was in his twenties, but he forgot that he was not in his twenties. He was scrambling around, completing passes, and making plays. In the moment we had all forgotten that he was old as shit. Eventually he tore his hamstring from all the running. We had no other options at quarterback, so he continued to play through the injury.

His grit was infectious. Defensively, though, we knew it was time for us to get another stop. And on 3rd and 8, Schwartz called for me to blitz the quarterback. I was supposed to hit the B gap between the offensive left guard and tackle, but the guard saw me coming and I ran right into him. He had at least a hundred-pound advantage, so instead of trying to go through him, I dipped my shoulder and churned my legs, wrapping all the way around the outside of the line, making him collide with the offensive tackle and leaving me a free path to the quarterback. I beelined right for him, pushing him and knocking him to the ground for a sack. The third time in two games and the Seahawks were forced to punt.

On the next drive, we needed another stop. There were only five minutes left in the game. I was covering the tight end when he began blocking. Without hesitation I added into the rush, pressuring Russell to throw the ball earlier than he wanted, resulting in an incompletion and a big hit from me. We forced the Seahawks to punt again.

With very little time left in the game, and down six points, our offense had an opportunity to drive down and win it. Josh McCown, torn hamstring and all, nickel-and-dimed our offense down to the 10-yard line. Everyone on the sideline and in the stands could feel it, we were about to pull off the upset and advance to the divisional round. On 4th and 7, Josh dropped back to pass, but no one was open. With no options Josh tried to scramble, but his feet looked like they were stuck in mud. The defense collapsed around his legs, bringing him to the ground, and it was a turnover on downs, ten yards from the end zone.

On the next drive, we were desperate to get the ball back for our offense, and we sold out on the run, knowing that the Seahawks were going to try to run the clock out. They ran the ball on first down, we stuffed it. They ran the ball on second down, we stuffed it. Anticipating them running the ball again on third down and not wanting to take any chances of giving us the football, especially on that side of the field, we called another zero blitz, leaving no defenders in the deep part of the field. Russell Wilson faked a screen and threw a rainbow ball to a wide-open D. K. Metcalf, who went up, caught the ball, got up, and waved goodbye to everyone, because with that completion, he knew, just like we knew, that our season was over, and so was my time with the Philadelphia Eagles.

As a defensive back your job is to read patterns. We read the patterns of receiver routes, the tendencies of a play caller, patterns of offensive formations, patterns of blocking schemes, etc. When you've played as long as I did, you get really good at recognizing those patterns. Even the patterns off the field. For example, every year the fourth and final preseason game for the Eagles will be against the New York Jets. I'm not sure why, only that it happens every year. I've noticed over the years that the same play gets run in every fourth preseason game. It's not a play you'll see played out on the field. It's a play that is run by the front offices of NFL teams against one or two players on the roster.

As I walked through the visitors' locker room at MetLife Stadium I watched my teammates go through their pregame rituals. The fourth and final preseason game was meant for the bottom-of-the-roster players who were trying to make a good final impression to team and league scouts before the league-wide mandatory roster cuts a few days later. I saw a teammate of mine in full pads heading from the training room back to his locker. I didn't remember his name because he had been hurt since the beginning of training camp and had spent most of his time in the training room. What was about to happen to him I've seen happen to a player in his position every single year. NFL teams cannot cut a player while they are injured. Oftentimes they will pay players a settlement of money to release them injured so that they can free up the roster spot.

The fourth preseason game provides the front offices with a unique opportunity to take advantage of a player's desperation to be on the team. The player usually gets injured early in camp and isn't able to get back on the field for practice or any of the preseason games. It's clear that he is not going to make the team and will be a victim of the final cuts. The player is stuck between a rock and a hard place. On one hand he wants to make the team he's on and believes that if he can just show what he can do then maybe he'll make a big enough impression to make the team. On the other hand, having not played in the preseason, no other scouts from around the league have gotten an opportunity to see them play, either, and won't sign anyone they haven't seen play. The player is desperate to prove himself. That's when the team trainers will ask the player if he thinks he's able to play, even if they know he's not quite ready. The player, seeing no other pathways to his dreams of making a team will say yes and agree to play even if he is still injured. They will allow the player to dress for the game, a silent agreement showcasing that the player is indeed able to play, but the teams are not dumb, nor do they want the player to get hurt. They have no intentions of putting this player in the game, they only want to save themselves from having to give a cash settlement to a player they have no intentions of keeping. They will let that player dress so that he is no longer declared as injured and they can cut him the next day with no strings attached.

I walked over to my teammate, whispering, "Hey, are you about to try to play?"

"Yeah, I need to get some film out there," he said with his eyes looking doubtful about what he was about to attempt. He was preparing himself to play a football game injured. I've done it before, and it is an absolutely terrifying experience. I don't want to crush his spirit, but I don't want to see him forfeit his rights out of desperation. "Bro, they are not going to put you in this game. They are going to cut you tomorrow, and you won't get your settlement," I said, looking him dead in his eyes. It's like telling a kid whose dream is to play in the NFL that he is not good enough. It hurt me to be the one to tell him, but I knew it hurt more to accept the news, especially when you were this close to the goal. After a little back-and-forth he gave me his final answer, "I hear you, but I gotta try." I ended my pestering and let him go back to preparing his mind for what he's about to attempt.

The game started and finished, and he never once touched the field. The very next day he was cut, without a settlement and his dreams were still deferred. I've seen this happen every single year I've been in the NFL. It has taught me to play the cards that I am dealt and to never leave my fate in anyone else's hands. It's easy to become a slave to one's own desperation, so I try to always remember that I cannot win a negotiation that I am not willing or able to walk away from. It's the reason I spent considerable time building businesses while still an active player. I didn't want to wait until I retired from the game to build something. By then it's too late. Malcolm Inc., my holding company, consists of businesses ranging from a clothing line, DAMARI, to Disrupt Foods, which owns just under twenty franchise restaurants, to real estate, to my production company Listen Up

Media. I realized that I needed options outside of football to build wealth and saw the need for my peers as well. That led me to create Broad Street Ventures, a venture capital fund focused on investing in tech companies and consumer goods. It was important for me to expose those around me to the opportunities I was getting to make good investments. I made sure we educated every investor on the importance of group economics principles and made sure they understood the investment strategy. We raised funds from Black athletes, entertainers, and other professionals and made Ralonda one of the general partners of the fund, making her part of the 1 percent of Black women in the space. Financial freedom is when you have enough options to never have to make a decision out of desperation and the only way for me to feel free was to invest in building options for myself. We may play a game, but the game will give you constant reminders that it's a business first.

It was March 2020, a few months shy of a year after I sat down with Mr. Lurie and Howie about renegotiating my contract. The time had come and Mr. Lurie, keeping his word, cut me and I was, once again, a free agent. In January, Morrisa decided that she could no longer live in Philly as we finalized our divorce, and she moved with Elle and Selah back to New Orleans. I acquiesced to the move because I wasn't sure where I'd be playing the next season. I might have to move to a new city and find ways to commute to New Orleans every week or every other week. I didn't know how I was going to do it, but I refused to be absent from my children. I called Ben to figure out what my options were. He explained that there weren't many. There wasn't a huge market for my services. The swell of money that was flowing toward safeties the season before had dried up. None of the teams expected me to be a free agent until 2021, per my contract, so no one was really looking for me, either. I had bet on myself by asking to go into free agency and it wasn't clear if it would pay off in my benefit. Ben asked me to make a list of places I might want to play. I wanted to go wherever was close to my kids. Ben asked, "What do you think about Dallas? Dallas needs a safety and they've got money to spend."

"Fuck no, absolutely not. I'll retire before I play for Jerry Jones."

"You sure?"

"Yes. I'm positive. What about the Saints?" We both assumed that they were set at the safety position and didn't see why there would be any need for me on the team. They had a young rangy safety in Marcus Williams and another consistent playmaker from Ohio State in safety Vonn Bell. Ben thought it wouldn't hurt to ask and reached out to the Saints. It turned out that the Saints were in a contract battle with Vonn and they were pretty far apart. Allegedly, under the advisement of his new agent, Vonn was asking for upward of $10 million per year, quite higher than what the Saints were willing to pay him. I was not looking to be the highest paid safety out there, that window had come and gone. I only wanted to be near my kids and keep my salary the same as it was with the Eagles, around $8 million per year.

When the Saints heard that I was available and the amount that I was looking for, they were in shock. Everyone was assuming that I was out of Philly because I wanted to be one of the highest paid safeties in the NFL, and that was never the case. In fact, I never asked Philly for any set number. I only told them I wanted to be paid more. I would've been happy with a $500K bonus, anything that let me know that they valued what I was bringing to the table and showed that they would honor their word. Vonn Bell is a great player, solid and consistent, but at that point in his career, he was not a $10 million safety. With a new path forward the Saints quickly snatched the offer that they had given him off the table and offered it to me: four years, $32 million, which I gladly accepted. Just like that, I could finally breathe again, knowing I would be able to continue to raise my children and be present for them consistently. It almost seemed too good to be true. I was heading back to where I started, to a familiar city, familiar team, and familiar fans, but I'd been gone for six years. I had changed dramatically in that time and my gut was telling me that coming home ain't always easy.

# 13

# FUN

*"Good friend, in the path I have come," he said,*
*"There followed after me to-day*
*A youth whose feet must pass this way.*
*This chasm that has been as naught to me*
*To that fair-haired youth may a pitfall be;*
*He, too, must cross in the twilight dim;*
*Good friend, I am building this bridge for him!"*

**—WILL ALLEN DROMGOOLE**

Almost three months into the pandemic, I was watching my daughters, Elle and Selah, play on the rock wall I had built for them at my home in Philadelphia, when I received a call from Darren Sproles. Excited for the opportunity to catch up, I answered.

"Yo, what's up with your boy Drew?"

"What you mean?"

"Go check it out, then call me back."

Clicking the link from one of the group chats, I watched a Yahoo! Finance interview where the host asked Drew Brees what he felt about those who may protest during the national anthem. "I will never agree," Drew said, "with anybody disrespecting the flag of the United States of America."

Believing Drew was always calculated and measured with his

words, I watched the interview repeatedly, trying to make sense of his comment. Drew spoke about how his grandfather's service in WWII was the reason he respected the flag. As someone who also had a grandfather who fought for this country and earned a Purple Heart, I was hurt by Drew's comments.

While I was processing all of this, texts and calls streamed in, asking what I thought. Overwhelmed with anger, grief, and confusion, I went into another room and hit record on my iPhone. I had already learned from the Players Coalition and the Kaepernick situation that the media can be unpredictable in how they'd represent my position, so I wanted to post my own thoughts on my social media platform. In the end I recorded two videos. Unable to contain my emotions, the first one ended with me telling Drew he should "shut the fuck up"; the second, though emotional, was more composed. As I sent both videos to India and Kristi to help me decide which one to post, Drew called, explaining that the question caught him off guard, that he understood his comments were problematic, and that he was sorry.

Though I accepted his apology, I informed Drew that because he had made his statements in public, he put his teammates in a position where my public silence would be seen as cowardice, if not betrayal, and that I would be honest about how I felt about his comments. Drew said that was fair, and we ended the call. When I checked my messages to see which video Kristi and India thought I should post, I was surprised to see they chose the one where I told Drew to "shut the fuck up." *Maybe this is the best way*, I thought to myself, and I posted it.

My phone rang five minutes later. It was India.

"Oh my God, why'd you post that one?"

"You told me to post the first one!"

Not realizing that I had sent the videos out of order, I had posted the wrong video. By the time I attempted to switch them out, the video had gone viral. Because this happened around the time our off-season program was supposed to start, the Saints were conducting our normal off-season programs virtually. The first thing Sean Payton did was hold a team meeting, addressing the situation. When Sean gave Drew the floor, Drew delivered an emotional speech that communicated his sincere remorse.

After Drew finished, Sean asked linebacker Demario Davis to speak. A fellow member of the Players Coalition, and a leader on the team, Demario was already on a media campaign to vouch for Drew's character in the days following Drew's initial comments.

"We all know Drew's character, what he's done, and who he is. Anyone who's not willing to speak to that is a coward!"

Amid the radio silence, Sean Payton then gave me the floor. As I was about to address the team, I realized that, though I had spent my first five years in the NFL on this team, most of the players on the call weren't here when I was, so this was a new team for me. Understanding Demario's comments were for me, I knew I was in hostile territory, but spoke my mind.

"With the exception of a couple coaches, I've known Drew longer than everyone. I know very well who he is, or at least I thought I knew."

Then I reiterated the same things I spoke with Drew about in our conversation—that though I still considered Drew a friend and believed his intentions were in the right place, believed him to be an ally, his comments in that interview challenged my own belief about who I thought I knew. Suddenly the hopes of returning to a warm welcome in New Orleans were as uncertain as the silence.

A few weeks after the tense team call, Drew invited the team captains to his home to decide what we wanted to do for training camp.

Walking up to Drew's massive home in the Garden District from my Uber, I realized that, in all the years I'd known Drew, I'd never been to his home. When I rang the doorbell, Drew answered with a smile. We dapped, hugged. He welcomed me in.

Over the summer, Drew and I had conversed multiple times, most of which were very uncomfortable. Even though we still cared for and respected each other, we treaded lightly. Due to the pandemic, Sean Payton wanted us to self-quarantine in the Loews Hotel all the way through camp and into the first few games of the season, creating our own bubble, like what the NBA players did down in Orlando. Some guys thought this was a worthy sacrifice. Others, like myself, were against it.

Joint custody of Elle and Selah already meant I didn't get to see them as much as I wanted to. I wasn't going to sacrifice any more time. I also didn't see how the league could survive an entire football season where protocols mandated that we stay six feet away from one another while our jobs were to tackle one another.

After we decided each player commuting back and forth from their home to practice was best, we headed out. As I walked toward the front door it occurred me that I didn't have a ride home. Given the awkwardness of my exchange with Drew, my anxiety regarding overstaying my welcome, and my own difficulty with asking for help, instead of telling one of my teammates I needed a ride, I walked to the corner of Drew's block to wait for my Uber.

At that moment Craig Robertson, who played linebacker for us, pulled up with defensive end Cam Jordan in the passenger seat.

"Hey, you need a ride?"

"Nah, I'm good."

"No, dog, we teammates. Get in."

Ahead of the Saints' special teams meeting during the first week of training camp in 2020, I had called Ralonda to see how she was doing and immediately noticed that something was off after she answered. "What's wrong?"

"I'll tell you later."

"Nah, tell me now."

She took a deep breath.

"I have cancer."

In full-blown emergency mode, I ran over to the special teams coach and asked if he needed me for this meeting.

"Nah, you're good."

Knowing I had forty-five minutes to talk, I returned to my call with Ralonda, who informed me about the lumps in her breasts that her doctor informed her were a rare form of cancer usually found in elderly women and something she needed to aggressively address. Thinking of something positive to say, I assured her that everything was going to be fine—words that may have helped me more than they did her, but after a few minutes of repeating the sentiment like a mantra, I was determined to support her and Joe the way they'd supported me.

After the chemotherapy took Ralonda's hair, and the double mastectomy took both breasts, her smile—brandishing the dimples in both cheeks—persisted. Two days after her surgery, Ralonda arranged follow-up calls with the athletes we had recruited to invest in the venture capital fund she and I had created. Though I initially fought her about working so soon after her surgery, my mother advised me not to treat Ralonda like she was dying, and that allowed me to shift the kind of support I wanted to offer to the type of support Ralonda needed. Within a year of her sharing the news of the cancer that could've taken her life, Ralonda was cancer-free.

Witnessing her resilience up close not only made me grateful to still have my friend, but the uncertain journey of her battle with cancer was yet another nudge that the game I devoted so much of my time to was coming to an end.

I remember the first game of the 2020 season at the Superdome, which normally held up to 74,000 people, being the quietest I'd ever heard it. With the COVID protocols mandating a maximum allowance of 750 people at the game, there were probably less than 200 — close family and friends of players, coaches, and staff, as well as the inactive players and practice squad players who were in attendance.

With a global pandemic, and an uncertain timeline of when things would end, there was too much money on the line for the NFL to just cancel the season. Also, many of the players couldn't afford to miss a year without a paycheck. So a deal was struck between the NFL Players Association and the NFL to continue forward with the 2020 season with stringent protocols, making sure that masks were worn on the sideline, that there was social distancing as much as possible, and that everybody did whatever they could to ensure that the season could be played in its entirety.

Our first opponent that season was the Tampa Bay Buccaneers, the year Tom Brady left the Patriots to join the superstar lineup with receivers Mike Evans, Chris Godwin, tight end Rob Gronkowski, and running backs Shady McCoy, Ronald Jones, and Leonard Fournette. As soon as he joined the Bucs, Tom automatically drew Super Bowl predictions, which was a problem for us, because we had Super Bowl plans of our own. A personal goal that year for me: make first team All-Pro. To accomplish that, I would need a combination of at least five interceptions, five sacks, and five forced fumbles.

After punting to the Buccaneers in our opening possession, Tom drove the ball eighty-five yards in nine plays, capping it off with a quarterback sneak from the 3-yard line. After trading punts, we tied the game up 7–7, with a touchdown by running back Alvin Kamara. On Brady's following drive, he overthrew his intended target and put the ball right into the hands of safety Marcus Williams. Our offense capitalized on that interception, scoring a touchdown three plays later, making the score 14–7. By halftime, we'd extended our lead to ten. To start the second half, Janoris "Jackrabbit" Jenkins snatched one of Tom's passes out of the air without breaking stride and took it all the way into the end zone. Now we were up 24–7. But even in a game where our defense blocked a field goal, intercepted the ball twice—returning one for a touchdown—we found ourselves up only seven points, but that's the Brady effect: no matter how well you think you're doing against him, if he's on the field, and there's time left, you can't count him out.

When the game was over, and we had won 34–23, I went right to Brady.

"Good job," he told me.

"Respect."

We knew we'd see each other again, as we were playing in the same division, and the next time we saw each other, we'd be on his turf. With no preseason, this was our first time playing each other, and I saw why, even in this defeat, his team was knocking on the door of a Super Bowl.

Heading into week 4 of the 2020 season, we were 2-1 and preparing to play the Detroit Lions. Studying Matt Stafford's game, I knew that anytime he saw that the corners played man-to-man coverage, he scrambled. Because I also knew that the Saints' defensive coach

Dennis Allen's game plan was to run the very defense Stafford would scramble against on 3rd and long plays, right before the opening drive I put him on game.

"If we get a third and long, don't call two-man because Stafford's going to scramble."

He nodded his head and walked off.

On 3rd and 10, the call came in:

"Two-man."

As soon as all of us ran the coverage, locking up our assignments, Matt scrambled for a first down. Livid, I looked to the sideline for eye contact but got none. When we got to the next third down, Dennis called a new blitz he had created that week. When you add new blitzes, a defense gets to practice them three or four times maximum, which means that you can't possibly practice them versus every formation and adjustment. You don't want to roll out the new things that you haven't practiced because you'll likely get new plays that you haven't seen. And that is exactly what happened.

In preparation for the game, our defense had discussed this one formation where the Lions' offense lined all three receivers on one side and put their running back on the opposite side. The route concept was sure to give this new blitz problems, and it was just our luck that they called that formation.

When Stafford snapped the ball, he immediately connected with receiver Danny Amendola, who created a big play that put them in scoring position. They would score on that drive. Unable to control myself, I walked over to Dennis Allen after the sequence.

"Stop calling that bullshit!" And walked away.

We won the game 35–29, but the next day Dennis called me into his office.

"We won a lot of games around here," Dennis started. "We played some damn good football. Not once has anybody ever questioned my call. I need you to buy in."

*I practice every snap. I'm here early, I stay late. Don't talk to me about buy-in.* At least that's what my face said.

"I need you to buy in to *me*."

It was at this point I understood that my role wasn't going to be the same as it had been. The very next week in practice, in our preparation for the Los Angeles Chargers, Dennis introduced a new defense for short-yardage situations. Instead of going with two safeties on the field, he would go with only one safety and replace me with a corner.

Chuckling at the idea of him running this play in practice, I thought to myself, *He better not call that shit.* Then, when we got to practice, he called it. Standing on the sideline, missing a rep, I walked over to the defensive coaching staff.

"So who was it in the meeting that thought we'd be better off without me on the field? I just need to know where to channel this energy."

Dennis Allen immediately spoke up.

"That was my idea."

"Cool."

Even with him calling it in practice, I figured this was a way of flexing his authority. I still didn't think he would call the play—until he did, effectively ending the longest active streak of 2,651 consecutive snaps, 300 more than the runner-up.

To throw salt in the wound, the Chargers converted on the play. After this play, I decided it was best to go about my business and do what I was told.

A few weeks following the game where Dennis Allen broke my consecutive-snap streak in 2020, I stayed behind, after everyone else had left, to watch tape. While watching, I realized that Dennis was a defensive mastermind. Let me explain why.

Quarters was the Saints' main coverage. As a safety, quarters is a difficult position to play because if the offense runs the ball, you're expected, from ten yards away from the line of scrimmage, to be able to make a tackle before a big run, but you're also expected to play the backfield if the ball is thrown deep. Essentially, you're expected to be everywhere at once, all the time.

The way Dennis configures the defensive line and manipulates the linebackers creates havoc for the offense without the expectations that the safeties be in two places at once. Though I admitted the scheme was phenomenal, revolutionary even, I was still frustrated by the lack of freedom we had to read what the offense was doing and adjust in real time. With the frustration becoming a distraction both on the field and off, I needed to think about my role on the team differently. That's when our senior defensive assistant, Peter Guinta, crossed my mind.

With forty-three years of coaching experience, thirty-one of them in the NFL, Guinta knew he had more to offer than what he was asked to give, but I never saw him pout and mope. No matter what role he took on, he executed it with enthusiasm and thoroughness. *If Pete figured out a way to find joy in the marginalized role he has*, I thought, *then who the hell am I to mope around, not talking to anybody, when I'm living my dream every day?*

After asking myself this question, I opened my notebook, where I wrote down all the goals for the year—make first team All-Pro, win the division, get number one seed, and ultimately win a Super Bowl—scratched all of them out, and wrote down the jersey numbers of three players: #23, Marshon Lattimore; #22, C. J. Gardner-Johnson; and #43, Marcus Williams.

My work with Marshon would be to help develop a consistent approach to his game. To my mind, Marshon was the best corner in the game, but played to his competition. When he played top-tier receivers like Mike Evans, he dominated, but if you put a lower-tier receiver in front of him, his motivation wasn't the same. Because Marshon was the kind of man who wouldn't respect those that he saw were too afraid to tell him what he needed to hear, I took it upon myself to hold him to that level of excellence every week.

Because C. J. Gardner-Johnson's hair was styled in free-form dreads like Kodak Black and he spoke with a thick Florida accent, coaches underestimated his intelligence. What they didn't know about C.J. was that he was a kinesthetic learner. Drawing up on a whiteboard what you wanted him to do wasn't enough. For the lesson to resonate, you had to physically take him through the movements.

An intellectual player that could go sideline to sideline, understood concepts, and memorized all the things we needed to do, Marcus Williams reminded me a lot of myself in my first tenure in New Orleans. Getting him to play outside of what the coaches told him to do and trust that he knew what needed to be done was going to be my work with him.

But before I could get Marshon, C.J., and Marcus to buy into me, I first needed to buy into all their damn handshakes.

———

In week 8 of the 2020 season, we faced Tom Brady and the superstar Tampa Bay Buccaneers for the second time. Coming into that week with their record being 6-2 and ours 5-2, the winner of this game would lead the NFC South.

Beating Tom twice in the season wasn't going to be easy, but since I embraced my new spot as a roleplayer, I played better. That week's game plan was all about matchups. Marshon would line up against Mike Evans. C.J. would line up against Chris Godwin. Janoris Jenkins would line up against the recent addition to their lineup, star receiver Antonio Brown. And I was lined up against Gronk.

Remembering when Gronk first came into the league ten years ago, in 2010, the Saints had a joint practice with the Patriots in my second year. On top of the weapons they had in Randy Moss and Wes Welker, the Patriots also had Aaron Hernandez and Rob Gron-kowski. Absolutely unguardable, Hernandez left every single defensive back we had in the dust. Gronk, on the other hand, was slow, unathletic, and without bulldozing the defender, he didn't know how to create separation. He'd only come to life when they moved one-on-one drills closer to the goal line. Every single time he ran his 265-pound frame into the defender, sending the defense stumbling, and then caught a wide-open ball for a touchdown. *There is no way he could make a career out of that*, I had thought. Ten seasons, seven Pro Bowls, and five All-Pro selections later, Gronk had already solidified himself as a lock-in Hall of Fame player. But none of that mattered here—because by halftime we were up 31–0.

In a game where Brady tried to throw his way to victory, they would run the ball only five times in the entire game. On 4th and 7, after a decent drive by Brady, with about a minute left in the third quarter, Tampa Bay was desperate to score. Lined up against Gronk, I knew he only liked to run a few route concepts, so I jammed him on his outside to where I had help.

While our defensive line was hunting Tom, he retreated from the pressure, throwing a rainbow. As it went up into the lights of the stadium in Tampa Bay, I thought, *Just catch the shit*. Pinning the ball between my hands and my chest, I registered another interception. And like we did after we took the ball away from every offense, we found the nearest camera, and this is when those handshakes became the return on investment, symbolizing an informal passing of the torch from me to my younger teammates.

In the divisional round of the playoffs in 2021, we knew we were going to see Tom Brady and the Tampa Bay Buccaneers again. Even though they brought the all-star lineup into the Superdome, we had all the confidence in the world because we had beat them twice already.

The first two times, Tom thought, because he had Antonio Brown, Mike Evans, Gronk, and Godwin, he could win by throwing the ball, but our defensive line refused to give Tom the time he needed to find his targets.

After the blowout, our defense figured the Bucs learned their lesson and would take a different approach—and we were right, shutting Tom out on the first two drives, and giving the ball to our offense to get us in field goal range twice for a 6–0 lead.

Then, on the next drive, Tampa Bay steadily moved the ball down the field, and on 3rd and goal on the 2-yard line, I was matched up against Gronk, one-on-one. Whenever they put Gronk in the red zone, he ran two routes: a fade or a slant. There's a difference between knowing the play and being able to stop it, but I thought I figured how to play it. Instead of using my eyes to read his route in real time, I attempted something that Roman Harper had taught me about having a "feel" for the game. Roman internalized the game so deeply, he developed an intuitive, almost spiritual, sense of how to play. He called this connection that couldn't be explained "the feel for the game." It was a moment when all your senses worked together to tell you what was going to happen, and you had to trust what you felt.

Watching tape before that playoff game, I noticed that when Gronk wanted to run a slant, he got physical. He'd run directly into the defender, then break off, and the ball would be right there. When he wanted to run a fade, he avoided the defender.

When Tom snapped the ball, Gronk released to my right leg, creating just enough contact for me to feel the slant. Absorbing the contact, I slipped underneath him, and just as I thought, the ball was right there. I dove and knocked it down, causing a fourth down.

Although we limited Tom on yards and opportunities, they protected the football, took what we gave them, and played a conservative complementary plan that ultimately won them the game 30–20. That same season, Tom won his seventh and final Super Bowl. When we walked off the field and got to the locker room, the entire room was silent. All you heard was the sniffles and mumbles of players crying and managing their frustrations. This was the fourth year in a row that the team fell short of the Super Bowl that we felt we were destined for. I was satisfied knowing that I had given every bit of knowledge I had to my teammates and had prepared myself to compete at the highest level. I knew that I had very little control over the outcome of the game, but I did have control over my impact on the game and those I played with. I wasn't playing for a Super Bowl, I was playing to make everyone around me better and it resulted in a season that was as much fun as any I had in my career.

Heading into the 2021 season, Drew retired, and after a promising start with quarterback Jameis Winston at the helm, leading us to a 4-2 record, he tore his ACL. Jameis's injury left the six-year veteran out of Northwestern, Trevor Siemian, to take over. We went on a five-game losing streak, coming out on the other end 6-7.

To secure a spot in the playoffs, we needed to win the last five games. But the Omicron variant of COVID struck our locker room in week 16. Exhausted by the protocols designed to keep us safe, and disregarding the recommendations from doctors, players agreed to relax the COVID protocols midway through the season, opting to test weekly instead of daily.

Preparing for our week 16 game against the Miami Dolphins, I noticed Trevor struggle during practice. When they took him out, I knew something was up, so to play the situation safe, I tested before I left the facility. In the twenty minutes it took for me to drive home, my phone rang. I had just tested positive and needed to return to the facility for another test.

By the time they'd completed the contact tracing, sixteen players would miss the game against the Dolphins, causing us to lose 20–3. Now we were in a situation against the Atlanta Falcons where, even if we won, we'd still need the 49ers to lose against the Rams for us to make the playoffs.

I knew the game against the Falcons would likely be my last game, but I didn't tell anyone because I didn't want my teammates to see me as having one foot out the door. My whole career, I'd given everything I had on the field, and now, with nothing left to give, this last season was going to be a gift to myself: no pressure, no drama; just the game. I would finish the season with one interception for a touchdown, one forced fumble, one sack, two QB hits, and seventy-nine tackles, three of which were for losses and five pass breakups.

When the game against Atlanta kicked off, we jumped out to a 7–0 lead. By the second quarter, we were up 17–6. The Falcons had the ball with about a minute left to play. On the first play of the drive, Matt Ryan threw a short pass to running back Mike Davis. Watching Matt the entire time and responsible for covering Davis, by the way Matt dropped back, I knew that he wanted to dump it off. When Davis caught the ball in the flat area of the field, I was in full stride, wrapping him up with so much force that when I hit him, we both ascended off the ground.

When the ball flew out of Davis's hands, our linebacker Kwon Alexander recovered the fumble for eight yards. Three plays later, we scored again, making the score 24–6. Though it seemed clear that this game was ours, we all wanted to check the score of the game with the Rams and 49ers.

Winning the Atlanta game 30–20, we immediately rushed into the locker room for the conclusion of the 49ers game that was now in overtime. Looking to decompress from the anxiety, I hit the shower, where backup safety Jeff Heath, also a veteran who played for almost as many years as I had, asked me a question.

"How many more seasons do you think you got in you?"

"This might be it for me."

The Monday following our week 3 win against the New England Patriots in 2021, my last season, I ask my oldest, Elle, a question.

"How would you feel if Daddy stopped playing football?"

Considering the question, she smiled.

"I would like that."

Because Elle and her sister, Selah, had watched me play football since they were babies, her answer surprised me. Elle was four weeks old when she attended her first game, a Wild Card playoff game against the Philadelphia Eagles in 2013. And when I played for the Eagles the year we defeated the Minnesota Vikings to be crowned the NFC champions, Selah was on the field for the celebration at two weeks old.

"I thought you liked the games and going to practices. Why?"

"Because we'd get to spend more time with you."

Confirming what I feared most, Elle's answer rocked me to my core. The divorce had already limited our time together; now football took even more of that time. Though I hated waking up to an empty two-bedroom condo, I hoped that maybe the cool things we did on Sundays would compensate for not being within arm's reach.

Whenever I think of my daughters, I think of their names. Elle Makena Jenkins's first name is from the French word *elle*, meaning "she" in English. Though the simplified spelling of "McKenna" suggests Irish roots, her middle name comes from the East African Kikuyu language and means "happy one." She, the happy one. Despite the challenges that came with watching her parents split at a young age, she embodies her name's meaning.

Selah Nola Jenkins, my youngest, is my twin. "Selah" is a Hebrew word found over seventy times in the book of Psalms, and signifies a musical break or pause, like an amen. Her arrival challenged me to pause and consider who I was before her birth and who I wanted to be after it. Her middle name is an ode both to the place I called home and also to the main character Nola Darling in the remake of *She's Gotta Have It*, played by DeWanda Wise. She's a beautiful, brown-skinned woman and an artist. More interested in arts than sports, like her sister, Selah is a thinker.

After answering my question, Elle smiled and walked away with her iPad, while I sat there, knowing my days in the league were numbered.

On the second day of my vacation with my parents in Accra, Ghana, in March 2022, my father handed his last Ghanaian cedi to the merchant selling kufis outside of the bustling market for handmade sculptures, jewelry, fabrics, and paintings, effectively spending all his money.

"Can't take it with you."

"Yes you can!" I blurted back. "It's not Monopoly money."

Always a sucker for a sales pitch, my father has never been one to consider the cost of things. Anything "new," "improved," or "organic," he'll spend his last dollar on it. With the season over, I was back in Ghana for the fourth time in four years. While my father blew his cash, my mom lived her best life.

The first day we got there, we spent the day at the polo club watching the Accra team play the team from Lagos, Nigeria. Watching my mother don the largest smile I've seen since the day I was drafted to the NFL, I reveled in her joy. *She's home*, I thought. She wouldn't let anything ruin this moment for her, not even my father, who could barely stand up after drinking a whiskey and champagne mix for four hours.

A couple days into our trip, Saints GM Mickey Loomis called. When Sean retired, in January 2022, I let him know I, too, considered retirement. With free agency around the corner, I had to tell Mickey when I got back home, but with him calling now, my mind was made up.

"I've got a ton of respect for you, Malcolm, and all that you've contributed to our team. I hope you change your mind, but I truly appreciate you and support you. Anything you ever need from me, just holler."

Sitting in the living room of the Airbnb, I said out loud with my parents in the room, "Welp, I just retired."

Equally as flat as my delivery was their response. There were no congratulations, no champagne popping, no "Well done." Just my father attempting to convince me that playing one or two more seasons ensured me as a first-ballot Hall of Famer. Not the one to consider the cost of things, he clearly had no clue or care of what a season or two felt like on the mind and body and spirit.

My mother tried her best to say something positive, but all she could muster was a question.

"What now?"

Considering her question in that moment, it occurred to me that because so many people depended on my football career, their identities were intertwined with my professional trajectory. For almost a decade, my mother was the president of the Malcolm Jenkins Foundation and had since become the president of the Professional Football Players Mothers Association, an organization filled with NFL mothers who supported their sons and one another as they navigated the world of professional football. I regularly heard stories of other mothers whose sons retired from the NFL, but their parents, still trying to live like their sons were still in the league, didn't.

Right in front of me, I could see the sudden change of identity pull on my mother's mind. It's that very fear that I needed to face. That last-second blink before making a tackle. The hesitation that whispers, "You think you're more than your jersey number?" Knowing I had given this chapter of my life everything I had, what life would look like from that point on was unclear—but I was ready for whatever lay ahead.

# EPILOGUE

Two days after the Super Bowl win against the Patriots in February 2018, we filed onto the double-decker buses parked outside of Lincoln Financial Field. When I won my first Super Bowl with the Saints in 2009, there were no drinks on the floats, and to make a last-minute liquor store run, I slid a few hundred bucks to a police officer. In a city famous for its Mardi Gras parade, the Super Bowl victory, the first in its history, drew a crowd of over 800,000 people. So for my second Super Bowl, I knew to be loaded with cases of cognac.

Like the images I challenged my younger teammates to conjure in their mind's eye earlier that season, as our buses traveled north on Broad Street from South Philadelphia, our imaginations were made real. In a city where fans never hesitated to tell us when we were fucking up, that parade truly felt like the city of brotherly love. Dancing down the 3.5-mile parade route all the way to the Philadelphia Museum of Art, and onto a platform next to the famed Rocky statue, we took the stage. With fans packed shoulder to shoulder, the entire width and depth of the Benjamin Franklin Parkway was awash in a sea of green. In that moment, I held the Lombardi Trophy high above my head, drunk with joy, satisfied in knowing that helping to bring another city its first Super Bowl was nothing short of legendary.

# ACKNOWLEDGMENTS

would like to acknowledge the people who have made this book possible and express my heartfelt gratitude to those who played a role in bringing this memoir to life. Their support, guidance, and contributions have been invaluable, and I am forever indebted to them.

Yahdon, my editor, you believed in this project and went above and beyond to make sure it was something I would be proud of. It was an honor to work with you and I'm glad I can call you a friend. Without you, this book would not be what it is today.

To Morgan Parker, I extend my deepest appreciation. Your presence and our conversations during those formative days of the project helped me find my voice and refine the essence of my story.

India, my manager and dear friend, you have been my constant source of encouragement and motivation. You always challenge me to step out of my comfort zone, and your belief in me, even when I've doubted myself, has many times been the gas I've needed to push forward.

Kristi, your support and guidance prepared me for some of the biggest moments and stages in my career. Thank you for being a constant sounding board and for the countless hours you invested in helping me bring my visions to life. I genuinely appreciate our friendship.

Calvin, I owe you a debt of gratitude for saving me from a potentially life-altering decision during my teenage years. Your honesty and genuine concern for my well-being truly saved me. Thank you for loving me enough to keep it real with me. You truly saved me.

To my teammates and coaches, you have been instrumental in shaping me both as a man and as a leader. The memories we shared have left an indelible mark on my journey, and I am grateful for the lessons and experiences we've shared that have cemented themselves as part of my legacy. We will forever be linked.

To my parents, Gwendolyn and Lee, your love and immovable support have been the cornerstone of my life. Your belief in me has shaped me into the man I have become. Thank you both for your examples of servant leadership and for instilling in me the values of hard work and family.

To my incredible children, Elle and Selah, you have been the inspiration behind this memoir. Many things have been written about who I am and what I've done. I wrote this book, so you have a story directly from me. If I teach you only one thing from my story let it be that I want you to live out the most expansive versions of yourselves. Never be boxed in by fears of failure or the opinions of those too scared to try. I love you both with every bit of energy in my body.

To my ancestors, I am constantly driven to make you all proud. Your love and courage continue to inspire me. I carry your legacy within me with utmost reverence. Thank you for sharing your strength with me.

Finally, to anyone I may have unintentionally omitted from this list, please know that your contributions and support have not gone unnoticed. My gratitude extends to each person who has crossed paths with me and has had a hand in shaping this memoir. Thank you all for your support, belief, and love throughout this transformative journey. Without each of you, this memoir would remain a mere dream.

# ABOUT THE AUTHOR

Malcolm Jenkins is an entrepreneur, executive producer, philanthropist, and racial justice advocate who is widely recognized as one of the NFL's greatest defensive leaders of all time. Over the course of his stellar thirteen-year NFL career, he has won numerous awards and accolades, including Super Bowl championships in New Orleans and Philadelphia as well as three Pro Bowl honors.

A true embodiment of the athlete-activist, Jenkins has utilized his platform to advocate for racial justice and equality throughout the country. As cofounder of the Players Coalition, an organization dedicated to addressing racial and social inequalities, he supports initiatives focused on criminal justice reform and education; through the Malcolm Jenkins Foundation, he creates youth development programs with community support. A frequent CNN contributor during the pandemic, he provided meaningful insights on racial and social issues as the first active NFL player to be a commentator on the network. In addition, he has published op-eds on policing, criminal justice reform, education, and legislation across several news sites, including the *New York Times* and the *Washington Post*.

Jenkins's exceptional leadership extends into multimedia and beyond. In 2018 he launched Malcolm Inc., a private investment and management company to serve his wide range of interests, including franchising, venture capital, and apparel. A newly minted art collector, he has an affinity for artists past and present from the African diaspora. He also cofounded Listen Up Media, a groundbreaking media production company dedicated to amplifying marginalized voices. By focusing on diverse narratives and authentic representation, Listen Up provokes meaningful conversations and challenges societal norms.

With his multifaceted contributions, Jenkins continues to be a passionate force for positive transformation both on and off the football field. A proud father of two daughters, Jenkins splits his time between Philadelphia and New Orleans. *What Winners Won't Tell You* is his first book.